A JOHN CATT PUBLICATION

BATTLE HYMN
OF THE
TIGER
TEACHERS

THE
MICHAELA WAY

EDITED BY
KATHARINE BIRBALSINGH

First Published 2016

by John Catt Educational Ltd,
12 Deben Mill Business Centre,
Old Maltings Approach,
Melton, Woodbridge IP12 1BL

Tel: +44 (0) 1394 389850
Fax: +44 (0) 1394 386893
Email: enquiries@johncatt.com
Website: www.johncatt.com

ISBN: 978 1 909717961
Set and designed by
Theoria Design

"Michaela is a trailblazer for schools that walk every word they talk. Few schools would be so open about their methods and values, and here teachers and school leaders can find the blueprint of Michaela's ambitions laid out in a series of fascinating personal accounts, written by the people who made it happen. This book, like the school itself, should catalyse debate across the UK about why and how we choose to teach our children."

Tom Bennett, Behaviour Advisor to the UK Department of Education, and founder of researchED

"This book explains how this iconoclastic Free School became unashamedly knowledge focused. You meet the pupils – they are happy, well behaved and incredibly knowledgeable. This school is driving social mobility every day."

Nick Gibb, Minister for School Standards

"This is an inspiring and thought-provoking read. The staff at Michaela have deconstructed English secondary education, and rebuilt it from the ground up, thinking only about what schools should do, rather than accepting what they usually do."

Andrew Old, teacher and blogger

"Michaela has only been around for a couple of years, but already it has changed the way many people think about education. This book explains how, and shows the incredible things that can be achieved by a small group of people with vision, energy and passion."

Daisy Christodoulou, Head of Assessment, Ark Schools

"They describe themselves as 'tiger teachers', giving poor children access to knowledge, rigour, testing and competition. As Wole Soyinka says "A tiger does not shout its tigritude, it acts." Those of you who still believe that a knowledge rich curriculum is not for the likes of poor inner-city children, should read this book and repent of your sins."

Dr Tony Sewell CBE, CEO, Generating Genius

"This collection of essays provides some fascinating insights into the Michaela world and what can be achieved with leadership, determination, and a willingness to challenge the status quo."

Dame Rachel de Souza, Chief Executive, Inspiration Trust

"My overwhelming impression on visiting Michaela was one of joy — joy in the teachers at being able to teach the subjects they love, unencumbered by bureaucratic irrelevance; and joy in the pupils, as secure knowledge gave them confidence, fluency and freedom in wholly new worlds. This is emancipatory education. I have rarely felt so optimistic about what state education might finally achieve for all."

Christine Counsell, Director of Education, The Inspiration Trust

"This book offers an insightful blend of evidence and personal testimony that is as compelling as it is heart-warming. Teachers at Michaela show a profound devotion to the children in their charge. One that views knowledge, high expectations and the privileging of community over the individual not as a form of restriction, but as a form of emancipation."

Carl Hendrick, Head of learning and research, Wellington College

"This book explains how the Michaela team are building a school which embodies a love of learning so consistently and effectively that it can be felt in every lesson, transition, and interaction. This book prompts its readers to re-assess the biggest questions facing our education system today."

Natasha Porter, CEO, Unlocked Graduates

"Full of life-affirming common sense which is tangibly helping liberate young people from disadvantaged backgrounds, enabling them to desist from the poverty of aspiration and thereby fulfil their potential, and in so doing get the best education — and preparation for life — possible."

Lindsay Johns, Writer, broadcaster and Head of Arts and Culture at Policy Exchange.

"This book should be banned. If a parent of a teenager gets hold of it, they'll ask why their son or daughter's school can't be as good as Michaela. And the uncomfortable truth is, it can. Every school can."

Toby Young, Director, New Schools Network

"Love them or hate them — and there are plenty of people who do both — they bring something fresh and unique to the English schools system. And in this fascinating book, they set down exactly what they do and how they do it."

Jonathan Simons, Head of Education, Policy Exchange

"Pioneers get shot at. Michaela's mission is to do things differently, to do things better, to make a difference to young people's lives and futures. Told with missionary zeal, this is their story. Michaela may be Marmite but we are a better school system for its existence."

Stephen Tierney, CEO,
The Blessed Edward Bamber Catholic Multi Academy Trust

"Michaela has re-written what is possible. I feel privileged to be a Headteacher in 2016 to learn from their examples."

Janella Ajeigbe, Headteacher, Churchill Gardens Primary Academy

"This book captures the impassioned commitment of the staff, some of the challenges, plenty of the remarkable successes and lots of the practical details. At the very least, it's a provocation to anyone running a school but, more than that, it's hugely impressive and inspiring."

Tom Sherrington, Headteacher, Highbury Grove School, Islington

"If, like me, you haven't visited the school, then read this book. It is packed with evidence-informed examples of pedagogy which is inspiring remarkable learning in Michaela's students. You dismiss the Michaela project at your peril!"

John Tomsett, Headteacher, Huntington School, York

"Michaela Community school succeeds because the focus is on absolute achievement by every child — no ifs no buts. Katharine Birbalsingh's leadership shines through on every page."

Kate Hoey, MP for Vauxhall

"Visiting Michaela was for me a life-changing experience. The triumph of progressive, child-centred education and all the follies associated with it had led me to despair that our inner-city children would ever be able to obtain the knowledge that they need for a successful and socially integrated life. In Michaela I saw that this despair is entirely unjustified, that good teachers can instil knowledge and discipline into every child, and that a school can be a happy and fruitful home to children of all kinds and all origins. This book lucidly explains the philosophy behind Michaela's approach, and its arguments are incontrovertible. Michaela is the model free school that all our schools should imitate."

Roger Scruton, writer and philosopher

For the children at Michaela who are extraordinary
And in memory of Michaela who inspires us all

Contents

There is one thing stronger than armies, and that is an idea whose time has come.

Victor Hugo

We are very proud to present these essays. The writings within represent over 20 teachers' views on Michaela. These ideas have been developed together as a team. The Governing Body and the staff have been working relentlessly for over three years to develop Michaela into the extraordinary school it is becoming. These teachers, guided by Katharine's vision and leadership, have created something very special that we hope others can read, enjoy and be inspired by.

Michaela Governing Body

Note: All pupil names have been changed to preserve anonymity.

Introduction: Free at Last

Katharine Birbalsingh

'Where is the rigour?' was what my friend and inspiration Michaela used to shout. Michaela loved to teach from the front. She liberated herself in her classroom by closing her door so that she could get on with what worked. She did things differently, and so do we.

Amy Chua, a Chinese American lawyer and author, explores her Eastern parenting style in her book *Battle Hymn of the Tiger Mother*, published in 2011. She talks about raising her children with tough love; we do the same with our children at Michaela.

After a three-year struggle, moving from Lambeth to Wandsworth and then ending up in Brent, Michaela Community School finally opened in Wembley Park in 2014 with a full intake of 120 year 7 pupils. The school currently has year 7, 8 and 9 pupils and accepts 120 year 7 pupils every new academic year. In 2020 we will have 840 pupils, which includes our 6th Form. There is a waiting list for every year group, and our lottery admissions process is administered by the Local Authority.

We faced a lot of opposition during those years setting up and when we first opened. The opposition is now less intense, but has not disappeared entirely. The hostility has never been from local families in any of the areas where we tried to set up; on the contrary, local families were always very interested in the idea of a school with strict discipline that taught knowledge, with many families desperate for a new school option. Our detractors have always been either local councillors or politicians, members of the NUT, the Anti-Academies Alliance or various political groups opposed to free schools; they would bus people in from around the country to infiltrate our parent meetings and disrupt them. They would surround our events or our school with pickets and shout abuse, even targeting our pupils. We have been lied to by authority figures in councils, broken into, and threatened with violence. This is no longer the case but, in the early days, the threats and abuse were so bad that I was scared to walk down the street, and at one stage, for many months, I became very ill from the stress. Times were tough.

The fighting stage of our struggle seems to have gone on forever. I used to joke that perhaps our detractors thought we were setting up a factory to build nuclear arms but in reality we were establishing a school in the inner city to serve deprived children. Setting up a free school is hard work, even without detractors. I would run into hairdressers in Harlesden waving flyers that we had printed with our own money shouting, 'Does anyone in here have a child in year 6?' I nipped into churches, mosques and temples, stood on street corners, outside primary schools and swimming pools.

Everyone in the steering group did, in various parts of London where we tried to establish ourselves, over several years in the rain, wind and sunshine. When we couldn't find a building in Lambeth, we went searching in Wandsworth, and when that didn't work, we went to Brent. We wanted our school to be somewhere in London where deprived children were desperate for school places. In the end, we were lucky enough to find our building in Wembley Park. There were so many obstacles that, when I look back, it makes it extraordinary that we ever opened at all. But open we did, and we have moved from strength to strength.

Tiger Teachers is written by the teaching staff at Michaela and these chapters reflect who we are: we have NQTs, Teach Firsters, unqualified teachers and teachers of 20 years standing, and there is a burning passion that unites us all. There is a spirit of resolution and revolution that runs through every chapter. Some chapters are quirky, some serious, but all are honest and heartfelt. Teachers who live and love the Michaela way have taken the time to write these essays. We have teachers who have moved across the country to join our school because they are that committed to what we do, and then we have teachers who have come from as far as France and Zimbabwe. Fadila Bettahar's chapter compares her experience of Michaela with the schools she has worked with in France.

Each chapter gives the reader a taste of what we are like as a school. The subjects of the chapters have been chosen because they illustrate how unlike other schools we are, or because they demonstrate how differently we see the world in comparison to most people in the educational establishment. Some readers may find much of what we say hard to believe. If that is the case, I suggest you come and visit, as guests often say that visiting clarifies so much for them. If you are open-minded enough to be reading this book, then maybe you can go a little further: you are welcome to come and have lunch with our pupils. We are open at any time to anyone, and we are the only school in the country, state or private, that is happy to have anyone visit at any time. The only people we do not allow in the building are those who are actively hostile; we welcome everyone else with open arms.

Even our own staff members have questioned our ways. Visit us and speak to Lia Martin, whose chapter is about how and why she changed her mind about Michaela, or read William Eastment's chapter on his thinking, having only just started working at Michaela. Without visiting, it is easy to think of no-excuses discipline as oppressive because you may never have seen it work. You would have seen it work in Michaela's classroom. Sadly, she passed away in 2011, but now we have our school. Visit us, and as Jonathan Porter says in his chapter, you will see how happy our children are. Michael Taylor's chapter explores the beauty of our 'Family Lunch.' Again, without visiting, it is easy to criticise. When you experience it, you might understand why our Family Lunch is preferable to the lunch experiences children have at most other schools.

When we first started setting up in 2011, one local parent in Brixton joined our steering group. She was white and middle-class, had two young children still at primary school and was really excited to be part of this thrilling new venture. However, a few months in, she took me aside and said she had to drop out because she was losing friends because of her involvement with our school. The social pressure to hate free schools, to hate our school, was too much for her. Unfortunately, she left us. CPD (Continued Professional Development) at Michaela tries to give intellectual confidence to staff who may be surrounded by friends and family who simply cannot understand what we do because it challenges so many mainstream liberal assumptions. Instinctively to many, what we do seems wrong, despite the incredible impact we have on our pupils.

Jo Facer describes CPD at Michaela: the various issues that we address straight on, how we encourage staff to think afresh instead of following the crowd or never thinking at all. I have a quote in my office by Muhammad Ali, 'The man who views the world at 50 the same as he did at 20 has wasted 30 years of his life.' We help staff to come to their own conclusions, while considering all of the facts. In the chapter titled 'Education, Education, Education,' Barry Smith explores some of the recent educational trends that are responsible for so much harm in our schools. We regularly discuss these modern trends in our CPD sessions.

The undermining of authority in schools and elsewhere is one of the most significant developments of the last 50 years. Lucy Newman explores this in her chapter. Hin-Tai Ting examines the concept of respect in society for teachers. Hin-Tai could have done his two Teach First years and then left to pursue an apparently more glamorous career but he, like many of our staff, chose teaching, because he finds glamour in transforming the lives of disadvantaged children instead.

You will read about our bootcamp from Joe Kirby and how we get our pupils in year 7 to understand what Michaela is about. From Brett Williams-Yale, you will read about kindness at Michaela, how happy our children are, and how the most striking thing to all visitors is not the level of knowledge of our pupils but their manners, kindness and self-confidence. I also include in one chapter the perspective of one of our many visitors, Doug Lemov, who articulates what makes Michaela different from the visitor's-eye view.

One of the reasons why those who hate free schools are so angry is because free schools are allowed to hire 'unqualified' teachers who have not undergone standard teacher training. Yet our private schools are packed with unqualified staff – meaning they don't have a piece of paper saying they have met so-called teacher standards. Jake Plastow-Chason's chapter compares normal teacher training to the training you get at Michaela. He knows the difference because he has experienced both types and he compares being taught through standard teacher training and being taught how to teach Michaela-style. Sarah Clear writes about what it is like teaching at Michaela without a qualified teacher status (QTS).

How we teach is very similar across the classrooms at Michaela, but is vastly different to how people teach in normal schools. Our teaching methods should become clear when you read Joe Kirby on knowledge, testing and memorisation, and Olivia Dyer on drill and didactic teaching. Katie Ashford's chapter on reading explains how we put literacy at the heart of everything we do. We believe teaching the Michaela way isn't just better for the pupils: it is also better for the staff. It reduces their workload and increases their impact, contribution and sense of purpose.

We want our teachers to have lives. We do not believe that the only way to be a good teacher is to give a few years to the profession and then drop out exhausted and burnt out. We believe it should be possible to teach over a lifetime. Jessica Lund's essay shows from a teacher's perspective what it is like to work at Michaela. Jo Facer explores the thinking behind 'no marking' which, of course, plays a big part in our drive to value work-life balance for teachers.

I am regularly amazed and gratified by the commitment shown by our staff and how much they love the school. We make mistakes all of the time, and no doubt we will continue to do so, but we are developing every day as we learn from our mistakes and from the evidence in front of us: the children. We fine-tune constantly, depending on what works, and as Sarah Cullen says in her chapter, 'The Devil is in the Detail.' We demand a lot from people, including our parents. Chashe Musarurwa's chapter explores her development as a mother and what she has learned about parenting from Michaela.

My own chapter explains our approach towards parents at the school, where we believe mindset is everything, and so we often work with some of our parents to encourage them to be better parents. We work with staff to help them question the nonsense that has been forced onto them by the system. Most importantly, we work with our pupils to ensure they have the kind of mindset that will make them resilient in the face of what the world will throw at them. Barry Smith discusses the importance of an elite culture in his chapter 'Top of the Pyramid.' Eton and Harrow do not have to make their pupils feel as if they can take the world by storm. We do. Katie Ashford's chapter explores how we support our SEN pupils to make dramatic progress. She describes how labels destroy children's lives. Dani Quinn's chapter talks about how crucial competition is for success.

To close, we include some direct quotations from pupils and visitors. Joe Allan's chapter brings together various examples of our pupils' work, and their own heartfelt testimonials and quotes. Katie Ashford's chapter gives some data on our pupils' progress.

We hope to persuade our readers to begin to question the orthodoxies in our education system, but Jo Facer's chapter 'What Are We Afraid Of?' describes how, despite evidence, some people will continue to reject reform in our education system.

This is why, finally, freedom from the system is the only answer, and why free schools are so important. If the current education system were performing well, then such freedom would not be necessary. As it is, nationally, with 17% of our children leaving school functionally illiterate and 22% leaving school functionally innumerate, only freedom from our current broken culture of low expectations will allow our poorest children a way out. We are not the only school daring to do things differently. Freedom is there for the taking for us all and we should embrace it.

On my office wall, I have the poem 'Caged Bird' by Maya Angelou. I challenge everyone in education to look up and dare to claim the sky.

> The caged bird sings
> with a fearful trill
> of things unknown
> but longed for still
> and his tune is heard
> on the distant hill
> for the caged bird
> sings of freedom.

Knowledge, Memory and Testing

Joe Kirby

The neglect of knowledge

Very few schools in England claim to make factual knowledge a top priority. When I started teaching in 2011 as an English teacher, I was told, 'English isn't about knowledge; it's a skills-based subject.' When I was observed, I was told that it was difficult to see any evidence of progress in my lessons, because my questions were focused on information retrieval, passive listening and knowledge quizzing. I was informed that knowledge isn't important, especially to Ofsted, and that I needed to focus on skills rather than on content.

'Don't ask so many closed factual questions,' I was advised; instead, I was told to ask higher-order questions. Knowledge was seen as lower order, and less important than skills. Perhaps English departments in 2011 were correct to think Ofsted preferred engagement and skills above rigour and knowledge. For instance, in a 2011 Ofsted report titled 'Excellence in English: What we can learn from 12 outstanding schools,' a subject leader described her view of English as 'getting out the plasticine and paint.' The same report eulogises picture books rather than classic literature: 'some of the Key Stage 3 units of work are innovative and highly distinctive. For example, younger pupils especially enjoyed the *Mr Men* unit of work.' In Ofsted's English handbook in 2011, there was not one single mention of grammar, vocabulary or spelling in the outstanding category. Instead, media, film and technology all received several lavish mentions.

English schools and their English departments still neglect facts and knowledge, worried about spoon-feeding or regurgitation. Instead, the aim is to develop 'transferable skills' such as analysis or evaluation, detached from specific content. From 2011, I taught units to year 10 and year 11 GCSE pupils on TV and Twitter for entire half terms, requiring no factual, grammatical or literary content whatsoever. I taught six-week units on short films, picture books, celebrities, chocolate bars and cereal boxes, all designed to engage pupils; none were designed to teach them substantial literary knowledge. Knowledge of the rules of grammar was not taught or practised extensively, but crammed into the odd starter to a lesson. As a result, many GCSE and even A-level pupils I taught could not accurately use full stops, commas or colons, and did not know the rules for using them. Without having automated accurate punctuation, and with a very shaky grasp of sentences, my pupils found it hard to produce articulate writing. The curriculum was eviscerated of extensive, rigorous knowledge, and classrooms had become fact-free zones.

Double disadvantage

Unzipping skills from knowledge fails. Scientists over the last three decades have come to a scientifically robust conclusion: critical-thinking skills require domain-specific knowledge. Teaching transferable skills devoid of factual knowledge makes little sense. As cognitive psychologist Daniel Willingham says:

> Data from the last thirty years lead to a conclusion that is not scientifically challengeable: thinking well requires knowing facts. The very processes that teachers value most – critical thinking processes such as reasoning and problem solving – are intimately intertwined with factual knowledge that is stored in long-term memory.

Science shows that learning and remembering facts isn't regurgitation: it is the route to understanding and critical thinking. Scientists have shown that transferable skills are not a promising route to academic achievement. Cognitive scientist Herbert Simon and his colleagues have cast doubt on the idea that there are any general or transferable cognitive skills. All cognitive skills depend on procedural and substantive schemata that are highly specific to the task at hand.

The consequence of reducing the knowledge taught, not just in English but also in the humanities such as History, Geography and Religion, is an entrenchment of the gaping achievement gap between richer and poorer pupils. Whereas over 90% of private school pupils get to university, less than 20% of pupils on free school meals get to university. Wealthier pupils pick up cultural knowledge from their families, family friends, holidays, libraries and trips to museums and theatres. Poorer pupils are doubly disadvantaged: they lack families who give them knowledge and then are denied knowledge by their schools. Lacking literary, historical, geographical and grammatical knowledge, it is little wonder they struggle to compete with private school pupils in academic GCSE and A-level exams. Many of my friends taught in the most disadvantaged communities in the country. Their stories resonated with the experiences I had in my previous school, as my pupils did not know very much at all. Many pupils didn't know who Shakespeare was, or whether Henry VIII was Queen Elizabeth II's son; many couldn't place England, their city, the USA or China on a map; most couldn't list the four countries that made up the UK, or name the date of one historical event. Another teacher told me her pupils thought Manchester was in Scotland, Wales was an island and the Romans came from Portugal. Many thought the Vikings and the Nazis were around at the same time. In another teacher's school, many pupils couldn't name the Prime Minister, but thought it might be Barack Obama or Gordon Blair. These are experiences that teachers in disadvantaged areas are having all round the country. These are troubling tidings for democratic society. As William Beveridge said, 'no democracy can afford ignorance among its citizens.' As Thomas Jefferson put it, 'if a nation expects to be ignorant and free in a state of civilisation, it expects what never was and never will be.'

Schools were teaching and assessing skills, neglecting knowledge, and then finding that pupils seemed not to know very much at all.

The Matthew effect

'To whoever has, more shall be given; but from whoever has not, even what they have will be taken away.' This haunting message from two thousand years ago comes from the New Testament's Book of Matthew. The Matthew effect is that advantages lead to further advantages: the rich get richer, the poor get poorer; the knowledge-rich get richer and the knowledge-poor get poorer.

It is a travesty that in England today, children from poor and illiterate homes tend to remain poor and illiterate. The achievement gap and the university access gap between rich and poor can be explained in part by the cavernous gap in cultural knowledge. Those who have lots of knowledge learn more knowledge and so achieve more; those who do not have lots of knowledge learn less and achieve less. Private schools take advantage of the Matthew effect, doubling up their advantage of selection with the advantage of a highly academic subject curriculum. Comprehensive schools in disadvantaged areas exacerbate educational inequality and unequal opportunity whenever they neglect or marginalise the powerful mathematical, scientific, historical, religious, literary, artistic and musical knowledge that could help their pupils achieve academically, understand the world and live fulfilling lives.

E.D. Hirsch, an American advocate of a knowledge-led curriculum, pointed out the Matthew effect decades ago. Hirsch writes:

> Breadth of knowledge is the single factor within human control that contributes most to academic achievement and general cognitive competence. Breadth of knowledge is a far greater factor in achievement than socioeconomic status. The positive correlation between academic ability and socioeconomic status is only half the correlation between academic ability and the possession of general information. That is to say, being 'smart' is more dependent on possessing general knowledge than on family background. Imparting broad

knowledge to all children is the single most effective way to narrow the gap between demographic groups through schooling.

For Hirsch, just as for us at Michaela, knowledge is a 'sure avenue of opportunity for disadvantaged children and combating educational inequality.'

There are many teachers and school leaders working hard in disadvantaged areas who have yet to apply the advantages of knowledge-led curricula, often because of a scientifically disproven stigma that teaching facts is 'lower order', 'passive' or 'spoon-feeding.' I have lost count of the number of conversations that my fellow teachers at Michaela and I have had, throughout all the years of our careers, with those who are sceptical about making knowledge the centre of the curriculum. In a comment that is far from unusual, one headteacher wrote online that 'knowledge transmission is a very limiting and limited view of teaching.'

Yet some still maintain that knowledge isn't marginalised in schools. To a teacher or school leader who claims that knowledge isn't neglected, I ask the following questions:

· Do you meticulously specify every concept that pupils will master in each year, along with precise definitions?

· Do you decide and organise every piece of knowledge in advance of every unit you teach?

· Do you sequence and revisit knowledge from previous units explicitly and systematically?

· Do you test pupils' knowledge of all of these facts multiple times, even after a unit has ended?

· Do you assess whether pupils have remembered those facts even a year later?

· Do you know to what extent pupils have remembered or forgotten the precise definitions of those concepts?

The answer to many of these questions is usually a stunned silence, and then a reluctant no to most or all of them.

The fact is that most schools, departments and teachers, after years of Ofsted marginalising knowledge in education in England, simply do not coherently or systematically decide on, drill or test many facts. Many school assessment systems, including the previous schools of every single one of my 30 colleagues, are based on skills descriptors. How many teachers agree with this, as we do at Michaela: all there is to intelligence is the simple accrual and tuning of many small units of knowledge that in total produce complex cognition? How many school leaders agree that if nothing has been retained in long-term memory, nothing has been learnt? How many agree that long-term memory is the dominant structure in cognitive architecture? How many agree with the teachers and leadership at Michaela that the best way to achieve the aim of complex thinking skills and academic achievement for pupils is not to teach and assess skills, but to drill and test facts?

There is a mismatch between what science has discovered about the importance of knowledge and memory in the mind and what teachers and schools are doing in their curricula and assessment systems. A coherent, sequential knowledge-led curriculum is a challenge to the tenacious orthodoxy of the skills-led curriculum and assessment regime.

Michaela's knowledge-led curriculum

We see a knowledge-led curriculum as a powerful force for academic achievement and lifelong fulfillment. Our motto, which we share with all pupils right from their first day at school, is that 'Knowledge is Power'; it empowers all children to achieve, choose their future and decide what legacy they would like to leave. We believe that broad cultural and historical knowledge improves all pupils' academic achievement, especially poorer pupils. Even the very weakest pupils can study the greatest books ever written, such as *Frankenstein, Oliver Twist* and *Animal Farm*.

All pupils deserve the chance to see Shakespearean theatre, fine art and classical music as accessible to them, not alien to them: access which richer pupils take for granted. Knowing about democracy, its origins, evolution and discontents empowers pupils to make their own minds up as citizens in politics, referenda and elections.

We believe that powerful mathematical and scientific knowledge empowers pupils to choose among the most competitive and selective vocations, such as medicine, finance, engineering, technology and law, as well as appreciating how the world works, in all its wonder. Only a cohesive, cumulative and carefully sequenced knowledge curriculum will close the wide vocabulary gap between the poorest and wealthier pupils, narrow the over 20% gap in GCSE attainment between poorest and wealthier pupils aged 16 and reduce the 80% gap between the poorest and private school pupils attending university aged 18. The reason we want all pupils to have secure subject knowledge is because we think it is the best route to social justice.

We select knowledge for challenge and coherence

How, then, are we to decide which knowledge to teach? At Michaela, we decide based on challenge and coherence. We prioritise the core academic and artistic subjects that help pupils understand the world and live fulfilling lives: Maths, English, Science, History, Geography, Religion, French, Art and Music. The subject knowledge we choose to teach our pupils to master is the most vital and the most challenging content.

The pupils we teach often arrive at school far behind, unable to read fluently or multiply. Many have a vocabulary of fewer than 6,000 words, while wealthier pupils often have one of over 12,000 words. The opportunity cost of teaching anything other than the most challenging subject content is high. Only the most challenging topics with the most stretching vocabulary, combined with high support so all pupils understand and use it accurately, will allow them to compete academically with the 96% of private school pupils who reach university. We dedicate extended teaching time for the mastery of grammar, spelling and vocabulary; these are the hidden bodies of knowledge that make for accurate writing. Our pupils already have vivid memories of reading some of the most complex and beautiful texts ever written: Shakespeare's *Julius Caesar*, Swift's *Gulliver's Travels*, Shelley's *Frankenstein*, Orwell's *1984*, Malcolm X's autobiography, Maya Angelou's autobiography, Duffy's *The World's Wife* and Mandela's *A Long Walk to Freedom*, to name just a handful of examples.

Our aim is to help pupils remember everything they are learning, and master the most important content. To this end, subject content knowledge is best organised into the most memorable schemata. So we organise History and English Literature chronologically. We start in year 7 with classical antiquity: in History we study Mesopotamia, Egypt, Greece, Rome and Roman Britain; in Religion, we study polytheism, The Old and New Testament, Judaism and Christianity; in English, we study Homer's *Odyssey*, Sophocles' *Antigone*, Aeschylus' *Agamemnon*, Euripides' *Medea*, Cicero's rhetoric, Seneca's stoicism and Shakespeare's *Julius Caesar*; in Art, we study Egyptian, Greek and Roman art, sculpture and architecture. Chronological, cumulative schemata help pupils remember subject knowledge in the long term, not for ten weeks or ten months, but for ten years and beyond. Those who have visited Michaela have seen our pupils' eyes light up with excitement – every subject we teach is inspiring.

We select subject knowledge to dovetail cohesively across and between subjects. At Michaela, our pupils remember year 7 as the year they learnt about Classical Civilisation. Across subjects, they are making exciting connections. Sacrifice, for instance, recurs in the stories of Abraham and Isaac in religion, with Agamemnon and Iphigenia, and Minos and Theseus in Greek mythology. Across English and Science, the planet Mercury is named after the Greco-Roman messenger god, as it is the fastest-moving planet that takes 88 days to orbit the sun. A dovetailed knowledge curriculum allows pupils to make limitless fascinating connections for themselves, and understand the ideas of democracy, dictatorship, tragedy, monotheism, sculpture, geometry and algebra from their early origins. In short, we select challenging, sequenced, coherent schemata within and across subjects, so that our pupils remember what they've learned for years to come. We are already seeing our pupils develop formidable, accumulative advantages from studying such a rigorous, sequential knowledge curriculum. How, though, do we ensure they remember it all?

The problem of forgetting

Forgetting is problematic in education. Many of us teachers achieved good grades in compulsory GCSE exams such as Physics, Chemistry, and Maths. Yet if you asked us to redo those exams tomorrow, we would undoubtedly struggle to achieve the same high grades. We've forgotten much of what we learned. Given the months and months of time invested, that seems a waste. Every teacher has had the experience of seeing a class grasp a concept perfectly in a lesson, only to have completely forgotten it when you mention it later in the year, with many pupils assuring you they've never heard of it before in their lives. I have been asked several times by exasperated English teachers: 'isn't it frustrating when they still don't remember how to use full stops properly?' It seems puzzling why pupils forget so much of what they've learned.

Over a century of research in cognitive science can help us understand how forgetting works. In 1885, Ebbinghaus drew sharp forgetting curves that showed that without revisiting, we forget new things we've learned very quickly. All of us have this experience often, such as when we hear the names of new acquaintances. School pupils also have this experience all the time, especially when learning ten subjects or more over a week in the dizzying secondary school timetable flurry of six subjects a day. Scientists have learned that the human mind forgets what it does not practise, revisit and consolidate.

So, when we grumble as teachers that pupils don't use punctuation properly, even though they've learned it, we need to ask ourselves the questions:

· Have they really learnt it?
· Have we really taught it with sufficient time, focus and attention?
· Have we sufficiently revisited it?
· Have we consolidated it in their minds?

- Have they mastered it?
- Have they automated it in their long-term memories?

It's no good grumbling about pupils' written ineptitude. Punctuation is complex, even the basics of using full stops requires lots of little chunks of knowledge to be automatic; to decide whether a sentence has a subject and a verb to avoid fragments and whether a sentence runs on into multiple, confusing independent and subordinate clauses, you need to know what subjects, verbs, independent and subordinate clauses are.

It may be automatic for us, but it's not for our secondary pupils. If we want our pupils to automate complex concepts, we need to ensure sufficient time, focus, attention, revisiting, application, consolidation, practice, usage and eventual mastery. As it stands currently, I'm unconvinced we do this for them, as sixth form English pupils' weak writing and History graduates' weak knowledge testify.

The testing effect

So, how can we help pupils remember what they're learning? From over a hundred years of research, there is a clear consensus from cognitive scientists who have studied the evidence. Extended practice, overlearning even after pupils know the material, and frequent testing, are the best ways to prevent forgetting and boost pupils' long-term memory retention. More than a hundred years of research has yielded several hundred peer-reviewed, replicated experiments that testify to this. In 2013, five cognitive scientists collated hundreds of studies to show that testing has a higher impact on learning than other techniques such as re-reading, highlighting or summarising. Testing has a high utility across tasks, formats, subjects, learner ages, learner abilities, outcome measures and retention intervals. It is one of the most effective study techniques in the research literature, according to these psychologists.

Cognitive psychologists have summarised the advantages of low-stakes or no-stakes testing:

- Testing improves long-term retention
- Testing identifies gaps in knowledge
- Testing causes pupils to learn more from the next study episode
- Testing produces better organisation of knowledge
- Testing improves transfer of knowledge to new contexts
- Testing provides feedback to instructors
- Testing encourages pupils to study

Over the last decade, 11 cognitive psychologists took over a hundred years of laboratory research and applied it to the classroom. Here's what they conclude in their book, *Make It Stick*: 'In virtually all areas of learning, you build better mastery when you use testing as a tool.'

Frequent testing helps pupils remember subject knowledge

At Michaela, we apply this scientific research on low-stakes testing in every single lesson. Every lesson in every subject at Michaela starts with a low-stakes, open-question recap quiz. Pupils get instant feedback, correct their mistakes and improve their answers, but no score is recorded, tracked or monitored. Testing is especially powerful for learning when kept low-stakes. What we've seen is that this creates enthusiasm and excitement among all our pupils, who feel motivated by learning, mastering and remembering so many tangible facts that they can find connections. Visitors can testify to the positive energy and momentum in lessons that remembering so much knowledge generates from pupils.

Let's imagine a normal six-subject day in the life of a Michaela pupil. They tackle written quizzes in History period one on five dates and events; period two on five concepts and definitions in Science; period three on five characters in a play in English; period four they have a map and locations in Geography; period five they have five mathematical problems to solve; period six they have a quiz on five themes in Art. They get instant feedback in every subject quiz so they know what to revise and strengthen that evening. They also have recap quizzes on what they learned in previous units, some from months and even years ago. Every moment matters at Michaela, so as they enter and leave lessons, they are being quizzed by the teacher with oral questions that they all reply to in a choral response. Every minute of every lesson is packed full of opportunities to revisit, consolidate and struggle against the sharp, savage forgetting curve.

Exams are heavily knowledge-focused at Michaela. We have multiple knowledge exams twice a year in every subject in February and July. We also have extended A-level style exams right from year 7, with extended essays in English and History for instance. Our knowledge exams allow us to test pupils on a massive range of broad, deep subject knowledge. In year 8 English classes, all our pupils, regardless of their level, encounter four knowledge exams twice a year with 36 questions on the context, themes, characters, plot, dramatic devices and quotations in Shakespeare's *Romeo and Juliet* and *Macbeth*; 36 questions on the context, themes, characters, poetic techniques and quotations of the six Romantic poets (Blake, Coleridge, Wordsworth, Shelley, Byron, Keats), including writing out the poems 'Ozymandias,' 'Auguries of Innocence' and

'Kubla Khan.' There are also 36 questions on the context, themes, characters, plot, literary techniques and quotations in Mary Shelley's *Frankenstein*; and 36 questions on every topic they learned in year 7, including Greek mythology, epic and tragedy, Roman rhetoric, Shakespeare's *Julius Caesar* and the poems memorised by heart: Kipling's 'If' and Henley's 'Invictus.' This is in one subject of nine.

It is a vastly ambitious breadth and depth of subject expertise that we are testing: as ambitious as I imagine the best public schools with academically selective intakes. What is more, the vast majority of pupils achieve excellent results in all of these exams – exams that if we asked our teachers to tackle across all subjects, most would struggle. The extraordinary breadth prevents teachers from teaching narrowly to the test, because the test samples vary broadly from the subject domain.[1] We save time on marking by using comparative judgement and grading pupils simply from A (excellent) through to B (good) and then to C (concerning) for each of these knowledge exams. This allows us to recognise excellence of effort and identify concerning lack of effort whilst avoiding high marking workloads and high teacher burnout.

Aside from their ambitious breadth, one major advantage of these exams is that they are cumulative. Cumulative knowledge exams are powerful for consolidating learning covered in earlier years and to prevent the pupil from forgetting it all. We want our pupils to remember all the Greek mythology they learned in year 7 for when they study the many allusions to it in poetry, from Byron's 'Prometheus' to Tennyson's 'Ulysses,' and the many references to the Roman Republic that they study in year 7 as they study Shakespeare into year 8, 9, 10 and 11, such as when Macbeth wonders if Banquo might become the Octavius Caesar to his Mark Antony; or what they learned in year 7 about specialised cells and year 8 about plant asexual reproduction and cloning when they study evolution and genetics in year 9. There are endless examples in every area of the curriculum.

We think very carefully about sequencing our subject curriculum and assessment models, evaluating them every year and improving them so that

---

1 'Domain' refers to the body of knowledge of the entire subject. For example, an essay on hubris in *Macbeth* is only testing a small sample of pupils' wider 'domain' knowledge of the play, what they know about that theme in those particular scenes: they should be taught a lot more about that topic (more quotations, dates, techniques, links) than could ever be tested in a single, one-off essay. Too many departments make the mistake of teaching only the *sample* – that which will be tested in the end of unit assessment or essay – and not the wider *domain*. By having knowledge assessments alongside in-depth essays, we assess both at Michaela.

we optimise the connections pupils are able to make within and between their subjects. We are already seeing powerful flow-over effects. Pupils' strong sense of chronology helps them locate unseen poems and literature. Their deep knowledge of Shakespearian themes, plots and contexts in English helps them to understand the end of the Tudor and the start of the Stuart dynasties in History. Their rich knowledge of Christianity and the Bible from Religion helps them understand many writers' preoccupations, from Chaucer through Milton to Blake and beyond. Their broad knowledge of Geography helps them understand, for instance, why Cyprus is contested by Christian Venice and Muslim Ottoman Empire in *Othello* and between Greece and Turkey in modern History; why Bolivia and Chad are both poor. Their wide-ranging, chronological knowledge of artistic and musical movements helps them understand the evolving story of Western civilisation, its interactions with other civilisations, its discontents and crises.

Many visitors and teachers express a wish that they had been taught at Michaela, seeing the missed opportunities for learning about how art, music, literature, religion, geopolitics, science, mathematics and language co-evolved over the centuries. Every one of our pupils remembers by heart three poems in year 7, three from year 8 and three from year 9; one of which we revisit as a whole year group to begin every assembly and every lunchtime. For my part, I learned one poem during my entire time at school, and to this day, over a decade later, it is still one of my most treasured possessions. Our pupils will keep the gift of poetry by heart for the rest of their lives, looking back on their time at school for years to come. We are ferociously ambitious for our pupils. We are certainly not narrowly teaching them futile, disconnected factoids, nor cynically training them to jump them through exam hoops for league table results. We see a knowledge-led curriculum as teaching them to remember broad, deep, subject expertise that will give them a lifelong curiosity and love of learning.

At Michaela, we see broad, in-depth subject knowledge not just as the firm foundation of learning, but as an ultimate ambition and intrinsic good. At university and beyond, we want our pupils to be contributing to the forefront of knowledge in Science, Mathematics, the Arts and beyond. Establishing, reinforcing and consolidating that sound, broad, deep subject knowledge is a vital priority for all our teachers in every subject. It is phenomenally useful that any new teacher who teaches any year 8, year 9, year 10 or year 11 class at Michaela knows exactly what they should all know well from their previous years' study. This shared foundation is what teachers utterly lacked in all the other schools we have worked in. Every teacher essentially had to start from scratch each year; so much seemed to have been forgotten, so little seemed to have been remembered, so little deliberately consolidated.

It does not have to be this way. At Michaela, we focus on designing our curriculum, lessons and exams with long-term memory in mind. We prioritise careful sequencing and dovetailing of subject knowledge. We ensure that every lesson and every exam week it is revisited, drilled and tested rigorously and relentlessly. In short, we aim to ensure that our pupils do not forget what they are learning for years to come, perhaps even for as long as they live.

The blind spot of many school curricula and assessment regimes is knowledge in long-term memory. For far too long, the teachers of England have been chained and encumbered by mind-forged manacles, a blinkered paradigm that sidelines and dismisses knowledge and memory as marginal or unhelpful. It is only when school leaders overcome the outdated stigma against drilling and testing extensive factual knowledge as 'regurgitation' that they will unlock the greatest academic achievement and intellectual potential in the minds of their pupils. The poorest pupils, most disadvantaged by the weak cultural capital of their parents, stand to gain the greatest advantages. At Michaela, we have seen that teachers can change pupils' lives through a powerful knowledge curriculum. Teachers of England, unite! You have nothing to lose but your chains.

Drill and Didactic Teaching Work Best

Olivia Dyer

While drill and didactic teaching are now second nature to me, there are many who consider such traditional methods to be the preserve of old, crusty, fuddy-duddy, elbow-patched, pullover-wearing public school teachers who really might drill and kill motivation. In fact, drill can thrill, and didactic teaching can result in children who are impassioned by your subject. In this chapter, I shall suggest ways to implement drill and didactic teaching in the classroom and argue why it works best by outlining and deconstructing four arguments to the contrary. As a Science teacher, I am going to give particular emphasis on drill and didactic teaching in Science.

We need to didactically teach knowledge and embed it into pupils' long-term memories through drill. Didactic teaching is the pedagogy of imparting immutable facts. At Michaela, we embrace the pedagogical view of the teacher as the fountain of knowledge, which is why pupils sit in rows facing the teacher. There is no guesswork at Michaela. Repeated practice of using this knowledge enables pupils to achieve automaticity. This practice is known as drill. Allow me to outline how drill and didactic teaching work best to teach the concept of density, or indeed any other concept, below.

Prior to this lesson, pupils would have spent a fortnight learning about the fundamentals of 'matter.' They would have learned that atoms are the tiny building blocks of all matter, as well as about sub-atomic particles. Pupils would have learnt that matter must have volume and mass as well as their definitions, by heart, through drill. When automaticity in more basic content is achieved, pupils can move more quickly towards more complex content. Pupils would be able to identify volume and mass as physical properties of matter and contrast physical properties with chemical properties. The teacher would have instructed pupils on procedures to calculate volume and pupils would have practiced these through increasingly challenging drills. Having mastered this, pupils would have learned how to calculate the volume of an irregularly shaped object by the displacement of a known volume of liquid and would have then carried out a practical doing so. Pupils would already have thorough knowledge of this practical method and the story of Archimedes, the scientist who discovered this method.

Whole-class recap

To begin the lesson, there is a whole-class recap on definitions memorised in the previous lesson. The teacher expects every member of the class to contribute. Drilling pupils on definitions produces learners who are proficient at the basic but fundamental subject foundations.

Teacher: State the two things that matter must have. One, two, three...

Whole class: Volume and mass!

Teacher: Identify the name given to the amount of space that matter takes up in a three-dimensional object. One, two, three...

Whole class: Volume!

Teacher: State whether mass is a chemical or physical property of matter. One, two, three...

Whole class: Physical property!

Teacher: State the person who discovered how to calculate volume by displacement. One, two, three...

Whole class: Archimedes!

Teacher: For a regular cuboid object, volume equals... One, two, three...

Whole class: Length x width x depth!

Teacher: State how many grams are in one kilogram. One, two, three...

Whole class: 1000!

Teacher: State how many millilitres are in one cubic centimetre. One, two, three...

Whole class: One!

The teacher cold calls pupils, asking them to recite the definitions learned in previous lessons.

Teacher: Mischa, define mass.

Mischa: The amount of space that matter takes up in an object?

Teacher: Almost! Said, can you help Mischa out?

Said: Instead of just object, we're meant to say that it's a three-dimensional object. Mass is the amount of space that matter takes up in a three-dimensional object.

Teacher: What do you think, Sam?

Sam: Miss, I agree.

Teacher: Can you articulate what you agree with, Sam?

Sam: That mass is the amount of space that matter takes up in a three-dimensional object.

Teacher: Excellent use of full sentences, Sam! The reason we are to refer to three-dimensional objects is because objects in the real world have three dimensions that are length, width and depth.

Individual recap

Pupils recap individually by answering questions in their exercise books, enabling the teacher to assess their own understanding of volume and mass. The teacher should circulate the classroom during individual recap to gather data on which pupils are making mistakes, and to assist the weakest with trouble spots. As the time for recap comes to an end, the teacher will choose pupils to contribute answers, whilst other pupils self-mark their work with a green pen.

1. State the common units of measurement for the volume of solids.
2. State the two things that matter must have.
3. Complete the formula used to calculate the volume of a regular cuboid object.
4. State the common units of measurement mass.
5. Define volume.
6. Define mass.

Whole-class reading

The teacher introduces the concept of density by nominating pupils to read sections of the textbook aloud. The teacher stops at natural points in the reading to clarify, restate or expand upon points raised in the text. The whole class chants key facts or procedures in order to aid memorisation. The teacher cold calls pupils, asking them simple comprehension questions, to ensure understanding and maintain focus.

Yasmine: The sixth physical property that we use to describe matter in a solid, liquid or gas state is the density of matter.

Teacher: Last lesson, we learned about five of the physical properties used to describe matter in a solid, liquid or gas state: compressibility, intermolecular forces between atoms or molecules, movement of atoms or molecules, volume and shape. State *all* six physical properties, Abdi.

Abdi: Compressibility, intermolecular forces, movement, volume, shape and density.

Teacher: Thank you, Abdi. Leah, continue reading.

Leah: Density is the mass of a substance per given volume.

Teacher: I say, you say: density is the mass of a substance per given volume...

Whole class: Density is the mass of a substance per given volume!

Teacher: Density is the mass of a substance per given volume. One, two, three...

Whole class: Density is the mass of a substance per given volume!

Teacher: Define density, Mischa.

Mischa: Density is the mass of a substance per given volume.

Teacher: Fantastic listening, Mischa. Joseph, take over from Mischa.

Joseph: This 'given' volume is most often one cubic centimeter, or one millilitre.

Teacher: So, density tells us the mass of a substance per given volume, which is usually one cubic centimetre. Density is usually the mass of a substance per what given volume? One, two, three...

Whole class: One cubic centimetre!

Teacher: I say, you say: density is the mass of a substance per given volume, usually one cubic centimetre. One, two, three...

Whole class: Density is the mass of a substance per given volume, usually one cubic centimetre!

Teacher: Next, Ashley.

Ashley: So, when we talk about density, we are talking about the mass of one cubic centimetre or one millilitre of a substance. The formula for calculating density is: density = mass / volume.

Teacher: To calculate density, density equals what? Kevin!

Kevin: Density equals mass divided by volume, miss.

Teacher: Thank you, Kevin. Aaliyah, continue reading.

Aaliyah: The most obvious way of finding the density of a material is to measure its volume and mass. The unit of volume can be cubic metres or cubic centimetres for matter in a solid state and litres or millilitres for matter in a liquid state. The unit of mass can be kilograms or grams. The most common unit of density is grams per cubic centimetre.

Teacher: Thank you, Aaliyah. I say, you say: density is measured in grams per cubic centimetre. One, two, three...

Whole class: Density is measured in grams per cubic centimetre!

Teacher: So, density is the mass of a substance per given volume, usually one cubic centimetre. The common unit of measurement for density is grams per cubic centimetre. Alexandra, continue reading.

Alexandra: This means that when we find out the density of a substance, we are finding out how many grams are in one cubic centre of that substance. It might be surprising to learn that the mass of one cubic centimetre of mercury is not the same as the mass of one cubic centimetre of gold, nor is it the same as the mass of one cubic centimetre of carbon dioxide.

Teacher: Look closely at Figure 3.36 to check out the masses of one cubic centimetre of different substances. Identify the substance with the highest density. Summer!

Summer: The substance with the highest density is gold, miss.

Teacher: Thank you, Summer.

Individual drill

These six short drill questions assess pupil understanding of what has been read and taught. If pupils finish, they are expected to memorise one or two definitions related to the lesson using the Michaela method, self-quizzing. The teacher will choose pupils to contribute answers, whilst other pupils self-mark their work with a green pen. An example of these drill questions can be:

1. State the unit(s) of volume for solid matter.
2. State the unit(s) of volume for liquid matter.
3. State the unit(s) of mass.
4. Identify the unit of density.
5. State the formula for calculating density.
6. Define density.
7. Self-quiz on density.

Whole-class instruction

The whole class looks at examples together. There are a number of ways to do this, such as instructing pupils to look over the examples in silence, modelling examples on the visualiser or board, instructing pupils to whisper an explanation of the example to their partner or nominating a pupil to read through the example.

Teacher: Imagine that you have cubes of solid gold, solid magnesium, liquid water, liquid mercury and carbon dioxide gas all held in an invisible cuboid container. Imagine that next to that you have a ruler and some scales. The length, width and height of each of these cubes equates to one centimetre. Therefore, all of the cubes have a volume of one cubic centimetre. However, put them on the scales, and you will find out that all of the five different substances have different masses. The mass of one cubic centimetre of gold is 19.7 grams, magnesium is 1.7 grams, water is one gram, mercury is 7.6 grams and carbon dioxide is 0.002 grams. This is because the atoms, molecules or compounds that make up some of those substances are closer together than the atoms, molecules or compounds that make up some of the other substances. This is density. Density is the mass of a given volume of a substance. The molecules or compounds are also composed of different atoms that have different masses.

The teacher can use the board and work through the procedure for calculating density.

Individual drill

Having explained the concept, the remainder of lesson time can be used to drill pupils to ensure that they can effectively complete taught procedures.

1.   The mass of a substance is 30 g and its volume is 120 cm^3. Calculate the density of the substance.

2.   The volume of a substance is 200 cm^3 and its density is 1.5 g/cm^3. Calculate the mass of the substance.

3.   The mass of a substance is 1 kg and its volume is 450 cm^3. Calculate the density of the substance.

4.   The mass of a substance is 45 g and its density is 0.5 g/cm^3. Calculate the volume of the substance.

[Another eight questions on calculating density.]

13.   Define the term 'density.'

14.   Identify the substance from questions 1-12 with the highest density.

15.   Identify the substance in Figure 3.36 with the lowest density.

16.   Self-quiz on 'density.'

Many educationalists, both past and present, have criticised the value of didactic teaching and of drill. Educationalists such as Dewey, Piaget and

Vygotsky believed that if teachers crafted learning environments carefully enough, they could pique the curiosity of children to the point that the children taught themselves. Rather than the teacher transmitting knowledge to children, this child-centred approach enabled children to pursue their own inclinations and interests. This shift in the view of the teacher as the fountain of knowledge to a facilitator of learning began in the early 1960s and is known as progressivism. When proponents of progressive education refer to drill and didactic teaching, they often use pejorative terms such as 'drill and kill' and 'rote learning.' It is often claimed that drill and didactic teaching take the joy out of learning, and that such methods are ineffective.

Progressive argument 1: Teachers should let pupils discover

The phrase 'think like scientists' is regularly mentioned. In a Science laboratory, progressive approaches would require pupils to discuss and hypothesise the expected outcome of an experiment, even if their underpinning scientific knowledge is shaky or relatively new, and then carry out the experiment to discover for themselves. A few pupils will be able understand through discovery, albeit with very basic understandings. The majority of pupils either fail to discover or develop misconceptions that are difficult to resolve, or worse, identify. Experts need to acknowledge that even the greatest scientists did not think like experts when they started out. They thought like novices. As Daniel Willingham explains, history has taught us that the most important scientific discoveries were made as a result of accumulating knowledge and experience over years.

Imagine the 30-year-old puzzle of the Rubik's cube. It would be every eager child's (and adult's!) dream to discover the secrets of solving the cube. However, only a tiny number are able to work it out for themselves, with the majority becoming bored and disenchanted within a few minutes, as my colleague Jessica Lund discovered. Then another colleague, who herself had been taught the methods to solve the cube, taught Jessica explicitly the algorithm involved. Jessica took the Rubik's cube to her form class and within days there were 20 children engrossed as they had been given the necessary information needed to complete the cube. There is a lesson to be learned here: give learners the necessary information and opportunities to practise, and their enthusiasm won't go to waste. Hattie's 2009 statistical meta-analyses show that minimally guided constructivism or discovery-based learning does not work best in improving pupil achievement. Much of the time, discovery fails to materialise, but with sufficient drill and didactic teaching, enduring success over time can be guaranteed.

Cognitive scientists such as Willingham, Adrian de Groot and Herbert Simon have studied experts in various fields and found that knowledge acquisition is key. The most important difference between the best and weakest chess players is the knowledge they have of typical chess positions. There are as many as 1000 different vent configurations that a chicken sexer must learn to competently differentiate between male and female chickens. These are feats of memory. Thousands of hours of drill and didactic teaching are needed to become an expert at something. This is what children are missing. There are no shortcuts to academic achievement: we cannot fast-forward time. Cognitive science findings from the past century should cause teachers to think about the opportunity cost of discovery-based learning.

Progressive argument 2: Teachers should talk less

Ofsted requirements around 2012 encouraged teachers to give children more autonomy in the classroom. In my initial teacher training, observation feedback based on Ofsted guidance would warn me to talk less, as imparting facts through talking was not believed to aid learning. In many 21st century Western schools, the teacher is no longer seen as the figure of authority; their role is to discuss ideas with children to enable them to construct new knowledge. Newly qualified teachers share comments in the staffroom and online such as: 'For my final NQT term, I am reverting back to group tables. I hope it will remind me that it is me that needs to stop talking.'

Concepts such as density weren't stumbled across, but were in fact discovered by, as put by Daisy Christodoulou, 'geniuses with exceptional insight.' There are reasons why reading methods such as 'Look and Say', in which pupils were expected to pick up the ability to read, resulted in a decline in literacy levels. Knowledge that was invented or discovered by geniuses is not instantly intuitive to school-age children. If this knowledge is not explained to pupils, they are left to discover for themselves and end up floundering.

Encouraging pupils to blindly guess and somehow discover scientific principles haphazardly for themselves, rather than explicitly instructing, will not aid pupil comprehension. Didactic teaching means teachers do most of the talking and, given that they are the fountain of knowledge in the classroom, what is wrong with that? For a long time, I felt extremely guilty about telling pupils things: I had been indoctrinated into a constructivist method of teaching. I was led to believe that children are more likely to make meaning of knowledge and remember it if they are involved in the discovery and construction of knowledge. This is untrue. Research, such as the 2006 Kirschner, Sweller and Clark study, found that when novices are learning new knowledge, learning is most effective when they are explicitly instructed. Pupils require clear explanations, worked examples and opportunities for purposeful practice. Didactic teaching works best to teach knowledge. How can we best embed knowledge into long-term memory? Drill, drill, drill!

Progressive argument 3: Drilling isn't real learning

As Joe Kirby explains in his chapter on homework, self-quizzing is the homework that we set all pupils at Michaela; every pupil drills the same definitions for hundreds of scientific, historical, literary and mathematical concepts each year in school. Many teacher friends ask similar questions such as, 'what will you do for GCSE?', 'how is drilling definitions going to help in essay subjects?' and 'how do you know if pupils have actually learned anything?'

The answer I give is always the same. Working memory is highly limited, with scientific research suggesting that young people struggle to hold more than five items in their working memory at any one time. Discovery-based learning requires pupils to sift through new information and this places heavy demands on working memory. The information cannot accumulate into long-term memory while working memory is being used. We have already seen the amount of knowledge pupils need to comprehend a single complex, abstract concept like density. Inflexible knowledge has only been introduced, accessed and understood on a surface level, compared to flexible knowledge, which can be accessed, understood and applied outside of the context in which it was first introduced. In order to commit inflexible knowledge to memory, pupils must drill concepts thousands of times. Memorisation through drill files knowledge into long-term memory and so alleviates working memory to enable pupils to apply what they know to a new scenario, be it a Physics examination, English literature essay or university admissions interview. As pupils drill the knowledge we teach, their store of knowledge will become increasingly flexible, as will their ability to use that knowledge.

A feat of long-term memory is that of the London cab driver. In London, cab drivers must commit an average of 34 months to studying the 25,000 streets in the world's most demanding training course for cab drivers, which is known as Knowledge of London. Hopeful cab drivers must pass at least 12 'appearances': one-on-one oral examinations where, without consulting a map, applicants must recite the shortest and most sensible route from one landmark to another. In order to prepare for appearances, applicants spend months motorcycling around London learning 320 specified routes. They then pair up with a 'call-over partner' who helps to drill and practise the routes that they have spent the last days, weeks and months learning. Much like the self-quizzing method at Michaela, pupils of the cab trade learn the route explicitly and then drill it thousands of times. Appearances get increasingly challenging; applicants may get asked questions about more complex routes to and from temporary events and theatre shows, which incorporate obstacles such as road closures, multiple drop-offs and even instructions to avoid road humps.

It is this constant drilling of inflexible knowledge that enables flexibility to happen, which explains how, over time, applicants can be expected to apply their knowledge of the streets to take into account a temporary event or road closure. Whilst they may never have been explicitly taught how to manoeuvre around that particular obstacle, they have such a wealth of knowledge about the streets of London in their long-term memory that they can easily come up with an alternative route. In contrast to drilling, discovery-based learning does not result in changes to long-term memory, therefore preventing pupils from accessing and applying knowledge to new contexts as London cab drivers are able to do.

Progressive argument 4: Drill and didactic teaching is boring

A Science teacher at another school who had heard about the drill and didactic teaching employed at Michaela asked me, 'do your kids hate Science yet?' Drill and didactic teaching can be boring if pitched and paced incorrectly, but so can progressive teaching approaches. In fact, drill pitched at a challenging but accessible level can leave pupils feeling successful, confident and able to conquer complex problems. Progressive approaches to teaching enable children to pursue their own inclinations and interests related to the lessons, which often end up as distractions. Willingham tells of such lessons where pupils baked biscuits with the recipe used by the American slaves who escaped the Deep South. Such a lesson would be promoted by progressive educationalists as good practice: a memorable, fun lesson in which pupils are engaged. However, it is likely that the baking element of the lesson would have dominated pupils' cognitive processes, with very little thought given to the American slaves who originally baked them.

In contrast, the sort of lesson supporters of didactic teaching advocate comprise frequent, challenging drills. Regular practice ensures that pupils experience satisfaction linked to successfully answering challenging drill questions and that they feel as though every second counts, making it highly unlikely that pupils will feel bored. As a result, drill and didactic teaching works at improving both academic performance and motivation, whereas a child-centred teaching method can side-track pupils from the actual learning and reduce subject comprehension. Far from seeing drills that kill motivation, visitors to Michaela see drills that thrill pupils who are, every day, growing in academic confidence and thriving at school.

Most teacher-training institutions in England subscribe to the progressive view of education, and so demonise drill and didactic teaching. This is highly problematic because most uninformed, unqualified teachers view teacher-training institutions as experts and do not question their doctrine. Would an undergraduate medical student doubt their professor? No. As a PGCE student, nor did I. In my experience, the conversations that dominated staffrooms were predominantly focused on 'talk-less teaching' and how to make learning discovery-based, engaging and fun because, as Barry Smith expands on, teachers were led to believe that this resulted in effective learning. It would have been considered blasphemous to suggest that progressive methods were ineffective. Despite the staggering evidence base in favour of extended practice drills, educationalists cling to these less effective teaching methods, having been indoctrinated into these progressive methods during their initial teacher training.

It is ironic that the teacher-training institutions that advocate education based around discussion and discovery are the very same institutions that indoctrinate unqualified teachers with their one-sided progressive values. Teachers are explicitly taught not to explicitly teach! Just because plugging constructivist pedagogies during your training year meant that you sailed through assignments and observations, it does not mean they work best.

Michaela's tagline is 'Knowledge is Power.' In Science, we are already seeing powerful, cumulative, compound effects of all our pupils' scientific knowledge. Our year 8 pupils can draw the atomic structure of 20 elements of the periodic table from memory. In my previous, progressively-minded school, many could not do this by the end of year 11. By the end of year 8, our pupils can balance complex chemical equations and connect them to complex processes such as combustion, rusting and photosynthesis. Our pupils can remember by heart hundreds of complex scientific concepts such as, in electricity for example, ions, amps, voltage, current, circuits, insulators, resistance and the interactions between them as directly or inversely proportional, explaining why. This is to name just a handful of concepts from our first year 8 knowledge organiser – and electricity is in itself just one topic out of six for year 8, in just one subject. We are hugely ambitious in the breadth and depth of subject expertise that we expect our pupils to master and remember across our nine subjects.

It is didactic instruction in rigorous knowledge of the intricacies of science that will enable our pupils to go and study Biochemistry or Physics at university, not jazzy, whizz-bang experiments undertaken with minimal guidance and maximum collaboration or 'co-construction.'

Pupils love knowing things. We should never underestimate the satisfaction our pupils gain from being taught an inspiring collection of wonderful facts by the most effective vehicles for subject knowledge transmission: drill, and didactic teaching.

How Reluctant Readers Learn to Love Reading

Katie Ashford

With a third of our pupils arriving at the beginning of year 7 with reading ages below their chronological age, there is much work to do to help them catch up as quickly as possible. A highly academic curriculum rich in literary masterpieces is utterly life-changing, but it is incumbent upon us to ensure that it is not reserved only for those who can already access it. If we want to be able to give every child the opportunity to read these enriching, broadening texts throughout secondary school, we must prioritise a rigorous, robust reading strategy that enables swift progress and engenders a deep, lifelong love of reading.

It is no secret that often those who excel in reading actually read the most, and that those who struggle with reading read least. Predictably, this leads to an ever-expanding gap between readers and non-readers. It's no surprise then that by the end of Key Stage 4, approximately 17% of 16-year-olds leave school functionally illiterate. If those who are furthest behind never get the practice they so desperately need to catch up, they will be left behind forever, academically malnourished, starting life on an uneven, bumpy playing field, with far fewer life chances ahead of them than they would otherwise have.

Perhaps more worryingly, the gap in reading success leads to a gap in love for reading. Every teacher knows a child whose reading was so weak that the thought of opening a book filled him with dread. The fact that most teachers have lost count of these kids demonstrates that the problem is profound. Children who dislike reading quickly get stuck into a perpetual downward spiral: can't read, hate reading; hate reading, don't read; don't read, can't read.

At Michaela, in an attempt to break the cycle, we have chosen to put reading firmly at the centre of everything we do. Our relentless focus on supporting the weakest readers to get maximum practice and optimal reading instruction has enabled them to make up to five years' progress in reading in just under a year.

Starting with the basics

Time is short and we have to make sure that every child has the reading skills they require right from the start. If a child has not learned to read by age 11, all is not lost. It can be turned round, but it takes time and patience. Getting the basics in place ensures that all pupils get the support they need right away.

We use a robust phonics programme and implement it as early as possible in year 7. If pupils struggle to decode, this typically means that they will find it hard to read and spell unfamiliar words. A good phonics programme will help pupils to overcome this quickly. In the first term of year 7, our weakest readers forgo French so that they can receive up to four hours of reading instruction each week. Once the basics have been embedded, pupils return to French and receive an extra hour of the language per week to make up for time lost. Our French teachers agree that studying a language is extraordinarily difficult – and often is not a priority – if one cannot read and write in English.

Reading across the curriculum

At Michaela, all teachers embed reading into their lessons. Our philosophy is simple: anything you explain verbally could be written down for pupils to read. Not only does this approach iron out the problems some teachers may have with off-the-cuff explanations of new or complex concepts, it allows all children to read hundreds or thousands of words every lesson. If every teacher does this, it means that, on an average day, the weakest readers at Michaela will encounter around 12,000 words.

The method is simple: every child receives a printed copy of the text. These are usually booklets produced by the Heads of Department. Each line has been numbered so that it is easier for every child to follow. Pupils place their rulers below the first line and are expected to follow along with the rest of the class. Usually, teachers will read the majority of the text aloud, asking every child to read a sentence or two at some point in the lesson, combining a cluster of techniques called 'Control the Game,' explained in detail by Doug Lemov in *Teach Like a Champion*. This keeps pupils highly accountable and ensures they follow along. If, when being called upon to read, a child does not know where we are, they receive a demerit as a reminder to stay on track. The cumulative effect of such high expectations during all lessons ensures that as close as possible to 100% of pupils read 100% of the words on the page every single lesson.

Michaela teachers read beautifully to children. Whilst children are frequently given the opportunity to read aloud, we recognise that teachers are usually the best readers in the room. Teachers model expression, projection and pronunciation of difficult words. When the class comes across a new or particularly complex word, the teacher simply pauses to say 'I say, you say' before saying the word clearly, and the kids repeat it back in unison.

If you ever come to visit Michaela, you will see how consistent this approach is. In every classroom, across the curriculum, this happens at some point every single lesson. Even in Maths, where pupils spend a huge amount of time practising and drilling themselves in core concepts and processes, many explanations are delivered through this medium.

The benefits are plentiful, as it gives pupils more access to more words in more contexts. Gradually, this builds pupils' vocabularies and gives them access to a broad range of new, high level words. This approach also enables pupils to see and understand how the same words can be used in a variety of different ways. For example, the word 'structure' has subtly different uses in English, as in the structure of a poem, sentence or novel, than in Science, in terms of the structure of a cell, atom or molecule. Seeing the same words in different contexts helps to improve pupils' understanding of the nuance of language. The cumulative effect of this exposure to such quantities of new words not only improves pupils' reading ability and confidence in reading but also their courage to express themselves using a broader vocabulary.

Reading for pleasure

Reading is not purely beneficial for learning. Its intrinsic worth is boundless, and we want every single pupil to benefit from the richness that a life filled with books can provide. To that end, we insist on broad reading during tutor time, after school and independently.

The trouble with reading is that it takes time to really get into it. It requires dedication and commitment, attributes that are often somewhat underdeveloped in the average 11-year-old. Tackling a classic or a book about a topic in which you have absolutely no knowledge or real interest seems overwhelming and, frankly, a bit dull. I rarely fancy delving into a compendium of historical battles, for example. But as an adult, I have a broad enough experience of reading that I can at least read around topics of varied interest and invest in the more niche aspects of my preferences at will. The problem for children – and in particular, the weakest readers – is that at such a young age one has had very few life experiences. Combine that with a disadvantaged start in life, having only visited a few places or having had little access to cultural knowledge, and a child's world view and range of interests can be limited. The consequence of this is that children rarely want to read things that push them out of their comfort zone. Let's face it, if you were 11, would you rather read the comically illustrated *The Diary of A Wimpy Kid* or the dauntingly complex *Wuthering Heights?*

To overcome this challenge, we treat reading as a habit. Daily reading of a broad range of texts gives children access to hundreds of new titles, topics and areas of interest that they may never otherwise have encountered. Our Class Reader programme, skilfully orchestrated and administered by my brilliant colleagues Jo Facer and Joe Allan, does precisely this.

Every day, in form time, tutor groups read the same book together with their tutors, in the same manner as we read in lessons with rulers on the page and everyone following along. A box of 33 copies of the same title are delivered to rooms (on an intricately scheduled basis, carefully sequenced and designed by logistical magician Joe Allan), and every day, during tutor time, everybody reads a section from the book. We have deliberately chosen titles that provide children with the most cultural capital, but also that offer the best characters, ideas, writing and scope. The intention of the Class Reader programme is to give children access to books that they would never otherwise read. Texts such as *To Kill A Mockingbird*, *Dracula*, and *The Hunchback of Notre Dame* rarely jump off the shelves in the average school library, but children are quickly amazed by these stories, quickly coming to see why they have endured for decades or centuries.

A further benefit of reading these texts as a class during tutor time is that weaker readers have a teacher to guide them through it. Rather than reading alone at home and struggling, a teacher is on hand to pause and explain new or difficult words and prompt pupils to explore important concepts or moral questions.

Our weakest readers stay for 30 minutes after school every day for reading clubs. Jo Facer, our Head of English, and Lia Martin and Sarah Cullen, two of our English teachers, guide these pupils through even more books. These titles, again selected and sequenced by Jo Facer, are deliberately intended to be more pupil-friendly, with titles that are a sort of halfway house between 'classics' and the books they'd pick up on their own. They tear through *The Red Pony*, *Fahrenheit 451*, *The Woman in Black* and many others. Again, these books are challenging for the less able readers, but with the support of their teachers, are made more accessible. Importantly, this means that the least able readers in the school are reading the most books with adults, and are reading even more broadly than other pupils.

Jo Facer came up with another brilliant idea of 'Friday Reads.' We found that lots of pupils, of all abilities, were struggling to choose books from the library. Jo suggested that we recommend our class one book every Friday. These are from all sorts of genres and appeal to a wide variety of interests. So far, we've had *A Tree Grows in Brooklyn*, *My Sister's Keeper*, *Gone Girl* and many others. We show pupils a picture of the front cover of the book, talk about it a bit, and then tell them where to find it in the library. At lunchtime, loads of kids turn up to grab one of the coveted 'Friday Read' books.

Following the Class Reader theme, we have lots of full class sets of books in the library that pupils can take out together and read in groups. These are called 'Team Reads.' These are a mixture of classics and modern novels, and pupils are welcome to come in to the library at lunchtime and read them together, or take them home to read and discuss. It's lovely to wander in to the library or the playground at lunchtime and see pupils huddled together, reading a book out loud to each other and sharing the experience.

Independent reading

Our pupils are all expected to have a library book with them every day. They read this in silence in morning tutor time and at home in the evenings. This gives kids the flexibility to choose anything they want to read. Interestingly, pupils often choose books related to the topics they are studying in lessons; so we see lots of kids reading about Ancient Egypt or Astronomy, for example. *Tracy Beaker* is still popular, but lots of our pupils challenge themselves to read more widely and push themselves out of their comfort zones.

We have been careful to select good-quality books for our pupils to read. You will never find comic books or magazines in the Michaela library. This is because we know that kids who want to read comics and magazines will nag their parents enough to source them outside of school. As ever, our philosophy is that, as a school, we have a duty to expose children to texts that expand their knowledge of the world.

To achieve this, we painstakingly choose every single book on our library shelves. Every single book our pupils select has been carefully considered. We always ask, 'what would a child get from reading this?' If the answer is a resounding 'not much,' then we simply won't put it on our shelves. This does not mean that our library is filled exclusively with dusty old copies of *Silas Marner* and *Middlemarch*, but rather that titles such as *Captain Underpants and the Perilous Plot of Professor Poopypants* fail to make an appearance. We like to think that we are somewhere between the two extremes, encouraging pupils to read great teen fiction titles such as *The Fault in Our Stars* and *Noughts and Crosses*, and challenging grown-up tomes such as *Life of Pi* and *The Blind Assassin*.

For our weakest readers, these strategies provide a platform for supporting them to become confident readers who continue reading broadly into adulthood. For the rest of our kids, who either don't have any difficulties with reading, or who already love it when they arrive at secondary school, it provides an opportunity to expand and develop their knowledge of the greatest works of literature. I relish the conversations I have with some of more able readers, whether it be discussing whether Gabriel Marcia Marquez's writing is all it's cracked up to be, or whether *Of Mice and Men* provides a better depiction of the Great Depression than *The Grapes of Wrath*. A school-wide culture of reading develops every child, regardless of the starting point, into a curious reader. They become someone who knows what they like and what they dislike, someone who can be both critical and complimentary, and someone who can engage with and someone who can, perhaps one day, even replicate great writing.

The impact of the combination of these strategies is massive. Our school feels like a place of reading, where children think and talk about books often, and where success in reading is the norm. No child is too shy to read aloud. No child fears or severely dislikes reading. No child avoids reading at all costs. All children read, every day. All children come to love it, see its wonder, and understand the power that books can have to change lives.

Marking is Futile

Jo Facer

We don't mark books at Michaela. We also don't let children write at length and then neglect to look at it for days. When Michaela pupils write, they receive feedback the very next day. We can give such swift feedback *because* we don't mark. Marking not only harms teachers' work-life balance, it also damages pupil progress. Marking is futile.

Marking has got out of control

Before Ofsted published a report entitled *Myths* in 2015 claiming that it 'does not expect to see any specific frequency, type or volume of marking and feedback,' marking was spinning out of control. Celebrated bloggers had come to advocate for marking as the cure-all: the panacea. Well-known educators claimed that if everything were going wrong in your classroom, at least marking pupils' work would definitely ensure they made progress. Other prominent edu-bloggers showcased ideas like 'triple impact marking', whereby a pupil's work was marked, improved, marked again, improved again, and marked a third time. Schools endorsed this too, with one large academy chain celebrating it as excellent practice. Teachers were marking books, essays, coursework, assessments; they were filling in assessment sheets, cover sheets, dialogue sheets. When they told a pupil how to improve, they were stamping books with 'verbal feedback given' to please the watchful eyes of the senior leadership team and Ofsted.

Despite the publication of this myth-busting document, teachers around the country are buckling under the weight of a hundred unmarked essays, with all of their Key Stage 3 books mouldering in a hallway or car boot, guiltily, over weekends and holidays. Twitter is full of teachers sharing their morning coffee beside a stack of neatly marked books, full of praise stamps, smiley face stickers and laboriously lengthy comments in rainbow colours. Marking feeds into the Boxer-complex of many teachers: the harder we work, the better we think we will be at our jobs. It comes from a well-intentioned place: in the most chaotic schools, marking is the only way teachers can give individualised feedback. Spending each lesson containing the chaos is not conducive to whispered advice over silent practice. There are marginal gains from marking, as evidenced by any teacher of coursework's laborious comments on draft 23 finally bringing candidate Y to the magic C.

Marking is not a panacea

Those who advocate marking do so through three main arguments. The first is that marking motivates children. How often have I heard: 'if you don't care enough to mark their books, why should they care enough to put effort into their writing?' Such comments stem from the initial assumption that teacher and pupil are equals, an assumption we at Michaela challenge; we are the professional experts, they are the children and novices. Secondly, some argue that marking enables teachers to know pupils better; yet the reading of every pen mark on a page is surely no one's chief guide to true understanding. Finally, they will argue on the basis of personalised and individualised teaching that marking is the best way to differentiate, as you can tailor your feedback, guidance, and even instruction to the individual child. I have seen examples on Twitter of written marking explaining how to use an apostrophe in each individual child's book who could not do so. Such labour-intensive personalisation of instruction, while being undeniably well meant, is misguided.

We have to ask ourselves, what is the impact of marking? At Michaela, we see every decision through the effort-to-impact ratio. Which decisions are butterflies – low-effort for teachers but high-impact for pupils? Which decisions are hornets – stingingly time-consuming for teachers and minimally effective for pupils? A number of years ago, some switched-on teachers were starting to clock that marking was a hornet – burdensome for teachers and ineffective for pupils. The first step was taken: the issue with marking was that pupils did nothing with that feedback. Thus DIRT was launched – Directed Improvement and Reflection Time. Teachers were spending eons of time marking, only to have pupils make the same mistakes over and over again. Like many a modern novelist languishing in the bargain basement of the local bookshop, teachers' painstakingly thoughtful comments were going unread. The focus shifted to ensure teachers gave pupils time to reflect on the marking, writing out corrections and explaining how they could improve. Hallelujah, finally marking was leading to improvement!

This was an illusion. Not only did such improvements sprawl into the aforementioned 'triple marking' madness, where teachers were now expected to mark the new writing and the corrections pupils had made using their feedback; but teachers began to realise that while their pupils may be improving, they were essentially writing the same comments in book after book after book. Moreover, marking policies and deadlines continued to be set by members of the senior leadership team, often teaching only a single class themselves, who simply had no understanding of the impact of this on teachers or, when alerted, simply dismissed complainers as lazy. Marking, always Sisyphean, had collapsed under the weight of its own contradictions.

Those who did prostrate themselves to worship at the altar of marking entered what we at Michaela call the 'hero teacher arms race.' Hero teachers are those in difficult schools who not only survive but also seem to thrive. They are the ones all the children love. Their classrooms are bastions of learning, a calm island in a tempestuous sea of choppy chaos. They aren't just marking in line with the policy; they are actually going *beyond* the policy. They are choosing to mark all weekend, all holiday, and every evening. They are choosing to mark books, quizzes, assessments, coursework and mock exams; even though marking only one of these would clear them for the 'every two weeks' remit. They tell themselves, and anyone who cares to listen, that they mark because they care. But all this does is create an arms race: another hero teacher comes along and wants to show they care even more. So what do they do? They mark even more. Without pausing to consider whether they make the right choice, hero teachers simply go above and beyond on every front. See a policy, do more than the policy. Many of these heroes go on to be swiftly promoted to the senior leadership team, where they express the desire for others to achieve excellence by doing more.

In such schools, desperate teachers keen to avoid the polar labels of 'heroes' or 'lazy' advocated 'icon marking' in an effort to comply with unreasonable marking policies. Yet many teachers began to suspect they had been duped: that marking was not a panacea. In fact, it seemed plausible that marking was actually making the children *worse at writing*.

When Michaela opened in 2014, the founding team pioneered another way. At Michaela, we don't mark any books, ever. We don't mark because we don't want hero teachers, we want a team. We don't want one shining star; we want all our teachers and pupils to shine. We don't mark because pupils are not customers and teachers are not slaves. We are not at the beck and call of our charges. At Michaela, we believe in personal responsibility: we don't serve children, just like we don't pity them for their disadvantage. We actually hold pupils back when we mark, because in marking we make the effort to spot the mistake for them, and we make the effort to correct the mistake for them. By not marking, we thrust this responsibility where it belongs: with the pupils themselves.

What we do at Michaela

At Michaela, we don't simply teach and ignore the writing. We are keenly aware of the gap between our pupils' writing and the writing of pupils at private schools. Many of our kids come to us unable to write for sustained periods of time, making errors in grammar and spelling, and writing garbled nonsense. Yet we have found that even these pupils do not require individualised feedback in their books to make progress in their writing.

Writing is high on the agenda: we are always looking for ways to help pupils improve their writing that are low effort, high impact. Without the tie of accountability for marking through traditional 'book looks,' where was the pressure to ensure teachers read the kids' books? I, myself, had found marking helpful previously as it held me accountable. I have to actually read what the pupil has written carefully if I need to put pen to paper to say something about it. Yet while this might have been essential, those 7am pre-intervention session Saturdays when I needed to clear the last 20 books to enjoy the semblance of a weekend when I returned home that afternoon, or the mid-week 9pm marking session when I just really, really wanted to sleep; actually, I had underestimated my ability to focus.

To begin with at Michaela, I couldn't get out of the habit of marking. I would spend two hours with about 60 books, circling and underlining when I couldn't resist, writing limitless notes to share with the class and photocopying paragraphs to get pupils to annotate their peers' examples. The comments I received on this kind of feedback were questions such as, 'would you want all teachers to be photocopying twice or three times a week?', 'is it worth the time getting the pupils to annotate a piece of paper they are then just throwing away?', 'what else could you be doing with that time?'

Of particular interest was the discovery of the pitfall of marking, pupil helplessness. Alongside my guilty red-pen circles, residues of six years of marking experience, I would also deliver whole-class feedback, delivering comments like, 'check you have put commas in the correct places.' This would recap on a recent grammar lesson that involved the rules of commas. In a school where no one else was marking, if I put the merest hint of a red pen on a child's book, my whole-class feedback was discounted as hands shot up.

'Why have you circled here, Miss?'
'You need a comma.'
'Miss, what about here?"
'You need a comma.'
'Miss...'
'Everybody listen! If you have a red mark in your book, please think about why it might be there. You might need a comma.'

It was infuriating, but illuminating. Marking distracts from instruction. It reduces the pupil's responsibility to really read, think, check, correct and improve what they have done. If they are reminded of what they know, they then have to go painstakingly through each line, assessing and finding where they must improve. And they can and do – even in year 7, even in the lowest stream. Marking, conversely, breeds over-dependence on the teacher.

After this experience, it was easy to convert to the Michaela way of helping pupils improve their writing. Let me outline what that feedback looks like.

I teach English, and four classes: each with between 28 and 32 pupils, so around 120 books in all. With two free periods a day, I could read my pupils' books any day. I read them after they have written an extended paragraph, which is normally once or twice a week. I read 60 books in about 30 minutes. As I read, I make notes: spellings lots are getting wrong, things they're all doing well at, and the main issues they need to improve. I note down anyone whose paragraph is especially impressive to reward with merits or show the class using the visualiser; I note down anyone whose work is messy to give a demerit to.

Our first aim at Michaela is to ensure our pupils are writing accurately, so spelling is at the forefront of the feedback we give. Before even talking about the paragraphs, I talk about spellings. There are usually between six and 12 in any feedback session. Taking advantage of the 'testing effect,' we teach explicitly and then test repeatedly to help pupils remember these spellings.

For example, I will say:
'Referring... referring... Who can spell referring?'
Hands shoot up.
'R-E-F-F...'
'Stop there – no.'
More hands.
'R-E-F-E-R-R-I-N-G.'
'Thank you! Referring has one F, and three R's. Lots of you muddled this up. Remember: referring: one F, three R's. One F, three R's. Say after me: one F, three R's.'
The children chorus: 'One F, three R's.'

Immediately after going through each spelling in this way or similar, I say: 'front of your books, one to eight.' And test them. Immediately. Straight after instruction, many achieve 100%, which builds their confidence from the outset. Reminding them that they may have got it right now but didn't when writing the paragraphs I read, I give them between one and three minutes to 'green pen.' This is where pupils choose the three hardest words, write them out, interleaving them (so not: 'referring referring referring' but 'referring repetition implies') and then checking them. The next day, I revisit these by saying 'back of your books, one to eight.'

This method of spelling is admittedly reactive. We therefore collate these spellings to improve both our spelling sequence (pupils learn 60 key spellings a year) and to improve our work packs, so we can hopefully explicitly teach these in future well enough that pupils will not get them wrong in writing.

The next step is to read out merits and demerits. We do this publicly, as always, celebrating those who have done well and visibly showing our disappointment with those whose paragraphs revealed a lack of effort. Merits are given for massive improvements in writing, as well as impressive insights or excellent expression. Demerits are issued for lack of effort, messy writing or presentation and poor use of space.

I then share the positive things I found. This may take longer for year 7 pupils; there are often pupils who are already far ahead in their writing and the gap is large for the rest of the class. Often, there is a whole-class misconception, and the best way to address this is to write what we call a 'Show Sentence' paragraph. For example, my year 7 pupils were very poor at linking their ideas together logically, so I spent the first part of the feedback talking through how I would structure my ideas in a paragraph. We take the first sentence from a pupil and then write it out, saying as we go improvements to that sentence. Katie Ashford gives an example of such a conversation about a *Macbeth* paragraph:

Teacher: Okay, so Charlie said 'Shakespeare combines alliteration, rhyme and chiasmus.' That was a great start. I'd like us to use a synonym for 'combines' to improve this sentence. Anyone have any ideas? Ushra?

Ushra: Shakespeare fuses alliteration, rhyme and chiasmus, Miss.

Teacher: Excellent. I really like the use of the word 'fuses' there. But now I want us to turn this into a Show Sentence. So what does Shakespeare fuse these three techniques to show? Turn to your partner for 30 seconds.

Once 30 seconds pass the teacher gets the pupils' attention again.

Okay, hands up, what does Shakespeare fuse these techniques to show? Ray?

Ray: Shakespeare fuses alliteration, rhyme and chiasmus to show the witches' sorcery.

Teacher: Love it! Can we use a synonym for 'to show' though, Ray?

Ray: Shakespeare fuses alliteration, rhyme and chiasmus to emphasise the witches' sorcery.

Other parts of the feedback include re-teaching. This can include the rules of commas or apostrophes or the kinds of appropriate comments we want them to be making in their analysis of literature. Contrast this with traditional marking. Seeing a missing apostrophe, we could write 'use the apostrophe accurately,' or we could give some extra examples; but the apostrophe is almost bafflingly complex, with at least five rules guiding its usage. If one child has misused an apostrophe, all can gain from overlearning these rules – and it is rarely only one child who holds such misconceptions. Re-teaching, and then planning into the unit additional practice drills, supports children to all write more accurately.

It must be said that a knowledge curriculum significantly aids this kind of feedback. In a skills-based curriculum, teachers are tinkering around the edges, looking for marginal gains, or quick wins through using connectives in English, for example. In a knowledge curriculum, improvement is easy for children to see: add more knowledge. The better the pupils know about plot, character, vocabulary, technique and context in English, the better their paragraphs will be. Rather than saying: 'could you analyse more?', which is impossible for many children who believe that what they have produced is analysis, you say: 'could you include [insert specific thing they know]?' You remind them of the context they have learned, the vocabulary, the techniques, and you ask them to combine this knowledge in their writing.

Following instruction, I then summarise the two key things pupils need to improve quickly (when we mark we might find as many as ten things the class could improve, but this is overloading for children and they often find it impossible to follow and remember every piece of advice), and give them around ten minutes to improve their paragraphs, circling all the while to give merits to those who are putting in maximum effort to improve their writing.

The onus is very much on the children to listen carefully and then improve their paragraphs. To begin with, a handful of pupils continued to express helplessness; these tended to be the least well behaved of the children. I would simply repeat the key pieces of advice, and express disappointment that they had not listened carefully enough. This is usually enough to quash any overdependence.

The second powerful tool at Michaela is in-class feedback. With an excellent behaviour system, silent writing for 25 minutes means I can see every child's work at least twice while circulating, giving them suggestions and tweaks while they write. This classic 'intervention at the point of writing' was always the aim in each of my previous schools, but it definitely takes a strong behaviour system to sustain absolute silence to the extent that you can spend some time with weaker writers. The same is true in all other Michaela lessons, including Maths where they intervene at the point of 'working out'.

Every classroom at Michaela also contains a visualiser. Rather than laboriously typing out paragraphs, we can instead thrust a book under the visualiser, and narrate what makes this pupil's paragraph good, and what they could improve on. Doug Lemov, in *Teach Like a Champion 2.0*, calls this method 'Show Call', and explains:

Show call is incredibly powerful accountability tool for writing. If you were to Show Call predictably, students in the class would feel a strong incentive to complete all writing with quality and thoughtfulness... Imagine if you went a step further and asked the class to analyse and revise [the student's] paper, suggesting specific revisions and edits. Show call enables a teacher to ask for precise, actionable analysis.

Once the book is under the visualiser, the teacher can lead the revisions and encourage pupils to green pen at the same time ('Hamza has misspelt Shelley! Have you? Tick every letter as I write it out: S-H-E-L-L-E-Y.' 'Elena has said "suggests," but can we think of a better synonym? Find where you have written "suggests" in your own paragraph. What can you change it to?' Cue hands up: 'Evokes?' 'Depicts?' 'Displays'?')

Alternatively, the teacher can use the visualiser to showcase excellent paragraphs. We also pre-empt pupils' difficulties with writing, and fill our units with example paragraphs written by teachers. The best way for children to get better at writing paragraphs is for them to see lots and lots of examples of excellent paragraphs. As the years go on, these teacher paragraphs are often accompanied by a brilliant pupil paragraph. We remind pupils as they write that they could be leaving a great legacy for others with their writing, if it is chosen to be included in the unit for the next year's pupils.

The crucial factor to bear in mind for making feedback useful is both the quality of that feedback and how timely it is. With traditional marking, teachers slog through ten pages a fortnight, laboriously writing comments on what to improve. Pupils then have to go back to that paragraph and remember exactly what they were learning two weeks ago in order to be able to action that feedback. Such improvements made in this way can only ever be surface-level. And the feedback the teacher scribbles in books can never be that high quality at 10pm on a weeknight, or they will soon find another profession.

At Michaela, pupils can improve the paragraph they wrote yesterday while it is fresh in their minds. Teachers can give thoughtful, focused feedback in a timely manner. Pupils have to take responsibility to make improvements to their own writing. As with everything that we do at Michaela, the responsibility is firmly placed on pupils, so that they become the masters of their own fate.

Homework as Revision

Joe Kirby

Reimagining homework

'I am the master of my fate! I am the captain of my soul!' 120 pupils from year 7 recite William Ernest Henley's 1875 poem 'Invictus' from memory in unison to begin family lunch at Michaela. 'Death, a necessary end, will come when it will come!' 120 pupils from year 8 simultaneously recite Caesar's speech on courage by Shakespeare at the end of their lunch break.

In years to come, an abiding shared memory that all pupils, teachers and visitors will have of Michaela Community School is the choral recital that pervades the school, from Shakespeare to 18th and 19th century poets. The lines are memorable, from Kipling's 'If you can keep your head, when all about you, are losing theirs and blaming it on you,' to Blake's 'Hold infinity in the palm of your hand.' So often do we revisit these poems, both in assembly and at lunchtime, the likelihood is that our pupils (and teachers!) will remember these uplifting words as long as they live.

Learning poetry by heart is just the most visible sign of collective memory at Michaela. Not only does each year group memorise the same poems and speeches off by heart so that all 120 pupils can recite them together in unison in assembly, every pupil also learns the same definitions for hundreds of scientific, historical, literary and mathematical and other subject concepts each year in school. This is the alchemy of collective memory: it turns short-term ability into long-term durability.

At Michaela, we have fundamentally reimagined the challenge of homework. As Steve Jobs put it, 'creativity is just connecting things.' We connect homework and revision. Our homework is a seven-year revision plan, from age 11 right up to A-levels. Our starting point was rethinking the challenges of homework and revision for pupils and teachers.

Challenges of homework for pupils

Homework is a tough ask for pupils. They start school at 8am and don't finish until 4pm. That's an eight-hour day and 40-hour week in lessons alone, before homework. Let's not forget that our pupils learn across a far wider breadth of domains than we teachers do. A typical day involves studying Maths, English, Science, Humanities, French and many other subjects, including Art, Music and sport. This is a variety so dizzying that most adults would struggle to concentrate on it for over six hours. Many secondary schools then expect kids to do at least an hour of homework after school, often more, especially before national exams like GCSEs and A-levels. Many schools draw up homework timetables so that pupils don't have too many subjects setting homework on the same evening. Many of us remember shedding tears in the evening over homework that we were struggling with as children. Homework turns 40-hour weeks into long, 45- or even 50-hour weeks. Although we know that in China (where pupils are some three years ahead of English pupils in Maths and Science) children work even harder than this, as do many children in expensive private boarding schools, homework is still a tough ask, especially of our poorest pupils whose home lives are sometimes not conducive to quiet study.

The paradox of homework is that the pupils with the most supportive parents benefit most from it, whereas pupils with the least supportive parents or most chaotic homes are least able to take advantage of its benefits. It therefore widens the achievement gap: wealthier pupils tend to practise more, and poorer pupils tend to practise less. What can be done about this practice gap exacerbating the achievement gap? Ideally, the weakest pupils would do the most homework, not the least, but this ideal is very far from the reality in most schools. The conundrum seems intractable.

We should have high expectations of our pupils' responsibility and work ethic, but we must also design our homework system thoughtfully, setting up all of our pupils to succeed.

Challenges of homework for teachers

Homework is also a tough ask for teachers. Teachers teach between 20 and 30 hours of lessons and form tutor time a week, and must balance that with their preparation, feedback, duties, meetings, department responsibilities, professional development and interactions with parents and pupils. On top of this heavy workload, homework demands that they set, explain, collect, check, mark, track, sanction and chase up the work that they ask of pupils. They must remember which pupils are absent when they set homework, which pupils are absent when they collect homework and which pupils are absent when the sanction (often a detention) is set. For teachers who teach several classes, and over a 150 pupils, keeping all these variables in mind becomes a tall order.

What does a teacher do about pupils who rarely hand in their homework? What does a teacher do about those who fail to record their homework properly? What does a teacher do about those who don't complete homework to a very high standard? Homework for teachers is rife with thorny issues. Compound that with the hundreds of micro-decisions that teacher have to make every day, on behaviour and misbehaviour in or around school, and you quickly see why so many teachers either stop setting or marking it altogether, or find it so hard to chase it up systematically enough, that many pupils end up not completing it at all, without consequence.

Challenges of revision for pupils

For many pupils, revision for GCSE exams is often crammed into a few weeks of the Easter break during year 11 or the start of that exam year. It is rarely coordinated across the school. Teachers think that their own subject is most important, and expect pupils to do some 30 minutes a night, mostly uncoordinated with other subjects.

Equally, pupils are rarely taught the best way to revise. There is a mismatch between how schools set revision and what the science suggests about revision. Schools often recommend re-reading, highlighting and underlining, which leaves pupils feverishly highlighting revision packs in lurid, fluorescent colours. Scientific research suggests, though, that re-reading, highlighting and underlining are not the most effective ways to revise. Instead, strong scientific evidence suggests practice testing and self-quizzing are some of the most effective ways to build durable long-term memory. This research is largely unexplored by many teachers, and only rarely shared with students. Underprepared pupils then underperform in exams. If, as teachers, we fail to prepare them, we are preparing them to fail.

Cramming is an ineffective way to revise, yet in practice many schools ratchet up intervention and pressure in the final years of school, rather than teaching successful revision habits from the first years of schooling. The science is unequivocal: cramming works for the short term, but does not build long-term memory. That explains why I can remember hardly any of my GCSE Physics or Chemistry, even though I achieved A* grades in the Double Award Science GCSE, and why I would almost certainly not get A* grades if I did the exams again now! As teachers, how might we override our pupils' natural tendency to cram before exams, to help them remember and not forget what they're learning?

The struggle of memory and forgetting

The science of learning provides a way forward. Over 100 years of scientific research into how the mind works provides insight that can help teachers and pupils succeed. Over 130 years ago, in 1885, Ebbinghaus studied memories and discovered forgetting curves. The human mind forgets things very quickly: over half of newly learned knowledge is forgotten within a matter of days unless it is revisited. This chimes with our intuition: how often have we been introduced to someone and forgotten their name within minutes if we do not revisit it? These studies have been replicated hundreds of times ever since.

Is memorisation all that's important in learning? No, but we should not underestimate its benefits. Cognitive scientists who study learning and the mind tell us:

> Long-term memory is now viewed as the central, dominant structure of human cognition. Everything we see, hear and think about is critically dependent on and influenced by our long-term memory... The aim of all instruction is to change long-term memory. If nothing has changed in long-term memory, nothing has been learned.[1]

In the last 100 years, scientists have studied how humans can remember what they would usually forget. The insights are fascinating. It turns out that distributing extended practice over time is far better for long-term memory retention than cramming massed practice. This has been tested and demonstrated in hundreds of replicable scientific experiments, across learning conditions (reading, listening, writing), student characteristics (age, ability and prior knowledge), materials (problems, texts and questions) and tasks (recall, comprehension and problem solving).

It also turns out that just revisiting and re-reading are not as effective for durable long-term memory retention as quizzing and testing. More than 100 years of research has yielded peer-reviewed, replicated experiments that show that practice testing outperforms restudying. Over the last decade, 11 cognitive psychologists took over 100 years of laboratory research on the testing effect and applied it to classrooms in a decade of applied research. Here is a summary of their findings: 'Use frequent quizzing: testing interrupts forgetting. In virtually all areas of learning, you build better mastery when you use testing as a tool. One of the best habits to instil in a learner is self-quizzing.'

These two insights – distributed, extended practice and practice testing – can be put to use in schools immediately, widely, at no cost, and to great effect. As we started Michaela, we started thinking: what would self-quizzing look like across a whole school? What if we combined revision and homework?

A seven-year revision plan

At Michaela, from year 7 onwards, homework is revision and self-quizzing for all pupils across all their subjects. Revision up to A-level lasts not seven weeks, nor

---

1   'Why Minimal Guidance During Instruction Does Not Work': Kirschner, Sweller and Clark

seven months, but seven years. It is a radical simplification. No longer do teachers have to think up, set or explain their own homework individually. No longer do they have to collect, mark, track, sanction and chase pupils' homework. No longer do pupils have to interpret all different teachers' homework intentions. There's just one simple strategy for revising and remembering knowledge across all subjects. Here's how Michaela's homework-revision ecosystem works: we combine knowledge organisers, knowledge books, practice books, class quizzes and practice book checks.

Knowledge organisers

First, all departments design knowledge organisers as a powerful revision tool. Knowledge organisers specify in meticulous detail the exact facts, dates, characters, concepts and precise definitions that all pupils are expected to master in long-term memory. They organise onto a single page the most vital, useful subject knowledge for each unit. We work hard to choose the most valuable content that we want all pupils to remember for ten years and beyond. At a single glance, knowledge organisers answer the question for teachers and pupils: 'what is most important for us not to forget?' Everything the pupils need to know is set out clearly in advance.

From creating knowledge organisers, we have realised that in secondary school, we expect pupils to remember vast amounts of required underpinning foundational subject knowledge. A casual glance through a year 7 pupil's Michaela knowledge book will demonstrate this.

In English, in grammar alone, we do not want them to forget the difference between nouns, verbs, pronouns, adjectives, adverbs, prepositions, conjunctions, clauses, commas, colons and semi-colons. Just knowing how to use the apostrophe correctly involves them distinguishing between verb-omission apostrophes like 'it's late', noun-possession apostrophes like 'the dog's collar,' and pronouns which must not have apostrophes such as: 'the cat ate its food.' Studying poetry, we want them to know the differences between metaphors, similes, symbolism and imagery, and sibilance, assonance, alliteration and onomatopoeia. In History, the definitions of autocracy, monarchy, royalty, democracy, republic, tyranny, authority, nobility, hierarchy, accountability, sovereignty, legitimacy and colony are just a few of the many concepts they are expected to navigate, and this goes for every subject.

Knowledge books

At the start of the year, all pupils are issued with a knowledge book to keep all their knowledge organisers in over the course of the year. There is one knowledge book per year, with a section for each subject. They are 80 pages long, so each core academic subject has between six and ten knowledge organisers per year. In English in year 7, there are organisers for myths, grammar, poetry, poems to be memorised, rhetoric, vocabulary, spelling and Shakespeare's *Julius Caesar*; everything they study that year. Organisers for all subjects are kept within one beautifully organised book for the entire year. All pupils keep these with them at all times in school, and take them home with them to revise each evening, weekend and during the holidays.

Practice books

Guided by a teacher, pupils self-quiz on one knowledge organiser from one subject every evening during term-time. For this, they use a separate practice book that they take between home and school. The practice book is just a standard exercise book. To 'self-quiz' means to memorise: they cover up one side of the knowledge organiser, look at the concept, write out the definition from memory (in a black pen) then self-check and self-correct any spelling mistakes, omissions or inaccuracies (in a green pen). They test themselves until they have learned it by heart for a minimum of 30 minutes each evening, to prepare for a written quiz in class the next day.

There is a timetable in the front of their self-quizzing books with seven nights for the seven main subjects: English, Humanities, Science, French, Maths, Music and Art. Every pupil in the year is revising the same subject on the same night. Everyone has the same seven-year revision plan. This is useful if pupils are absent for a day or two, or longer term; they still know exactly what revision to do, precisely which subject to prioritise, every day. Self-quizzing becomes an automated, daily habit for the long term.

Class quizzes and checks

Next, the day after pupils self-quiz on a subject, they are tested and their practice books are checked. The check aims to ensure that 100% of pupils complete their self-quizzing every night. That's a high bar, and here's what we do to help all pupils to reach it.

Teachers check the practice books to see if the self-quizzing practice is of sufficient quantity and quality. On quantity, pupils must complete at least one page of self-quizzing for prep, with no spaces left on the sides or at the top or bottom of the page. On quality, it must be neat and accurate, with all spelling mistakes corrected.

We set a weekly in-class quiz, so we can see precisely whose self-quizzing is ineffectual, and support them to improve their revision. Teachers simply sort these into three piles: those who have struggled, those who have passed, and those who have excelled. We support those who regularly struggle in class, and stretch those who excel with extension challenges.

As self-quizzing is the same revision strategy each evening across all subjects, it becomes an automatic routine. Our average is 98% quality completion. In our second year, out of the weekly 1200 hand-ins for our 240 pupils over five days, an average of just 20 instances were of insufficient quality. We minimise homework incompletion because of the immediate consequence: pupils do a 30-minute self-quizzing catch-up session that day if they do not complete it the evening before. We track those who struggle and contact their parents to support them.

Online

We also put all subjects' knowledge organisers online, using a free website and smartphone app called Quizlet. This means all pupils have the knowledge we most want them to revise available online and on their phones. They can revise anywhere, anytime, at their fingertips, in their pockets, even without the internet, on the tube, on the way to school, on the way back from school and during evenings, weekends and holidays. Quizlet turns knowledge organisers into digital flashcards, quizzes and tests with feedback. Once uploaded, every pupil who ever comes to the school can use it to revise independently of teachers' effort, and it requires no marking whatsoever.

Cover and Detention

There are also some advantageous side effects of sharing knowledge organisers in knowledge books and teaching pupils the habit of self-quizzing. In cover lessons, non-subject experts can supervise a lesson of self-quizzing revision. No Michaela teacher ever has to email cover work or forms in when they are ill or absent. Pupils simply self-quiz for the lesson and test themselves on previous terms' or units' topics, writing from memory, self-checking and self-correcting, to remember what they have learnt.

Another positive side-effect we have found is that detentions at Michaela, instead of writing pointless lines, apology letters or reflection sheets, can utilise silent self-quizzing from pupils' knowledge books. The same happens when pupils are called from lessons or in isolation for an afternoon or a day. Pupils' resentment is reduced because they can see that they are still learning lots of useful content, especially if a supervising teacher quizzes them at certain intervals to keep them focused on revising. Equally, pupils with long-term absence have their knowledge books and online quiz app so that they can avoid falling behind and keep up with their peers.

Coordination

This homework and revision ecosystem does require considerable coordination. Departments must agree on and create a one-page organiser for each unit. Teachers must check all pupils' practice books and quizzes weekly and set detentions if the self-quizzing is not done. Here's what we've found valuable about this strategy: it's long-term (spread over seven years up to A-level), habitual (always the same strategy every day), yet still subject-specific (one subject's content to focus on each evening), collective (all pupils in the year do the same subject on the same night), research-based (based on 100 years of cognitive science), inexpensive (a few exercise books per year per pupil) and minimalist (one sheet to photocopy for each pupil for each unit).

Most of all, it makes a dramatic impact on learning. In lessons, teachers can count on pupils knowing facts, concepts and definitions with lightning speed. Memorisation provides a very sound foundation for broad, deep subject expertise. Ask Michaela teachers, department heads and pupils, and they will tell you how happy they are with the simplicity and impact of self-quizzing as our coordinated homework and revision strategy.

Complications

That isn't to say we have not experienced complications. One is a short cut and another is an unintended consequence. We keep asking ourselves: 'what question do we not want to hear the answer to?' That turned out to be: 'what if pupils are gaming homework?'

Most pupils tend to minimise the effort they put in, especially after a long, eight-hour school day. Many pupils, once they understood how the system worked, found ways to take shortcuts. They'd just copy out a page rather than actually self-testing and rigorously learning by heart. This wouldn't fulfil the spirit of the homework, but it would fulfil the letter of the practice book check.

To overcome this obstacle, we used the testing effect. The next day, we'd test pupils to hold them accountable. It was soon very clear who was revising well and who was taking shortcuts. Those who passed and excelled at the test had revised well; those who had taken a shortcut did not.

The other problem we encountered was unintended consequences. As we initially awarded merits for the number of pages, pupils were spending more time on quantity of written pages than on quality of revision, actually testing themselves and revising until they knew the content by heart. We removed the perverse incentives to produce higher quantity written copying at the expense of quality revision by removing the award of merits for two or more pages.

The complication still remained that setting the 'target' of one page meant that some pupils aimed to write one page and finished revising as soon as that was complete, rather than spending time aiming for 'automaticity' of knowledge recall. No system is without its disadvantages, but we do our utmost to mitigate these by creating a strong culture around self-quizzing. Teachers explain why it's important and useful, teaching pupils the science behind the strategy. They explain the benefits of 30 full minutes of self-testing every day: those pupils who do this will have 100 hours of revision over five years up to GCSEs and achieve highly. Those who take shortcuts will be 100 hours behind and will not achieve highly. We constantly remind and reinforce the intrinsic benefits of self-quizzing properly.

Lastly, a complication that remains thorny is that the pupils who are furthest behind, although they require the most practice, often do the least. To some extent, daily self-quizzing catch-up ensures they do the minimum of 30 minutes a day. However, we do not want them to do just the minimum when we should be aiming to help them achieve the maximum.

We considered running a self-quizzing club after school for these weaker pupils. We have not done so, partly due to the impact on teacher workload, and partly because it reduces pupil responsibility, making them less likely to be the habit of independently self-quizzing during the long holidays when they need to rely on their own work ethic. Instead, we over-narrate and over-rationalise the benefits for them whilst contacting parents so they help their child take responsibility for working hard and catching up. If homework isn't done, parents are required to attend a meeting with the Headmistress where she will hold them to account. We also put in place support for pupils in the two areas of homework beyond memorisation: in reading and Maths practice.

Maths

Why extra Maths practice and not, say, Science or English? Maths is the most abstract and complex subject. Even number is an abstraction – decimals, fractions and percentages are hard to grasp; algebraic, statistical and probabilistic manipulation of numbers are meta-abstractions. Pupils who arrive at school in year 7 are sometimes unable to do the most basic of calculations such as adding and subtracting accurately, let alone with very large numbers, negative numbers or complex decimals and fractions. Without a very strong foundation in number, pupils' working memories become easily overloaded in more complex Maths such as geometry. Maths is a gateway subject to many other subjects like Biology, Chemistry, Physics, Psychology and Economics; many degrees and careers, from engineering to finance to science (and even teaching) are ruled out without a secure grasp of mathematics.

So what is the best way to organise Maths homework and revision? Online Maths programmes hold the promise of providing a low-effort, high-impact homework-revision strategy. Maths teachers do not then have to create the huge banks of questions and answers required for extended practice. Nor do they have to mark all the answers that pupils produce. Online Maths websites have huge volumes of questions online and mark them digitally, automatically. They also often run reports that allow teachers to display daily rankings of pupils by effort, time and number of questions answered accurately. We display Maths rankings every day during break time. These daily effort rankings are very, very powerful motivators. So powerful, in fact, that some pupils, in their bid to top the rankings, started waking up at 4am to complete extra Maths, until we reminded them that sufficient sleep is vital!

One complication of dependence on technology is uncertainty. Sometimes, a pupil's internet at home will go down for a day, or several days. Sometimes, the website goes down for a day and pupils cannot log on. Sometimes, pupils will use these pretexts as excuses, and it is hard to distinguish a lazy excuse from a genuine reason. To reduce uncertainty, we create as pre-emptive a culture as possible. We provide an after-school club with computers and the internet every day from 4pm to 5pm so pupils without reliable internet at home can complete their online Maths homework. We also open this club during their lunch break to maximise pupils' chances of completing the work expected of them.

We expect all pupils to hand in written workings on paper every day, so that even if there is a glitch in the website's logging system, they have proof of their homework. We've found the benefits of combining online Maths with written workings the best strategy. This is better than online-only, which is tech-dependent, or written-only which limits pupil work to that which the teacher can mark each day or that which pupils can peer-mark in lessons. With online Maths, pupils can work hard on almost limitless Maths practice, to consolidate their mastery of this most abstract of subjects.

Reading

Reading is a top priority at Michaela. It improves pupils' writing, accuracy, spelling, vocabulary, grammar, knowledge, attention and memory, as well as expanding their interests, imagination, curiosity, horizons and sense of adventure. In every subject, even Maths, pupils read subject content in lessons, so that they read around 10,000 words every day. They also read classic novels in tutor-time every day, many of which they would not choose to read at home (when they first arrive, at least!). They read some of the most challenging, enduring and inspiring novels every written, that have stood the test of time: in year 7, *Dracula, Gulliver's Travels*, the *Hunchback of Notre Dame, Treasure Island, Robinson Crusoe, The Three Musketeers*, to name just a few; in year 8, *Silas Marner, Of Mice and Men, The Pearl*, the *Diary of Anne Frank* and *To Kill A Mockingbird*, for example; in year 9, for instance, *Wuthering Heights, David Copperfield, A Picture of Dorian Grey, Catcher in the Rye*, the *Great Gatsby* and *Things Fall Apart*. Our ambition is that all pupils will have read 100 classic texts by the time they leave school, including complex Russian novels such as *Crime and Punishment* and *War and Peace*. All our pupils arrive every day with a book from our library that they take home to read and must have on them in school at all times.

Reading is one way we ensure that those pupils who need it most do the most instead of the least. We hold reading club after school four days a week from 4pm to 4.30pm, so that we guarantee that our weakest pupils read for two hours extra every week. Pupils and teachers say that this is one of the most magical times of their school day. As a result, their minds completely change from when they arrive in September hating reading; by the end of the year our weakest readers love reading.

For homework, we have experimented with many trials of different approaches, from reading logs to multiple-choice tests, open-answer quizzes, sanctions, vocabulary logs and incentives-only without sanctions. We have learned a great deal from our mistakes along the way.

We began when we opened Michaela with reading logs. Pupils had to read a book of their choice each evening and complete a summary of what had happened in a minimum of three sentences. There was a detention for those who were not complete and high quality. We found that this system had the unintended consequence that pupils were choosing easy books they'd already read and scrapping in their reading logs on the bus at the last minute. Many weren't reading for even as long as they were writing for, which wasn't the point.

We moved to a system of class readers that every pupil in the class read, and a multiple-choice question on the plot the next day, with a detention for those who answered incorrectly. But it turned out pupils were being put in detention even though they had done the reading, because the question was just on one part of the chapter. Pupils were also telling others what had happened so they could pass.

So we moved to a system of class reading set each evening with four open-answer questions in tutor-time the next day, with a detention for anyone who got 0% or 25%. This made it hard to game. It required quite a lot of work for teachers to write four questions for each evening, and it still didn't guarantee that pupils were reading widely, broadly and happily of their own accord, so that they read independently in holidays. Sanctions were proving to have too many perverse incentives.

One pilot we experimented with was using vocabulary logs. Pupils can optionally keep a little vocabulary book where they write unfamiliar words they encounter, the sentence to contextualise them, and the definition from an online source. If they write ten words, sentences and definitions, they are awarded three merits. Writing five words and sentences are compulsory for selected reluctant readers, to set a high minimum bar and encourage the habit of reading every evening. Those who do more than five earn a merit, those who do ten earn three merits, and those who do less are given a 30-minute catch-up detention where they self-quiz on their subjects. It was enthusing avid readers without ceiling effects, and encouraging less avid readers to do at least 20 minutes reading each night. Pupils really enjoyed seeing their vocabulary clock up, too. However, it was burdensome on teachers to check for sufficient quality, so we have culled this initiative for all but those furthest behind in reading, to ensure that the weakest readers do the most reading.

As Tim Harford puts it, 'success increases with the number of experiments.' We are still running pilots, still designing experiments, still making mistakes, and still learning lessons from them. Drawing the right lessons from complex, fast-changing challenges like pupils' home reading habits is hard. We now run 'pre-mortems' before introducing new initiatives and attempt to anticipate the implementation dip, perverse incentives and unintended consequences. Learning from evolutionary problem-solving, we keep searching for solutions, trying new variants in an adaptive process of trial-and-error, variation and selection. We have not found an optimal design for home reading habits yet, but I am optimistic that our approach is yielding valuable insights.

Accumulative Advantage

When Einstein was asked what the most powerful force in the world, he said, 'compound interest.' The greatest benefit of our knowledge curriculum and homework-as-revision strategy at Michaela is its compound, cumulative effects on learning, motivation and academic achievement.

Consider that we prepare Michaela pupils to revise for GCSEs for 500 hours in core subjects over five years: 100 hours in English, 100 hours in Maths, 100 hours in Humanities, 100 hours in Science and 100 hours in French. Consider that we teach Michaela pupils how best to use those hours: not blithely re-reading, blindly copying, mindlessly underlining or thoughtlessly highlighting but carefully self-quizzing, self-checking, self-correcting and self-testing. Consider that every teacher who teaches Michaela pupils in year 8, year 9, year 10 and year

11 will know exactly what pupils are expected to remember from previous years, simply consult the ten knowledge organisers in the subject for each preceding year.

The benefits of such collective memory are hard to overstate. 480 pupils from year 8 to year 11 share the subject-specific mnemonics shared with them in year 7, and can revise collectively rather than just individually. 480 year 8 to year 11 pupils can together recite the three poems they learned by heart in year 7 ('If', 'Invictus' and 'Ozymandias') and year 8 ('Auguries of Innocence,' 'Kubla Khan' and 'London') which improves their insights into any new literature they encounter. Choral recital also cultivates a strong school ethos. As psychologist Jonathan Haidt says, chanting in chorus builds trust and gives a sense of uplifting unity, making everyone feel like a family.

Researchers in education have long established the Matthew effect: 'To whoever has, more shall be given; but from whoever has not, even what they have will be taken away.' Reading and learning begets cumulative advantages for learning and reading. Success creates virtuous cycles, where readers learn to read faster, with deeper comprehension and broader knowledge. Knowledge is sticky, and accumulating knowledge sticks to prior knowledge like webs. The word-rich get richer, while the word-poor stay poor. Similarly, the numerate accumulate early advantages to accelerate in numeracy, while those who are innumerate fall further and further behind in numeracy. Advantage begets advantage; disadvantage begets disadvantage. Every day, teachers in England see the Matthew effect in action in mutually reinforcing, often vicious cycles.

Every day, Michaela teachers see the Matthew effect in action in their lessons as a virtuous cycle. Pupils begin to accumulate advantages once their teachers give them vast amounts of knowledge rich in cultural capital. As pupils revise and quiz themselves on this knowledge, their advantage over others who do not begins to accelerate. As pupils do Maths revision every day, all year, their numeracy accelerates. Since they bring a great deal of prior knowledge to year 8 from year 7, new knowledge sticks as it fits within their existing knowledge webs, or, as scientists put it, knowledge schemata. Pupils also read so much every day, both at school and at home, that their reading ability also accelerates. They know that every lesson and every day, they are learning and revising tangible subject knowledge rather than abstract and nebulous 'skills', and feel themselves remembering more than they ever thought possible. They feel more and more motivated to learn more. They experience increasing success; they feel increasing curiosity to learn, achieve and succeed all the more. Memorisation is invaluable as homework because of the collective memory and cumulative advantages it gives our pupils.

No-Excuses Discipline Changes Lives

Jonathan Porter

"Listen, you little wiseacre: I'm smart, you're dumb; I'm big, you're little; I'm right, you're wrong, and there's nothing you can do about it." – Harry Wormwood

Matilda was one of my favourite novels as a child. I loved the story of a precocious young girl succeeding in spite of her good-for-nothing parents. It's an essentially romantic story, which speaks to the innate goodness of children in spite of the feckless and fallen adults that surround them. Matilda's eventual triumph is in spite of, and not because of, the adults around her. The most well known of which – the aptly named 'Miss Trunchbull' – is a parody of the punitive Victorian schoolmistress, now much aped in literature and film. We all know these images; they retain a powerful and pervasive effect on popular consciousness.

As is so often the case in such instances, there are good reasons for this. School life in the past looked very different to how it does today. Corporal punishment (although perhaps not the 'chokey') was common and little or no provision would have been made for those with special educational needs. Historians of the period like Jonathan Rose in *The Intellectual Life of the Working Class* have suggested that around a third of pupils, from different social classes, considered discipline during their time at school to be 'too severe.' My own father bitterly resents being beaten with a slipper simply because he was left-handed.

However, as so often in the great pendulum swings of history, a natural correction to what had been, at times, an unfeeling system has been a disastrous undermining of the traditional forms of authority. Rousseau's fantastical notion of the noble savage (although he never used the term himself), and the inevitable goodness of children, had burrowed its way into the guiding philosophy of our teacher training establishments and, indeed, wider society. This was despite, of course, Rousseau abandoning all of his own children to orphanages.[1]

In the decades since the Second World War we have increasingly seen adults, like Rousseau, balk at their responsibilities to correct ordinary adolescent behaviour. This is the philosophical spectre that haunts debates about discipline in schools. It is the reason that so many schools gave up on detentions

---

1   A baby at the Paris Foundling Hospital in these years had only a two-thirds chance of surviving its first year and only a 5% chance of reaching maturity.

completely, preferring nomenclature which appears to be less authoritarian or, in many cases, blaming the poor behaviour of the pupil on the teacher.

We must be clear: discipline is not a dirty word. When the rules that govern our interactions with each other are brought down, we are brought down with them. Kindness, gratitude and empathy are not intrinsic and brought down by institutions. The contrary is true: they depend upon them. Kindness, gratitude and empathy must be taught by parents and teachers and learnt by pupils. Over time, these actions become our habits and our habits become our character. As Aristotle said, excellence is a consequence of ingrained habits. It is as true of our kindness, gratitude and empathy as it is of football, chess or computer programming.

The vast majority of schools recognise this to a greater or lesser degree. Most schools acknowledge that there has to be some consequence for behaviour that falls short of the community's expectations.

The consequences

The problem is that the systems that exist currently are evidently not working. Indeed, the ambient level of behaviour in Britain's schools is poor.

On one hand, you have what we might call the 'big ticket' behaviour. This is the really serious physical, verbal and emotional abuse which is much more common than many are prepared to admit. The National Association of Schoolmasters Union of Women Teachers (NASUWT) surveyed 5,000 members in March 2016 and found that nearly half of teachers had been subjected to some form of verbal abuse. More than 1 in 10 said a pupil had physically assaulted them.

But it's not just the 'big ticket' behaviour that we should be concerned about. For many teachers it's the low-level disruption that really sticks in the craw. This is the shouting out, the answering back and, in the present day, the constant fear that the next time you tell off little Jonny, little Gemma will record you getting all hot and flustered and post it all over social media.

In Ofsted's 2014 report on behaviour in English schools it found that up to an hour of learning was being lost each day. That's a staggering 38 days per pupil, per year. The report says that this is 'deeply worrying... not because pupils' safety is at risk where low-level disruption is prevalent, but because this has a detrimental impact on the life chances of too many pupils.'

Nor are these statements overblown. We know from a paper published by the National Bureau of Economic Research (NBER) on the long-term effects of disruption that 'exposure to a disruptive peer in classes of 25 during elementary school reduces earnings at age 26 by 3 to 4 per cent.' Sadly, though, this is a story that is being played out in thousands of classrooms across the country, and which has been most recently brought to public attention because of popular fly-on-the-wall documentaries such as *Educating Essex* and *Educating Yorkshire*. The story is often the same: one charming but unruly pupil, often from a troubled home, disrupting the learning of the other 30. If you have taught in classrooms like that, as I have, you know just what a challenge that is for the teacher. You cannot help but sympathise with him, and, often, even with the pupil in question.

However, we must also sympathise with the other 30. These are the pupils who turn up on time, every day, who listen attentively in lessons, who do their homework and who really just want to get on and learn. They are the silent majority in Britain's schools.

To compound matters further, the effects of poor behaviour are probably most damaging in schools where the pupils are poor. These children are doubly disadvantaged. Not only are they more likely to come from turbulent or unstable homes where consistency, routine or even high expectations may be in short supply, but they might also be served by teachers who will not preach what they would practise with their own children. Some teachers expect their own children to do their homework or put their hand up before speaking in class, yet they hold other people's children to different standards. Some of these teachers believe in different standards for different pupils.

This is the specific context in which 'no excuses' discipline must be situated:

1. A system where the ambient level of behaviour is poor.

2. A system where poor behaviour disproportionately damages those pupils on the margins of our society.

What makes no-excuses discipline different?

So far we have seen, first, how traditional forms of authority in schools have been gradually eroded and, secondly, what the consequences of that philosophical turn have been: a mixture of serious physical and verbal abuse and the ambient 'low-level' disruption that is pervasive in Britain's schools. We should be under no illusion as to the moral urgency of this. If you are poor you are much more likely to be in a classroom where the limited amount of learning provided for you by the state is taken away from you because adults in your life – parents and teachers – are abrogating their moral or professional responsibilities.

If you've followed the argument so far and agree with my characterisation of the status quo, then you are likely to be someone who advocates strict discipline. You might put pupils in detention for swearing. You might have a 'late detention' where pupils who are late to school are kept behind at the end of the day. Or, if you're really strict, you might have a consequence for pupils not bringing their stationery to school. You will also have a series of incentives, too. Most of these run on some sort of point-based system which allows teachers to give our credits or merits, or even cold-hard cash such as Vivo points – a system which allows pupils to buy items at the end of the year. This system of 'carrot and stick' is pretty typical across schools in the country, even if it is inconsistently enforced.

The problem with such a system is its inherent ambiguity. What is 'strict'? And who decides? My 'strict' is not necessarily the same as your 'strict.' Some schools will insist that pupils can all bring the correct equipment to school; other schools think this is too much to ask, particularly of its poorest pupils. Some schools think it is right to sanction pupils for calling out. Other schools argue that to do so would stifle pupils' innate creativity, and would crush the confidence of its pupils with anger management issues.

Where Michaela differs from the merely 'strict' schools is the level of expectation and the consistency with which those expectations are applied. First, we set the bar extremely high. We expect our pupils to turn up to school on time. We expect them to turn up with the correct equipment, we expect them to not disrupt other pupils' learning but, crucially, we expect *every* pupil to do so. That is what 'no excuses' means. It means that the same rules will apply to you whether you're rich or poor, black or white, two parents or no parents at all. Because the argument I want to set out here is that if you are not a 'no excuses' school then you are, necessarily, a 'some excuses' school, where you are prepared to flex the rules, on occasion, to adapt to the background of a particular child. You believe in different standards for different pupils.

How does this work in practice?

Well, a classic example of this would be a boy who arrives with you in year 7 from primary school. We'll call him Tom. He's had a disruptive upbringing, his dad is nowhere to be seen and his mum struggles to control him and his brothers. To a large extent, they do what they want: they swear at their mum when she tells them to eat their dinner, they stay out in the park well after dark, and, occasionally, they use violence both in and out of school to get their way. Most schools in challenging areas have pupils like this.

A 'some excuses' school argues that Tom's background explains why he behaves like he does. Of course, they are right. It is no coincidence that Tom throws chairs around the classroom: he's had precious few positive role models, his dad's nowhere to be seen, and he's grown up with few of the boundaries that have nurtured his middle-class peers.

What is at stake here is whether you think Tom is capable of changing. We do. But also whether you are prepared for Tom's behaviour to affect the learning of the other 30 pupils in his class. We aren't.

The way this works in practice is very simple. We treat Tom just like we would treat any other child in the school. When he arrives in year 7 we give him a pencil case with all the things that are required for a day at Michaela: two black pens, one green pen, one blue pen, a 30cm ruler, a HB pencil, an art pencil and a rubber. If Tom loses one of these items, which he surely will, he's able to go to the stationery stop at the beginning of school to buy a new item himself. The items are cheap: 10p for a pencil and 20p for a pen. Tom has to learn that losing these items will cost him money and is also inconvenient. Getting new equipment means he has to queue at the beginning of the day. If he arrives to his form without one of the pieces of equipment then his form tutor will put him in detention during his lunch break. His tutor will make sure to remind Tom why we have the system that we have: if there were no sanctions then every teacher would have to give Tom a pen at the beginning of a lesson and, more importantly, Tom would never learn to value his possessions or the organisational habits he will need in later life.

The other place this works in practice is in the classroom. Our expectation is that pupils should be silent unless they've been asked to answer a question or work with their partner. The reason for this is because pupils hate ambiguity. If you tell a class to work quietly, what you get is a range of opinions from silent through to very loud. What you see in classrooms like this are teachers constantly reminding pupils to keep the noise down by shushing them and, intermittently, having to shout over the din. It's a common feature of supposedly quiet classroom environments. The problem with it is that it invariably leads to pupils getting into trouble. What's worse is that it really isn't their fault: the teacher did not make the expectations clear enough from the beginning. When you think about it, how quiet is 'quiet'? At Michaela, we remove this ambiguity by expecting silence, unless we've asked otherwise. Usually this would be to answer a question or to work briefly with a partner. Most pupils like this. They recognise what people have recognised for centuries: that it's easier to concentrate when there aren't people chatting next to you. Our autistic pupils revel in it. For them, the ambient noise in their primary schools made concentrating very difficult indeed. However, a few pupils, like Tom, find this difficult. It's not that they can't work in silence, it's just not a habit.

The only way to change these habits is constant reinforcement and encouragement: celebrating those pupils who put their hands up before speaking and sanctioning those who do not. What excellent teachers do is catch Tom being good. When at first he does put his hand up, he is suitably recognised: 'well done, Tom, for putting your hand up before speaking. It's so important that we don't disturb other pupils' learning.' Tom is reminded why the rule exists at all. It's not arbitrary; it's there to allow everyone to be taught well together.

Sometimes Tom's bad habits from primary school get the better of him. He turns to the pupil next to him to whisper the answer to a question that he was desperate to answer himself. I don't want to know whether Tom knows, I want to know whether his partner knows. I've deliberately asked her because I'm concerned that she's not been concentrating. What am I to do? At Michaela, the answer is simple. It's a demerit. I explain to Tom, 'Tom, we can't have 30 people speaking all at the same time; it would be chaos. That's a demerit.' Again, I narrate the behaviour and explain why it is that he cannot behave in this way. This is important. To impose a sanction without explaining the reason for it would be like a policeman on the street giving you a fine but not telling you what it's for. It's one of the reasons why no-excuses discipline, badly done, can be very bad indeed, and is something I will return to later.

For the vast majority of pupils, this mixture of carrot and stick is enough to change their behaviours. They start with us in year 7 barely able to maintain eye contact, shake hands or put their hands up in class without shouting out. Within a few weeks they've completely transformed. If Tom disrupts the class again, and gets two demerits, he'll find himself in detention. It's easy to overstate how punitive this really is: half an hour in silence catching up with missed work or getting ahead of the rest of the class. There are writers' camps in Shoreditch that are more disciplinary.

What about those pupils who continually push against the system? What happens if Tom continues to disrupt his class? The response of the teacher is simple and exactly the same each time: 'Tom, you are continuing to disrupt the class, you've had two demerits already. I can't allow your behaviour to affect other pupils' learning. Please stand outside.' It's not mean. It's not cruel. It's not vindictive. It's professional. It's straightforward. It's 'no excuses.' I've not made a special exception for Tom; I've held him to the same high standards as everyone else. This time, he's not been able to reach those standards and so he'll work for the rest of the lesson elsewhere. Because as much as I desperately want Tom in my lesson, I cannot allow a minority of one to affect the majority of 30.

This is what no-excuses discipline looks like in practice. It's the belief that Tom is capable, over time, of reaching the same standards as everyone else. To hold him to a lower standard because of his background, as even many 'strict' schools would, would be to acknowledge that there were 'some excuses' which prevented him from behaving. It would be to have different standards for different pupils, and to run the risk that a minority set the level of behaviour for the majority. We, at Michaela, believe this is profoundly wrong.

So let us spell out the advantages of this system. Why does a 'no excuses' discipline approach change lives?

No-excuses discipline means all teachers can teach

One of the great challenges in teaching at the moment is recruiting and retaining teachers. The reasons for this are complex, but one thing that drives teachers away from schools, and particularly schools in the most challenging areas, is the anxiety and the waste that come with poor behaviour. In my training we used to call it 'the Dread': that feeling when you wake on a Sunday when you know that, not only are you going to spend most of the day creating a card sort, but that year 8 will spend Monday ripping it up.

There are those who will tell you that the reason for bad behaviour in classrooms is because of the teacher's poor planning, their inexperience or their lack of charisma. There is some truth in this. Pupils do behave better with teachers who set work that is pitched to the right ability. Pupils do behave better with teachers that make them laugh. Pupils do behave better when they feel that reciprocal bond between teacher and pupil. We all know teachers who have that magical ability to get it just right and to bring even the most subversive pupils in year 11 to heel.

However, our system response cannot rely on all of our teachers being exceptional planners, exceptionally humorous, or building exceptional relationships with their classes. Not everyone can be exceptional.

No-excuses discipline means that all teachers can teach, not just the exceptional, because it creates a consistent culture of sky-high expectations throughout the school. All teachers and all pupils know where they stand because it removes the ambiguity, which is so often the root cause of classroom disruption. By insisting on silence in classrooms, unless the teacher has asked for talking, pupils and staff know exactly where they stand. Every pupil knows they have to wear their uniform correctly. Every pupil knows they have to complete their homework. And every pupil knows they have to put their hand up before speaking. Pupils that can remember their equipment, complete their homework and put their hands up are recognised, and even rewarded. They get badges, certificates and the whole panoply of praise that is justified for those who have made a real effort.

Most importantly, the teachers know where they stand as well. When they are forced to sanction pupils for falling short of the school rules it's not personal, it's the system. And the system exists to allow everyone to work and learn together.

Of course there will always be teachers within these systems who are exceptional. But the success of our systems should not be judged on how they help the strongest teachers but on how they help the weakest. No-excuses discipline means that all our teachers can teach – even the nervous, the inexperienced and the uncharismatic.

No-excuses discipline means all pupils can learn

Let's go back to Tom. How does no-excuses discipline improve his life?

Tom's primary school teacher met with our Special Educational Needs Co-ordinator (SENCo) before he joined Michaela. The year 6 teacher reported at length Tom's difficulty with authority, his difficult home life, his emotional issues, and that he found it difficult to remain in the classroom. He would storm out when angry, and could not read or write for long periods of time. He would not be able to cope with silence in the classroom. Conversely, he disliked 'time outs' and detentions, reacting negatively to reprimands. She recommended that he be excused from a full school day, suggesting letting him leave at 1:30pm in order to meet his needs.

It would have been easy for us to take that teacher at her word. We could have excused Tom's behaviour or said that we were not going to hold him to the same standards. We could even have excused Tom from a full school timetable and a full education because he found it difficult to read and write. The problem is that this becomes a self-fulfilling prophecy: the more Tom is out of lessons, the further behind he becomes. The further he falls behind, the less motivated he becomes. Before long his behaviour deteriorates so much that it's questionable whether he can be taught with the rest of his year group at all. It's one of the ironies of the 'no excuses' model, which is often attacked for removing disruptive children from lessons, is that its proponents actually want to include disruptive pupils as much as possible.

We chose not to follow his primary teacher's advice. We didn't take him out of lessons and we didn't make exceptions for him because, in the past, he had displayed negative behaviour in response to discipline.

We should be under no illusions as to what a difficult thing that is to do. We know that Tom will struggle to reach the expectations of the school and we know that, at times, we, the adults in his life, will have to use our authority in a way that may temporarily upset him. Every time we tell off a child for behaviour that falls short of our expectations, this is what is happening. We are causing temporary discomfort because we know, in the long run, that it's the right thing to do.

It is something that we must do, though, because the alternative is so much worse. If we cannot change Tom's behaviour, we allow who he is now to define who he will be. There is nothing loving or optimistic in that whatsoever. Conversely, we believe that Tom is capable of taking responsibility for his behaviour himself.

Sure enough, Tom found it tricky at first. He spent the first three weeks of year 7 in and out of detention like a yo-yo. He cried a bit and, even now, he turns around from time to time. But he's on a full timetable rather than leaving at 1:30pm, he is polite and well mannered to teachers and pupils, and, most importantly, he's really happy. Now he can learn, now he can experience success – real, meaningful success.

The rest of his class benefit, too. The other 30 pupils, the silent majority of pupils in Britain's schools, haven't had to suffer a disrupted lesson because of the behaviour of one child. At the moment, Tom's behaviour is meeting the expectations of the community; he brings the correct equipment to lessons, he does his homework and he puts his hand up before speaking in class. However, he knows that the rules that apply to his class apply to him, too. If he can't behave according to the class rules, he must leave the class, and that is the right thing to do. We cannot allow our expectations for the vast majority of 30 to be dragged down by the behaviour of a tiny minority of one, however much it anguishes us at the time. Exclusion, whether inside or outside of school, should not be a dirty word.

This is a utilitarian approach that is common in public policy but which is so rarely seen in education. When there is a finite amount of money to spend on new cancer drugs, the National Institute for Clinical Excellence (NICE) has to make difficult decisions that decide how the greatest good can be achieved for the greatest number. Many expensive life-saving cancer drugs are not available on the NHS because the cost-benefit ratio is simply too great. NICE is forced to make rational, if desperately difficult, decisions based on what will lead to the greatest good for the greatest number. I think schools should too.

What is the evidence?

When it comes to the evidence for the 'no excuses' approach the best we can say is that solid conclusions are hard to draw. In the main, this is because of weak correlational data and extremely limited sample sizes. The number of schools that have tried a 'no excuses' approach is, globally, small and in the UK, almost non-existent.

In the US, where 'zero tolerance' systems were introduced in some charter schools to respond to widespread school-based violence, there is some data to suggest that extremely high rates of exclusion are negatively correlated with academic achievement. There is also anecdotal evidence of pupils in these 'zero tolerance' charter schools violently pushing back against a system that they perceive to be unsympathetic or uncaring – schools where teachers are not able to form the natural bonds which are the basis of any reciprocal relationship.

Routinely, what we see in critical pieces of 'zero tolerance' systems in the US is a system imposed on pupils without any narration of the reason for the system's existence. It's not difficult to see how this would erode trust between teachers and pupils. A justice system that arbitrarily arrests its citizens without explaining to them the reason for the arrest will hardly endear itself to the community. The same is true of school behaviour systems. If teachers do not explain to pupils why the rules exist – and encourage them to consider what the school would be like without them – then they are unlikely to be trusted by the pupils. As in society, no school behaviour system can function without the consent of its pupils, however begrudging they might be.

In this sense, then, there appears to be a marked difference between the way zero tolerance has been practised in the US and how its champions in the UK understand it. The most up-to-date survey of the evidence available is Didau and Rose's timely book *What Every Teacher Needs to Know About Psychology*:

> There's no reason why 'no excuses' [in the UK] has to equate with being punitive and making children suffer. Instead it can be seen to be holding children account for their effort, attitude and behaviour. If 'no excuses' results in relatively minor but *consistently applied consequences* [my emphasis], maybe those being 'punished' would feel differently... How we behave is a matter of choice. Students need to be helped to make good choices sometimes, and will benefit from being reminded of the consequences of poor choices.

'No-excuses discipline' – as it is practised at Michaela – is about just that: creating a system of consistently applied consequences that are proportionate to the misdemeanour in question. As long as our pupils know that certain choices will always result in certain consequences they are much more likely to invest in a system which, they know, is there to help rather than to hinder.

We think that is the reason why, at the time of writing, with 360 pupils, we have only had one permanent exclusion. Small examples of low-level disruption, such as shouting out in class, are dealt with quickly and proportionately and not allowed to grow into more hostile confrontations that can soon spiral out of control. We have a handful of pupils who have been in bad habits for so long that they at first struggle to rise to our standards. When, from time to time, they disrupt others' learning, they are taken out of lessons and internally excluded. However, we sweat the small stuff so that disruption of lessons becomes practically non-existent.

Conclusions

There are reasons why discipline, authority and punishment have become dirty words in the contemporary education debate. Genuine abuses in the past have alloyed with the Enlightenment project, and the Romantic view of the child. Rousseau and his 20th Century followers have consistently sought to emphasise children's innate goodness, a condition that, they argue, is gradually tarnished by the strictures imposed on children by institutions and their Trunchbull-like overseers.

I have rejected that view here. Rousseau, the man who once said that 'reading was a plague on childhood,' has himself been a plague on childhood. His philosophy fuelled a progressive view of behaviour management after the Second World War that has created appalling conditions for teachers and pupils in schools.

I set out to show how 'strict' behaviour management systems have tried to respond to this, often with some success. However, without denigrating the good work that has already been done, we, at Michaela, think schools can go further. We believe that 'no-excuses discipline' can be genuinely life changing.

The reason for this is because the alternative to a 'no excuses' school is a 'some excuses' school – where we allow children's circumstances to define who they are and what they can be.

Every teacher will have taught a pupil like Tom. And every school and every teacher has a choice. They can make excuses for Tom and say that kids like him are incapable of a full timetable, and that kids like Tom will never bring the correct equipment to schools, or be able to put their hands up without first shouting out. My argument is that this is the 'some excuses' school; a school that presumes that because he always has then he always will.

No-excuses discipline rejects this. It says that teachers should be able to teach: all teachers, not just those whose planning is perfect, or are charismatic or who have established their reputation over 30 years. Most importantly, no-excuses discipline works for pupils. A few pupils may not yet reach the sky-high expectations of the school. Occasionally, the most loving thing for the majority is for the disruptive pupil to be asked to leave the classroom. Exclusion should not be a dirty word. We cannot sacrifice the one shot that 30 pupils have at a good education because of one pupil's injurious choices.

No-excuses discipline doesn't lower expectations of children from tough estates by presuming that such behaviour cannot be changed. It stands resolutely by the belief that children and young people are capable of understanding why communal rules need to exist, and it contends that those pupils have the ability to make good choices rather than bad ones. It is a hopeful vision of all pupils realising their potential. That is why no-excuses discipline changes lives.

Bootcamp Breaks Bad Habits

Joe Kirby

Bootcamp breaks the bad habits of a lifetime

Bootcamp at Michaela is audacious. It is a brave school leadership team who will dedicate seven entire school days entirely to year 7 and trust other year groups with an extra seven days of the long summer holidays. We are convinced that it is worth the investment of time, because we have seen over the past three years how life-changing bootcamp can be.

Bootcamp is a military metaphor, conjuring up images of militant discipline, arduous drills, meticulous order and harsh, intensive training. It is well worth speaking to British or American army soldiers about their experiences in bootcamp recruit training; very often, they talk about it with reverence and veneration. For instance, J.D. Vance grew up in a part of America rife with poverty, unpredictability, divorce, violence, abuse, drug addiction, obesity and blame. Aged a (self-described) 'pudgy' 18 he joined the US marines. 'They'll teach you discipline,' he was told. It was 'a life-defining challenge.' 'Life had taught me I had no control: psychologists call it learned helplessness,' he writes. 'Every time I learned to do something I thought impossible, I came a little closer to believing in myself. Every interaction was a revelation. I had never felt empowered with such responsibility. I had underestimated myself. I'd never see things the same way again; I'd changed my whole perspective. If I had learned helplessness at home, the Marines were teaching willpower.'

Some of our teachers have brothers or relatives in the British army, and they all testify to how discipline can be life changing. One Michaela teacher writes about it here:

> Michael began to get into trouble at school when he was 11. By the time he was 13, his behaviour had escalated into physical fights and aggression both at school and at home. Michael began to take drugs and occasionally deal them. He would leave school during the day and get drunk with much older friends. His mother would often have to go and collect him, unconscious, from a local park. Michael was expelled from school after school. His parents re-mortgaged their house in order to send him to two private schools, but still he was expelled from both within weeks of arriving. He was sent to a child psychologist. He was told he had 'anger issues.' He passed just three GCSEs.

It was Michael's idea to join the army. From the moment he arrived at the recruitment office, he was sternly reprimanded: 'STAND UP STRAIGHT! GET YOUR ELBOW OFF THE DESK! GET YOUR HANDS OUT OF YOUR POCKETS. WHO DO YOU THINK YOU ARE?' After registering, as he left, he said: 'that's exactly the kind of discipline I need. I'm going to love this.' He was right; Michael flourished in the strict discipline of the army. Their standards are high, and Michael has gained a strong sense of pride and self-respect from meeting those standards. He has been promoted time and time again. The army taught him discipline that changed his life.

There are parallels with what Michaela bootcamp does for inner-city children. Responsibility, self-discipline and willpower are exactly what Michaela teaches kids, and much else besides.

Brent, where Michaela is located, is one of the most deprived boroughs in the country. Around 25% of children in year 6 (aged 10) are obese and its households are some of the most overcrowded in London. Many of our pupils arrive not knowing how to read words, how to multiply and divide single-digit numbers, how to tell the time or how to use a knife and fork. Many children tell us when they start school that they hate reading; some cry when asked to read aloud to an adult or asked to do single-digit addition sums. Many arrive in terrible habits, struggling to make eye contact or have a conversation with an adult. Personal hygiene leaves a lot to be desired, to put it mildly. One hapless culprit in the first week of year 7 defecated in a urinal. When I asked in one of the first assemblies how many have short tempers, 80% of the 120 pupils in the year put their hands up. When I asked how many had been told they had anger management issues at primary school, over 50% put their hands up. Some had a track record of bullying, threats and aggression towards other pupils. A few had threatened their mothers at home with violence. When told on arrival at secondary school to interact more politely, many of them snarl, smirk or sneer, having ignored teachers for years at primary school.

'Street' demeanour and macho, misogynist slang are intensified by peer pressure. In shops, some of these children have been caught shoplifting, throwing food at shopkeepers or hurling drinks at other customers. Texts on social media groups are surprisingly venomous insults – 'I hope you burn in hell, ***** – and sexualised, even at 11 years old. Blame and excuses are default reactions to reprimands, such as 'it's not my fault!' or 'he made me do it!' Casual racial slurs proliferate. At first, our pupils are overheard calling each other 'blick' or 'milky bar', insulting their complexions. Mendacity seems prevalent, it appears that some of these children have learned that lying adamantly and refusing to admit responsibility is the best way to avoid punishment, which has served them well with parents and teachers long before. Making the minimum, lazy, slouchy effort in lessons and in homework is an automatic reflex for many on arrival. We have a tough intake. There are some very bad habits that some of our pupils have been in, some for seven years or more, some for an entire lifetime.

Bootcamp teaches pupils the mindset and habits to succeed at school

In all of the many schools we have taught in as a team of teachers, induction for new year 7 pupils lasted one day at most, and was rushed, stressful and scary for the youngest year group. They were often jostled, harried, hustled, bullied and intimidated by those pupils much older than them. Teachers were so busy firefighting on all fronts with all year groups that they had the least time to nurture and protect the youngest cohort. As a result, many year 7 pupils start school terrified and terrorised, and in future years go on to inflict this intimidation on new pupils, stealing or hiding their bags, blazers or kit.

By contrast, at Michaela we take the most time for our youngest pupils, with 7 days to set them up to succeed in their first steps on the start of their seven-year journey at secondary school – without any older pupils at all. We recognise that they have to navigate the new demands of some ten different teachers and 120 pupils in their year group. This is very different to their primary schools, where they tend to have one form teacher all year and sometimes only 50 children in their year group. Bootcamp gives the new kids seven days to adjust these new challenges and rise to our high standards.

In bootcamp, we teach pupils what is required to succeed at Michaela and in life. On their first day at school, we teach pupils about our ethos and our routines. We start with an assembly from the Headmistress. Katharine Birbalsingh is candid: 'you are so lucky to be here. Our standards are very, very high. It is your responsibility to change your habits from primary school: your future depends on it!' We are meticulous in teaching them our routines. We teach them how to enter a classroom and time them in competitions so that they can do so in under 30 seconds. 'Every second counts,' we tell them. We teach them how to hand out their books; each row works as a team to hand out books and sheets and booklets in five seconds. We tell them that in other secondary schools, it takes longer than five minutes to hand out books. We tell them that we save hundreds of hours of learning before their GCSEs with such careful attention to detail.

We teach them that silence in lessons is golden, that it helps us listen and helps us learn. We teach them how best to listen in lessons, with the teacher's instruction, using SLANT. SLANT is an acronym that we learned from Doug

Lemov, a school leader from a US Charter School network, Uncommon Schools. We've adapted it so that it stands for Sit up straight, Listen, Answer questions, Never interrupt and Track the teacher (or text, or speaker) – tracking meaning making eye contact. We love mnemonics! We teach them explicitly how to be polite: using STEPS – saying 'sir' or 'miss', saying thank you, excuse me, please, and smiling. We demand the very highest standards of politeness from pupils in every interaction with any teacher or adult staff member.

We do not tolerate snarls, sneers or smirks. We reprimand these instantly, sternly and insistently. We do not accept blame, excuses, or manipulative tears as justifications for disruption, rudeness, selfishness or negativity. Instead, we hold children to account for the polite manners and professional behaviour that we would expect of our colleagues and our own secondary-age children. We teach them how to speak in whole-class discussions in lessons and in public using SHAPE – speaking in full sentences, using our hands well, articulating and projecting, and making eye contact with the audience. We also teach them exactly how to perform their role responsibly in family lunch.

On their second day of school, we teach pupils about the high standards of behaviour that are now expected of them. We teach them all our school rules, the consequences that follow from making wise choices, and the consequences that follow from making unwise choices. We explain in minute detail what we give demerits for and what we give detentions for. We clarify precisely how to avoid detentions. We tell pupils how to behave in a detention so there is no ambiguity, confusion or lack of clarity. We teach pupils how best to respond to a demerit; not by arguing, sulking, protesting, complaining or grumbling in the moment, but by staying calm, practising patience, keeping their self-control. We teach them exactly what to do if they feel that a demerit or a detention is unfair: they must find the teacher later and explain. We also tell them that the teacher's word is final, and will not always be perfect: for learning to work for everyone, sometimes imperfect decisions must be taken swiftly. We give them lots of scenarios and together as a class we discuss how best to react. We share stories about self-control and teach them why it is so useful and so important for learning and in life. We explain how exercise, nutrition and sleep are linked to self-control.

We tell our pupils that the reason their teachers at Michaela are so strict and so tough on them is because they care about them so much, because they believe in them so much, and because they love seeing them succeed and improve and achieve. It is our intention that this positivity, warmth, care and tough love pervades every interaction we have with pupils in school, even when we are disciplining them. One of my favourite lessons in bootcamp is teaching them our philosophy of stoicism. We explore the wisdom of Marcus Aurelius, Seneca and Epictetus: 'it's not events, but our judgements that disturb us'; 'anger is weakness; self-control is strength'; 'do not complain: think your way through difficulties.' It is a breathtakingly empowering philosophy for kids who often have been surrounded by a paradigm of blame and excuses their entire lives. It gives them control of their choices, reactions, responses, habits and, ultimately, their destiny.

On our year 7 pupils' third day of school at Michaela, they learn about habits, responsibility, equipment and attendance. We read stories of irresponsible choices and stories of pupils who have become increasingly responsible in year 8 and year 9. We read about the habits that will help them succeed at school: attending every day, arriving punctually, self-testing, self-checking, and self-correcting. We set out explicitly and in precise, meticulous detail, the exact requirements of their pencil cases, their workpacks, their uniform; all their school kit. We label all their folders and pencil cases and ensure that they have everything they need to start secondary school subjects, down to specifying the optimal number and colour of pens (two black, one green, one blue for annotation and self-checking in lessons). There are bans that we explain on clutter, highlighters, bendy rulers, clicky pens, colouring pencils, pencil sharpeners and shavings, which saves so much wasted time later in the year. 'No logos!' we explain. In uniform, there are bans on jewellery, makeup and branded logos on any bags, scarves, gloves, coats, kit, even glasses. Such decisive and attentive simplicity upstream saves hours downstream, and allows children to be children without getting into costly, competitive, commercial brand-war escalations.

On their fourth day, we teach pupils about intelligence, knowledge, learning and their unique self-quizzing homework. We tell them that no one is born automatically smart or stupid and explain the science behind how the mind learns. All our pupils from day four of school know the concepts of long-term memory, working memory, automaticity and overlearning. They understand the importance of practice, the power of quizzing for long-term memory, and why we recap so much in lessons and revise so much – so that we don't forget what we've learned. We tell them stories of sports athletes and musicians who have used the power of deliberate practice to improve and achieve great success, and together in class we explore the lessons we can learn from their lives. On homework, our standards are 100% of pupils completing homework 100% of the time to 100% of expected quality. This sky-high bar means that it is vital for us to be absolutely crystal-clear on precisely what will receive demerits and detentions, and what meets our standard of quality homework. In meticulous detail with guidance, instruction, examples, non-examples, modelling and extensive practice, we teach them exactly what we expect of them for their homework.

By day 5, we start to explore kindness and integrity. Our starting point is a lesson on bullying, its terrible, lasting, damaging ramifications, and how we all collectively have the responsibility to create a zero-bullying school that has zero tolerance for bullying: bystanders stand up, speak out and let a teacher know. Sharing is caring – there's no such thing as snitching at Michaela – and telling teachers is the kindest, most courageous thing to do because it helps another pupil to realise, learn and improve. This is a difficult message to grasp for those children made fearful of snitching by playground bullies in primary school.

Like all the ideas we teach them in bootcamp, it requires continual reminders, reiteration and reinforcement over the weeks and months ahead – but bootcamp is where teachers have the dedicated time to teach this vital message up-front, before subjects begin. We read stories about kindness and explore several ways of demonstrating kindness, compassion, generosity and consideration: by writing thank you notes, by greeting adults and guests politely, by holding doors open, by tidying up after ourselves in lessons and lunch, by taking turns in conversations, by helping out other pupils. We share more scenarios of what to do if a friend or sibling or another pupil is struggling. We discuss what to do in case they see others being unkind to a Michaela pupil outside of school.

On day six, we build up to taking the whole year group to sport by the end of the day. We start by teaching them about trust. All teachers all year draw on the shared analogy of the trust bucket: trust is like a bucket of water: easy to spill but harder to fill. We teach them the simple truth and the hidden, invisible secret of life: 'if you don't build trust – and especially if you undermine it – no one will trust you.' We teach them the Michaela pyramid. We don't want them to just avoid demerits and detentions and try to avoid getting caught making the wrong choice – that is the lowest base of the pyramid, where lots of people linger and few succeed; we don't want them just to want merits and rewards; we want them to build trust, to work towards a great future, to automate good habits, to reach the 'top of the pyramid' and contribute to the world and leave a great legacy in their lives.

Day seven, the last day of bootcamp, focuses on gratitude and perseverance. Like every day of bootcamp, the day begins with an assembly on the core themes of the day – on day 7, persisting when it's difficult, and remembering not to take things for granted – themes that run through all interactions between teachers and pupils. We teach the pupils the importance of gratitude, and explain to them all the things they should feel grateful for. We teach them what scientists have discovered: that practising gratitude makes people feel more optimistic, energetic, enthusiastic and happy. We help them notice the many reasons they have to feel fortunate. For one, there are 120 million children worldwide who do not have a school to go to, and who do not have the chance to learn about the wonders of science, art, literature, maths, music, history, religion, geography and languages. We explain that it is easy to forget how lucky we are and take our parents, siblings, families and teachers for granted. So many pupils that our teachers have taught around the country, take for granted the privileges of their brilliant lessons, uniforms, equipment, computers, meals, subjects, teachers and tutors.

We tell Michaela pupils every day of bootcamp (and beyond) how important it is for us to be appreciative rather than ungrateful and unthankful – otherwise, we lose opportunities and people will not want to be generous with us. We tell them how lucky we should all feel to be a part of a school that is so strict and caring, where they have teachers who are all experts who love their subjects, a school that is peaceful and calm in lessons and corridors, and where they can make mistakes without fear of sneering, jeering scorn, where they can learn and work hard without negative peer pressure that trying hard isn't 'cool.' We explain exactly what gratitude means for them: they must be considerate in the corridors and in breaks; they must not bring chewing gum into school that could ruin the place; they must not scribble graffiti on school books or booklets. We tell them to be considerate of future generations of Michaela pupils who would like to enjoy the same privileges they enjoy: for instance, using computers at lunch and after school to do their online subject quizzing practice.

The last day of bootcamp is also about perseverance. Throughout the week, we memorise two poems that are central to Michaela's mindset: William Ernest Henley's 'Invictus' and Rudyard Kipling's 'If.' All week, at 7:30am in the yard in the morning, at 8am in assembly, at 12:30pm when lunch begins, and at 1:25pm when lunchbreak finishes, the entire year 7 cohort chants the lines that have become part of Michaela's organisational DNA. Imagine 150 pupils and teachers cheerfully chanting in unison, with beaming smiles, loving learning and loving life:

> If you can force your heart and nerve and sinew,
> To serve their turn long after they are gone,
> And so hold on when there is nothing in you,
> Except the will that says to them: 'hold on'!

We teach pupils the story of Nelson Mandela, who persevered through a long and difficult struggle for freedom and democracy, who showed great courage, persistence and endurance, whose favourite poem was 'Invictus,' which inspired him when times were toughest, and who overcome all obstacles to become a great world leader.

We show pupils how to apply the life lessons of Mandela's story to their own lives; that they should overcome their own difficulties, setbacks and frustrations with courage and perseverance, that they shouldn't give up if they meet with failure; that both triumph and disaster are illusory imposters, that they should stay positive and keep trying and working hard, even, and especially, when they encounter tough times.

Bootcamp gives all teachers and pupils a shared repository of enduring wisdom, virtues, values, guidance, stories, paragons, parables, lessons, poems, quotations and mantras. Here are some of our memorable mantras that teachers continually remind pupils of at certain choice moments throughout their time at school:

- 'Winners never whinge; whingers never win.'
- 'Fail to prepare; prepare to fail'
- 'You control your emotions; your emotions don't control you'
- 'It's great to be grateful!'

Here are some of the quotations in our collective memory reservoir that we teach pupils:

- 'Success is never final; failure is never fatal; it's the courage that counts'
- 'Habits become your character; your character becomes your destiny'
- 'Anger is weakness; self-control is strength'
- 'If there is no struggle, there is no progress'

In bootcamp, we frontload many of the life lessons that pupils will experience their tutors and teachers teaching them over the coming months and years ahead. It sets our pupils up for success at school and in life, changing the bad habits of a lifetime for good.

	Day 1	Day 2	Day 3	Day 4	Day 5	Day 6	Day 7
Lesson 1	Routines	Rules	Responsibility	Intelligence	Bullying	Trust	Gratitude
Lesson 2	Family Lunch	Consequences	Equipment	Knowledge	Kindness	Arrival	Opportunities
Lesson 3	Reading	Self-Control	Habits	Learning	Integrity	Community	Perseverance
Lesson 4	Culture	Stoicism	Attendance	Self-Quizzing	Technology	Sport	Mandela

Bootcamp teaches pupils to understand exactly why we do everything we do

How do pupils respond to such startlingly high standards, such strict reprimands, such intense drills for handing out books and entering lessons, and such fearsome intolerance of excuses and irresponsibility?

They raise their standards; they start believing they are capable of more than they thought possible before; they shed their bad habits of complaining, arguing and making excuses; they feel empowered. Pupils who react to reprimands with tantrums and tears soon learn swiftly that staying calm and stoical is a far better way to earn respect and avoid reproach. They actually start to enjoy themselves. They enjoy trying to beat their 30-second record time for entering their classroom as a form. They enjoy the competition with other forms, and knowing that their new personal best of 24 seconds beats and outcompetes all other forms! They enjoy knowing that they have reduced the time taken to hand out their books from five minutes in primary school, to 30 seconds on day 1 in rows, to an astounding five seconds by day 7. They enjoy being praised for earning hours and hours and hours of extra learning by improving on their collective routines. Everyone enjoys improving; everyone enjoys succeeding; everyone enjoys teamwork when it works well; everyone enjoys being encouraged and recognised for their improvements. Every teacher is out and about during transitions, filling the corridors with warm, encouraging positivity and palpably enthusing excitement: 'Every second counts! Every moment matters for learning!' '100% attendance so far Talik, great stuff, keep it up!' 'Love that smile, Sasha, lovely energy!'

Of course, seven days aren't enough to break all the habits of a lifetime. Many of the children have been in bad habits for seven years of primary school or more, and not all will transform within seven days, seven weeks, or even seven months. However, what is remarkable is quite how many do change within seven days. The vast majority of pupils settle swiftly to feel happy and proud of the school, their knowledge and how much they have changed. So many of our pupils, even the best-behaved pupils who wouldn't ever think about swearing, or rolling their eyes at an adult, now tell me that in primary school they were naughty, rude, disrespectful and dishonest. So many pupils have told me that they hit other pupils, siblings and even teachers. So many of them have undergone a fundamental transformation in their personality, mindset and interactions. It is as if they are completely different people, and within a few days. Why is this?

I think there's something very powerful about collective norms. Take lunch for example. Every pupil — all 180 — looks at the teacher leading a lunchtime topic in total silence. No one shouts rudely over the silence or insults another kid under their breath. Rudeness is completely abnormal. Interrupting is completely abnormal. Unkindness and insults are completely abnormal. Peer pressure is reversed from negative pressure to disrupt and bully; instead, we harness positive peer pressure to conform and comply with beautiful, golden, collective, respectful silence in lessons and set times in lunch and break. It is a natural human tendency: we are social animals who like to conform. We don't want to face disapproval of the group and so we tend to do as others do. If 200 others around you are silently, reverently listening, you tend to go with the flow of the stream rather than swim against a strong tide of approbation that inevitably follows from breaking the taboo against disrespect. There is a strong, unconscious gravitational pull that grounds pupils who disrupted lessons in primary school. There, it may have been contagiously normal to shout out or slouch or distract others. At Michaela, pupils concentrate hard in lessons, which are mostly silent and always focused. The norms of respect and obedience are positively viral. Michaela pupils do what all teachers ask them to do on the first time of asking, and if they do not, they are instantly, authoritatively challenged on it. Following instructions first time, every time, was so far from being normal in my last school as to be unthinkable for most pupils. By contrast, it is replying rudely to a teacher's instructions at Michaela that is unthinkable.

One of the most fundamental parts of the bootcamp and continuing professional development (CPD) we run for all teachers before the year 7 pupils arrive is about narrating the reasons behind why we do everything we do. This goes for every single detail. It is not obvious to a pupil why we have such strict rules on the small details such as silence, jewellery, makeup, haircuts, logos, table manners, taking turns, following all instructions, not interrupting, not slouching, not reading without rulers, not arriving late, not making excuses, not avoiding eye contact, not mumbling in conversations or in class, and so on, for the thousand detailed expectations that we set out in bootcamp. Many pupils in the first few days have asked me questions like these: 'Why do we all have to read with rulers? I don't at home!' or 'Why can't we have logos on our coats? My friends in other schools can!'

We want all pupils to understand exactly why we do what we do, and we have seven days as a team of teachers to achieve this for our new pupils. We strive to explain the rationale behind the deliberate decisions we have made, and to make that rationale clear, rational, logical and even emotionally appealing. We share an exciting big picture vision with them: when they are 18, they will have the choice of the greatest universities and most fulfilling careers in the world ahead of them. Once pupils know the logic behind our expectations – that they are purposeful, designed to give them advantages over their competitors and to boost their long-term success and lifelong happiness – they are happy to accept them and willingly strive to meet the sky-high standards. Soon, pupils begin to understand that the rules are not arbitrary and hateful, imposed because teachers want power over them or because we dislike them. Almost all pupils grasp that it is precisely the opposite: we are tough on them because we care about them, because we love seeing them succeed, because we want them to achieve, because we believe in them, and because we are prepared to take the tough choice to hold them to the highest standards that we would want for our own children. For pupils to grasp this, all our teachers must also understand the rationale behind all of our expectations clearly, to be able to explain and narrate it. Even teachers who have only just joined the school.

Bootcamp is highly effective for new teacher induction

Teachers new to a school, even experienced teachers, have a tough assignment. They have hundreds of new pupils, teachers and staff to get to know. They have hundreds of rules and consequences to remember. They have hundreds of details to remember, and they have to be able to make hundreds of choices every day, as well as often having to justify those choices, aiming for consistency with the choices being made by other teachers round the school, especially on fairly emotive judgement calls like giving detentions. Teachers new to a school feel overloaded with all of the complex new systems they have to get their heads around the behaviour system, the teaching and assessment system, the IT and data systems, the timetabling and rooming system, the duty rota, the pastoral tutoring and registration systems. The complexity is ferocious. Toughest of all, they often teach year 9, year 10 or year 11 classes who have been at the school for two, three or four years longer than them and who know the systems and the people in the school far better than the new teachers themselves do. The challenge of establishing credibility and authority in the first half-term in a new school for any teacher new to the school, however experienced, is intense.

Bootcamp provides a strong, secure and sound foundation for inducting new teachers into the school. For a start, there is extensive time: they have seven full days with year 7 pupils who are also new to the school. This allows new teachers to get their bearings on the details that established teachers in the school take for granted: teachers' names; which teacher is on which floor and in which classroom; expectations of pupils in lessons and around school; computer network, email, registration, behaviour system and photocopier logins. The 60-page bootcamp booklet created for pupils, with 28 lessons on routines, rules, consequences, equipment, uniform, bullying, technology, attendance, punctuality and more besides, doubles up as a new staff induction handbook, with details, rationales, questions and scenarios set out in advance. As soon as they are recruited, new teachers are given this handbook, months in advance of starting. Reading the 60-page guide so far in advance sets them up for success at explaining all the rationales to new pupils. This in turn sets them up to successfully establish authority with older year 8 and year 9 pupils that they teach and interact with around the school. Bootcamp, a seven-day training regime for new pupils, is also a seven-day training regime for new teachers.

Alongside the carefully designed schedule of pupil lessons, we sequence the staffing of lessons very carefully, too. New teachers only observe established teachers for the first day; they do not teach at all. They deliberately practise some decontextualised drills on the core routines that help us achieve 100% focus from 100% of pupils in 100% of lessons, such as our routine for silence ('3-2-1'-and 'SLANT'), and our instructions for tasks: 'You have 30 seconds to write the title in your exercise books in silence; ready ... go!'

By day two, they teach a lesson and receive instant and extensive feedback from an established teacher. On days three to seven, they teach two lessons a day. After the first lesson, they discuss in depth the feedback and priorities to act on for the next lesson later that day. I seek feedback from teachers each September about how to improve for next year, so we can hone teacher induction and the new staff CPD programme during the preceding two staff training days and those precious seven days of learning. We still have a great deal to learn and to improve.

One of the things that I am most passionate about, and one of the many things that I think makes Michaela unique, is that every single teacher knows every single child's name at Michaela. We tell all teachers that it is a requirement that they learn all pupils' names. This is phenomenally powerful. It is astounding and impressive for pupils, seeing all teachers making the effort to learn every single one of their names. It impresses on them that their teachers care so much about them that they are prepared to memorise and remember all their names. This goes not just for the 120 pupils in year 7s who arrive in the first week of September, but for the 240 pupils in year 8 and year 9 who in 2016 arrived a week after, when bootcamp had ended. So many pupils have pointed out to me how astonishing it was that the new teachers knew their names, even on their first day back after the summer! How is it possible?

We use digital flashcards on an app so that all teachers have at their fingertips, in their pockets, the chance to quiz themselves on pupil names and photos whenever they want, anywhere, anytime. This will become harder as we grow from 360 to 600 pupils, and it may take longer for new staff – a half-term instead of a week, perhaps – but it makes a huge difference. There is no stronger demonstration of how much our teachers care about our children than they effort they put in to know their names. Pupils feel genuinely cared for and not nameless, especially as all teachers can use their names (perhaps one of their most prized 'possessions') in corridors to encourage and infuse them with positive energy. Equally, it establishes teacher authority in every interaction: instead of saying, '*You!* Come over here', it is ten times more powerful to say: 'Raekwon! Come over here.' It demonstrates and demands instant, reciprocal respect. There is magic in a school where all teachers know all children's names: an alchemy that turns potentially negative or hostile confrontations into glowing, positive and sometimes transformative conversations. Simply put, the kids feel loved.

Bootcamp gives departments time to resource the curriculum

Bootcamp also gives departments time to develop their curriculum and improve their resources so that every single lesson is effective, whether taught by a grizzled veteran or an unqualified novice teacher. Heads of Departments have nine days (including two staff inset days before bootcamp) to allocate units amongst established teachers to improve. Teachers take an existing unit for each year group, and work to strengthen the clarity of questions, the sequence of recaps, the challenge of extension questions, the precision of explanations and examples or the selection decisions on knowledge organisers. New units are also assigned to be written and resourced, with a focus on quality sequences, text, questions, exemplars and organisers. Some departments also use this time to write exams for the biannual exam week in January and July, planning, resourcing and printing far ahead into the year so that nothing is a mad, scrambling rush at the last minute. Part of the reason our ambitious curriculum in all subjects is improving year-on-year is that we dedicate extensive amounts of time, including the first nine days of each year, to focusing on it, discussing it, sharing feedback on it and improving it.

This extended resourcing and subject CPD, explained by Jo Facer, allows teachers plenty of time to hone their own curriculum knowledge and subject expertise. It boosts the authority with which they meet incoming older pupils who themselves have developed fearsome accumulated subject knowledge after years of Michaela teaching. Again, many year 8 and year 9 pupils have told me that they are impressed on being taught by a teacher new to the school, with how much they seem to know about their subject. Kids love being taught by experts. Teachers often come into teaching because they love their subjects. Bootcamp invests a week to declutter all distractions, foregrounding a relentless focus on rigorous subject teaching and effective, enduring knowledge transmission for the rest of the year. Here is how one Head of Department puts it:

> Bootcamp is a lifesaver for the subject: it gives us two entire weeks to get all the curriculum decisions made, to get all the resources written, to get all the booklets and organisers finalised, to get much of the printing and photocopying done for the full half-term so that nothing is being done the weekend before or the night before. It makes for a far stronger start to the year than if we didn't have it.

When we started in 2014 with our first bootcamp, I thought its major advantage was that it changed pupils' habits. By 2016, now that we have run bootcamp three times, I've seen that there is another, equally important advantage: not only is it life-changing for pupils, it is a game-changer for teachers, too. Because our teachers – all our teachers, even those who have never taught before or who are brand new to Michaela – are calm, confident, refreshed and energetic right from the outset, as opposed to stressed, fraught, hassled and frazzled in the first week, the pupils are also calm, settled, happy and confident in their teachers' care: they know they are in good hands. Bootcamp gives teachers new perspectives on authority, on discipline, on detail, on consistency, on expertise, on detail, on candour, on feedback and on alignment, as testified by Sarah Cullen and Will Eastment's chapters, both written after just one week at the school.

When school leaders visit, they often ask us: 'what's the one thing that we can learn and take away from Michaela that would work even in an established culture, without starting from scratch like a free school?' There is no silver bullet to creating a happy, successful school, and I'm certain that we at Michaela will make many mistakes and encounter many setbacks over the coming years. I am equally confident that we will overcome them. I once read that the first week is the most important week of the school year. My experiences so far have taught me that this is absolutely right. If there is one Michaela idea that might have a profound impact on other schools, it is establishing an extended September bootcamp induction (perhaps not just for year 7 pupils) that teaches pupils the habits they need to succeed. We have found bootcamp to be life changing for our children: it changes their life chances and propels them well on the way to achieving their highest aspirations.

Authority in Action

Lucy Newman

In many schools in England, authority is a rarely uttered word. Instead of authority, many teachers laud building relationships with their classes. While positive relationships are vital for a successful school, they cannot be the only basis of authority. For new teachers or supply teachers, authority based on relationships alone is especially liable to break down. The more a school depends on relationships for authority, the more within-school variation there is, and the wider the gap between the behaviour in the classrooms of veteran teachers and novice teachers; the more disruption there is in supply lessons.

Charlie Carroll's book *On The Edge*, telling of his year as a supply teacher in English schools, unveils the consequences for children and supply teachers if they exist in a vacuum of adult authority. He was disobeyed, shouted at, sworn at, insulted, abused, threatened, intimidated and persistently bullied by aggressive pupils. Such abuse sounds shocking, but it is in fact widespread: according to the Department for Education, in 2014 alone, 8,000 pupils in England were excluded for assaulting teachers. Even more shockingly, in many cases little or nothing is done about this assault. 43% of education staff said they have had to deal with physical violence from a pupil in the last year, according to a 2016 survey by the Association of Teachers and Lecturers. Ultimately, you get what you tolerate: school leadership teams get the misbehaviour in schools that they tolerate from their worst behaved pupils.

A cornerstone of our beliefs at Michaela is our conviction that adult authority must insist that all pupils follow all teachers' instructions, first time, every time.

As a left-leaning teacher, I began my career with a strong distrust of adult authority, but after my experiences teaching in deprived inner-city schools I now see things differently. When adults do not have authority in the classroom, there is a power vacuum that is filled by the children. Hannah Arendt argued that: 'where the adult is not in a position of authority, peer group authority will rule.' If a child is controlling the classroom, it is highly unlikely their goal is to improve their classmates' long-term life chances. Any pupils who quietly want to learn lose out when louder, more disruptive children derail lesson after lesson.

The decline of authority in many schools has not led to great relationships but to mayhem. Children suffer from the lack of authority. Arendt argues that 'by being emancipated from the authority of adults the child has not been freed but has been subjected to a much more terrifying and truly tyrannical authority, the tyranny of the majority.' Who has authority when the adults lack it? Often, it is bullies.

Children in England are unhappier at school than their peers in almost every other country. One international survey showed that widespread bullying is causing huge damage to children's wellbeing. An estimated half a million ten to 12-year-olds are physically bullied at school. According to a study by the Children's Society, they found that 38% of children surveyed had been hit by classmates in one month alone.

The disorder and indiscipline rife in schools creates the conditions where bullying can persist. The power vacuum in corridors and classrooms leaves vulnerable children susceptible to being bullied. Where there is no adult authority, there is chaos and pupils suffer. As psychologist Jonathan Haidt writes in *The Righteous Mind*, paraphrasing Marcus Aurelius, 'you don't help the bees by harming the hive.' Just like bees, children need the healthy hives of orderly schools and calm classrooms to learn, achieve and thrive.

The lack of authority in schools impacts on pupils from disadvantaged backgrounds most, who need to catch up with their peers where there are gaps in knowledge, numeracy and literacy. As a child, I went to a state school in Leicester where 50% of pupils did not pass their GCSEs, and where there were many pupils from disadvantaged backgrounds. On the whole, we behaved for some teachers sometimes. I may have mucked around in lessons, but when it came down to it, I could cram for exams at the last minute and do fine. This had nothing to do with the school I attended, but was because my educated family at home supported me. I was ahead of many of the other pupils before I even arrived at secondary school. Many of my peers had parents who spoke little English, or parents who could not help them as they were working multiple jobs, or didn't want to or know how to help. Those children suffered in ways that I did not. They could not afford to waste even a minute messing around in lessons. But I could. On results day, I opened an envelope full of A grades whilst they left school with nothing, many of them hardly even literate. An authority deficit was one crucial factor that deprived them of their potential.

Authority at Michaela

At Michaela, we highly value adult authority and children's politeness and respect. All pupils are expected to follow all instructions from all adults first time, every time, without argument or protest. Whether they are interacting with the Headmistress, a Deputy Head, teacher, office staff, caterer or cleaner, the same expectations are demanded of children: respectful, polite interactions with all adults at all times.

A visiting Head of Year once asked me the question: 'Are they ever rude?' One of the most remarkable things for me working at Michaela is that the children are almost never even impolite. At Michaela, to be rude has been made taboo; for the vast majority of pupils, it is unthinkable. The visitor said his school had a consistent system of consequences in place but the big difference, as he saw it, was that it did not have the culture of adult authority.

The pupils' respect for authority at Michaela stems from a strong culture of adult hierarchy and is supported by strong staff consistency. Authority is based on the adult's role as a professional and not the relationship alone. We recognise that teachers are adults, pupils are children and that every classroom works best when a benevolent adult is in charge rather than the most assertive child.

This culture creates strong, pervasive norms. No adult tolerates rudeness or disrespect. Clear consequences are calmly, consistently and predictably given by all staff. Politeness is reinforced every day in every interaction – we nip any signs of disrespect in the bud, such as sneering or scowling. If any pupil is slightly rude around school, there is a reaction of disappointed shock from the adult. Equally, teachers constantly encourage and recognise politeness and kindness from pupils. As pupils leave lessons, they often say, 'thank you for the lesson, Miss!' Teachers thank pupils for their gratitude with mantras of positive reinforcement such as, 'it's great to be grateful' and 'it's great not to take things for granted.'

Moreover, to be strict is not to be cruel or uncaring: adult authority is actually kind. All Michaela teachers try to embody 'tough love' in their interactions: they are tough on pupils and demand only the most polite interactions, but they do so with positivity, love and belief in every single child's potential.

During new staff induction at Michaela, the leadership team give three starting ingredients for teacher authority: names, knowledge and certainty. First, all the new teachers learn pupils names. This makes an enormous difference in interactions with pupils. Children feel as though every single teacher really cares about them personally, because every teacher has made the effort to learn and remember their name. It also makes giving reprimands much stronger for all teachers, because they can use the pupil's name rather than weakly saying 'you there!'

Secondly, teachers need to know their subject and curriculum knowledge inside out to establish authoritative expertise among the pupils they teach. Our children in year 8 and above have already learned an astonishing amount of knowledge, as Joe Kirby has outlined in more detail. The children test their new teachers, referring to previous texts and concepts and asking about links to catch them out. New teachers, armed with the previous year's knowledge organisers, are able to rise to this challenge and refer to prior learning with confidence.

Thirdly, new teachers are trained to teach and discipline children with decisive certainty. We acknowledge the uncomfortable reality: children sense uncertainty, see it as weakness and often exploit it. We want there to be no difference between novice and expert teachers. During bootcamp, our new teachers observe the rules being meticulously explained and explicitly taught to new pupils, which reduces the possibility of them enforcing non-existent rules or not catching misbehaviour we sanction.

Many people fear authority, but children are much happier in a calm environment where boundaries are clear. Moreover, we also take care to balance authority with kindness. We encourage healthy conversations about punishments. We teach the pupils explicitly how best to question teacher: after the lesson, and politely. It is vital the teacher does not spend time in the lesson having a conversation about a demerit when they should be teaching the other 30 pupils. We tell pupils regularly why we are so strict: it is because we care about their future, we care about their long-term happiness. Teacher authority is about purpose, not power; our purpose of helping pupils to live happy, fulfilling lives.

We acknowledge that teachers are fallible. We admit our limits. If a child is upset at a decision, we give the analogy of being the referee at a football match: 'I am the classroom referee, and my word is final – I can't promise to make every decision perfectly – no one is perfect – I may make mistakes; but that decision still may stand.' The referee's word has to be final or the game disintegrates.

Research shows there are certain conditions that make pupils happy to follow authority and strong leadership. People tend to be happy to follow when they see that their group needs to get something done. At Michaela we explain to pupils why we are so strict; we care about them and want to help them be the best they can be. Haidt writes that 'people do not resent authority when they feel part of something.' As we explore in our chapters on kindness and family lunch, Michaela forges a strong family community.

Freedom

There are those in education who value negative freedom: freedom from adult authority, freedom from rules. In our schools, we too often give children negative freedom to misbehave, to choose if they do or don't want to learn, and too often it is at the expense of their own futures. The most important freedom for our pupils is the positive long-term freedom to choose a lifelong career of their choice. It is our job as adults not to allow children to be ruled by their short-term desires. Short term, for 13 years of schooling, children learn to suppress selfishness and interact with empathy. Long term, this allows them to live a fulfilling life for many decades in society. For many children, every minute in school is vital for them to overcome the poverty of their upbringing. It is shocking that 17% of 16 to 19-year-olds have problems with literacy. It is shocking that in 2015, 47% of children left school without even five A*-C GCSEs including English and Maths. There is nothing truly freeing about pupils who leave school illiterate and unqualified after 11 years of being 'free' from listening, concentrating, learning, self-discipline and academic achievement.

I want the pupils I teach to become adults who genuinely change the country and the world. Whilst they are young, children are learning and growing. There will come a time when they, as adults, should have a different relationship with authority. Paradoxically, the teacher's authority is integral to ensure that the child grows into an adult who has the power to question authority in wider society. To change society, to improve it for the better, you need to be able to succeed in national exams and to be able to understand your cultural inheritance. If our children are deprived of strict, benevolent adult authority in the short term at school, longer-term throughout their lives as adults they will not be able to question political claims in elections, referenda or debates – nor will they ever become revolutionary thinkers, writers or leaders.

When Boris Johnson, then the Mayor of London, visited Michaela, in a History lesson he gave the date of Constantine's converting the Roman Empire to Christianity as 312AD. A pupil put up his hand and politely but firmly said, 'I believe it is 313AD, sir.' This 11-year old from Brent corrected the Mayor of London. The pupil knew he was right – and he was right. He had confidence. He had conviction. This Michaela pupil from one of England's most deprived boroughs had the courage and confidence to challenge the Eton and Oxford-educated Mayor of England's most powerful city, because the adults at Michaela have the authority to teach him.

Why Don't We Respect Teachers?

Hin-Tai Ting

'Those who can, do; those who can't, teach.'
— George Bernard Shaw

'Why on earth are you a teacher? I still don't understand. You could've done so many things and you chose to become a teacher.'
— Multiple pupils from my previous schools

I watched the 2015 BBC documentary 'Chinese School' with fascination. Among the many scenes of interest, one theme was clear: the highly experienced Chinese teachers had absolutely no behaviour management techniques whatsoever. They didn't wait for full attention, nor did they impose any sanctions for low-level disruption. The average NQT, trained in the UK, would've done a better job quietening those rowdy classes. However, the fundamental issue wasn't one of teacher training or teaching skills: instead, it was clear that the Chinese teachers had simply never experienced any behaviour like this before. That whole area, which takes up so much CPD, ITT, and teacher headspace here in the UK, hardly even exists in China!

In a study from 2009, Caldarella et al researched over 500 Chinese primary teachers' perceptions of difficult classroom behaviour. The unanimous response was that *pupil non-attention* was both their most frequent and most troublesome behaviour issue. Less than 1% of the teachers viewed non-compliance and disruption as a frequent occurrence. In contrast, it hardly needs saying that a teacher in an English school would be lucky to have non-attention as the most troublesome behaviour in their classroom.

In China, teachers don't have to worry about sanctioning poor behaviour. Instead, pupils listen. Pupils thank you for your lesson. Pupils act towards their teachers just how they act towards their doctors. Pupils even jump to clean up the classroom for their teachers, without being asked. In other words, in China, pupils respect their teachers.

What a contrast to England. Teachers in English schools are not respected by their own pupils in their own classrooms. To most teachers, this statement doesn't need defending – it's a fact lived out every day. The 2005 and 2009 Steer reports on behaviour disagree: 'the overall standard of behaviour achieved by schools is good and has improved in recent years.' Nonetheless, in 2014, even

Ofsted (who observe schools at their best) recognised the bleak reality. The report 'Below the radar' identified a culture where 'teachers have come to accept some low-level disruption as a part of everyday life in the classroom... pupils too often demonstrate a lack of respect for staff by talking across them or taking too long to respond to instructions.'

It seems, then, that teachers in England tolerate disrespect from their pupils. Many teachers might balk at this description, despite agreeing that they face disrespect on a regular basis. Who would want to tolerate disrespect on a daily basis? Don't most teachers fight against disrespect with warnings and sanctions and detentions? Everyone concedes that pupil-teacher relationships in China are much rosier than in England, but isn't that due to deep-seated cultural factors, rather than what teachers tolerate, surely? I used to think this way, too. Pupils were disrespectful to me, but I reasoned that this was simply part and parcel of teaching hormonal adolescents in the inner city.

Then I visited Michaela. I arrived for my first visit just after the school day had finished. Even then, on entering the school in my suit and tie, most of the (decidedly inner city and teenage) pupils greeted me with eye contact, warm smiles and sincere greetings. I was amazed. More importantly, I was wrong. Disrespect does not have to be the norm. Tragically, as Ofsted have observed, it has become the norm in British schools. Moreover, we have exacerbated the problem in the ways we most commonly deal with disrespect.

Take a look at the advice from Bill Rogers, the source of much widely praised behaviour management CPD. If you've been on any behaviour CPD, you've probably heard of Rogers, and if you haven't then you have undoubtedly heard his strategies, which are widespread across behaviour management literature. The advice we value can reveal the real issues we face. Some of Rogers' top tips:

1. **Take up time:** after giving an instruction to an off-task pupil, divert your attention from them and let them obey your instruction in their own time – perhaps by walking away or focusing on another pupil.

2. **Pause direction:** similar to the above – after you have asked for a pupil's attention, pause, so that they have some time to respond to your attention, meet your eye contact, and focus on what you're going to say.

3. **Partial agreement:** after a pupil disputes something with you, agree partially with their sentiment and give them the benefit of the doubt, and then redirect them to the task they should be focused upon. For example: 'okay, maybe you were talking about the work, but it's too loud and you two should be on question 2 by now.'

4. **Focus on the primary behaviour:** if a pupil reacts badly to a correction or a warning, don't react to this 'secondary' behaviour, but instead divert focus back to the primary behaviour that you were trying to correct in the first place.

5. **Forced choices:** if a pupil is not following your instructions, instead of just repeating your instruction, force them to choose between two options you determine. They can either choose to do what you say, or they choose to receive a particular sanction. For example: 'Either you work silently, or you're moving seats.'

Some of these should be familiar to you, and if so, I expect that you even use them as part of your regular behaviour management. I'm not questioning how effective Rogers' techniques are in the classroom. In fact, in previous schools I used these techniques regularly myself: they were helpful in minimising confrontations and refocusing pupils upon their learning. So what's my problem with them?

On closer inspection, the very reason these strategies work well is because they are designed to work in classrooms where pupils do not intrinsically respect their teachers. They are techniques designed to get pupils' compliance without ever challenging pupils' deep and entrenched disrespect. Indeed, they are techniques presupposed upon a lack of deep respect for teachers.

What makes me say this? Let's think carefully about the assumptions that lie behind each strategy. When we give pupils take up time or pause direction, we essentially allow pupils to pout and delay before complying with our reasonable requests. During take up time, they might roll their eyes or smirk behind our backs, but that's not deemed important as long as they eventually get round to obeying our instructions. When we extend partial agreement to pupils, we essentially allow pupils to lie disrespectfully to us without any consequence – in fact, we can even collude in their lies: 'okay, maybe you were talking about the work, but let's work silently now.' When we focus on primary behaviours and ignore secondary responses, we essentially allow pupils to answer back disrespectfully without facing any consequence for it; pupils aren't challenged when they answer back or roll their eyes or tut or sigh, 'as long as they get back to the learning.' When we present pupils with forced choices instead of simply expecting to be obeyed, we essentially remove respect as the key reason for listening to a teacher and replace it with pupils' naked self-interest. Pupils choose to listen, not out of any respect for their teacher, but out of fear of negative consequences.

In short, behind all of these strategies lies this prevailing logic: pupil learning is the key priority, so ignore pupil disrespect, don't make it an issue and let pupils save face so that they will eventually co-operate and focus on the learning. Indeed, these strategies all work because they ignore the lack of respect that is so endemic among British pupils. We can barely imagine challenging disrespect because of the great effort it requires and the emotional confrontations that we fear will result. So instead we have sacrificed our own expectations of respect for the sake of easier classroom management. Once we see these strategies working in terms of pupil learning, we stop realising what they've made us give up. There's an undeniable yet perverse logic to it: focus on pupil learning, stop expecting pupils' respect, and their behaviour towards you becomes easier to accept, easier to swallow, and thus easier to manage.

Whilst working in my previous school, I vividly realised that I had unwittingly bought into this mindset during a conversation with a poorly behaved pupil. I'd sent him out earlier in the lesson for continued distracting behaviour. I went out, armed to the hilt with Rogers' techniques:

Teacher: I'm talking to you, please listen to me. Yes, you might have found the task difficult, but that doesn't mean you should distract others. [Partial agreement]

Response: [*Angry protestations that he wasn't being distracting, that I was clueless, that I was picking on him.*]

Teacher: You were making jokes about her, I saw you, you were being distracting.

Response: [*More of the same protestations, thrown in with tuts, eye rolls, walking to and fro in the corridor.*]

Teacher: You said this about her, which was distracting.

[*This dispute and his responses repeat for several minutes – 'focusing on the primary behaviour.'*]

Teacher: I need you to listen to me. Either you do the ten minute detention I'm setting, or you leave and I will have to report your behaviour to your Head of Year. [Forced choice.]

At this point, a widely feared and respected Head of Year turned up in the corridor and correctly perceived me as being out of my depth. Her very first reaction to him: 'stand up straight, stop leaning against the wall, take your hands out of your pockets, stop making that tutting noise, look at me when I'm speaking.' His demeanour changed instantly. After quizzing him further, with warmth yet strictness, he soon 'chose' to do what I said. After he re-entered my classroom, the Head of Year then took me to task, 'He shouldn't be speaking to you like that, that's disrespectful. Especially that tutting noise he makes when you're talking. Don't let him get away with that.'

Her advice was invaluable. It kick-started my dissatisfaction with Rogers' strategies; especially when I realised that I hadn't even heard his tuts, or noticed his disrespectful posture, or consciously clocked the disrespect in his talking back. By focusing on the learning, ignoring secondary behaviours, giving partial agreement and so on, I had lost not only my expectations of respect, but also my ability to even pick up on disrespect. What's more, it wasn't the most effective way of dealing with this difficult pupil.

After this impromptu episode of CPD with the Head of Year, I began to have more fruitful relationships with pupils when I made it clear that their disrespectful behaviours were totally inappropriate. When I made it clear that I deserved their respect as their teacher, their growing respect naturally changed our relationship for the better. Perhaps most importantly, I started to see that I was doing my pupils a disservice when I enabled them to grow so disrespectful toward others.

I asked earlier whether teachers truly tolerate poor behaviour in schools. Schools across the country build their behaviour policies on the bedrock of Rogers' strategies. As I have shown, those strategies, at their very core, both tolerate pupil disrespect and make us blind to it at the same time. Furthermore, the very existence of Rogers' strategies proves the widespread existence of pupil disrespect across the country, too. The reason Rogers advises teachers to ignore secondary behaviours is precisely because pupils are responding disrespectfully. The reason Rogers advises teachers to force choices and to give take up time is precisely because pupils don't respect requests. So while these methods may get pupils to learn in the short term, over time, they will undermine respect for teachers in schools.

Thankfully, there is an alternative, and it doesn't have to mean teaching in China. Jonny Porter's explanation of no-excuses behaviour management outlines precisely what we need; stop tolerating such disrespect and stop making allowances for it. As Jonny describes, narration, again, is key and at Michaela, we stamp out disrespect not from a purely authoritarian basis – 'respect me because I am the adult!' – but instead out of a desire for our pupils to become respectful citizens. When disrespect occurs, a common reply might be: 'you never roll your eyes at someone. If I rolled my eyes at Ms Birbalsingh, she would fire me instantly. That is such a bad habit!' Pupils get it. Of course they do – it's mere civility that we're teaching. Tragically, it's terrifying that so many teachers, myself included, have been taught to ignore eye rolls, tuts, sighs, answering back, all in the name of focusing on the primary behaviour and stressing behaviour for learning. If we're not even teaching civility, what's the point in teaching our pupils anything else?

There's a frightening societal turn to this, too. Pupils learn not to respect teachers at school. The natural consequence: they become adults who don't respect teachers as a profession. Given the proliferation of poor behaviour in English schools, we have become a society where teachers are not respected.

One might object that this is simply semantic wordplay: 'respect' for a profession (i.e. regarding it well) – and 'respect' towards authority figures (i.e. obeying, complying with) signify slightly different things. But this is to draw too large a divergence between the definitions of 'respect,' which are naturally tightly linked. When you frequently disobey someone's wishes, you reveal your fundamental lack of regard for that person. A pupil may say they 'respect' a teacher – they may acknowledge that the teacher works hard, that they teach well enough, that they do an important job for society. However, if in the classroom that pupil doesn't consistently listen to and do what their teacher says, their attitude certainly isn't one of 'respect.' Pupils who don't fully obey their teachers are disrespecting them, and nothing will suddenly make them grow to respect their victims in adult life. They might pity them, or feel guilty concerning them, but the war for respect was lost a long time ago.

One might also object that teachers are actually widely respected in society. But the evidence for our disrespect can be found across society. In my teaching experience prior to joining Michaela, I have had pupils from every key stage puzzling over my career choice. Their confusion emerges when they hear that I went to Oxford University and have solid academic credentials. 'So why on earth are you a teacher, sir? You could get a far better job!' My former pupils simply could not believe that teaching could be an attractive career path for highly qualified graduates. It is hard to feel part of a respected profession when you are on the receiving end of such incredulity.

Moving beyond my own experience, you've probably seen Taylor Mali's inspiring spoken word 'What Teachers Make.' It's a rightly popular poem of praise to teachers and all we do, but it actually begins as a reply to a rude dinner party guest who asks 'what's a kid going to learn from someone who decided his best option in life was to become a teacher?' Mali's need to defend and extol teachers, however eloquently he does it, reveals the lack of respect we receive. In contrast, there don't seem to be any viral videos of doctors or nurses having to defend their career choices at dinner parties.

Zooming out to look at the wider culture, the very existence and popularity of Bernard Shaw's 'those who can't, teach' quote paints the brightest picture. If this quote didn't chime with wider perceptions of teachers in the UK, it would never have been said, nor become so popular. Contrast Bernard Shaw's quote with sayings from China: a quick Google helped me find a page featuring over

60 'proverbs for praising teachers.' To pick one, you could describe a teacher as 诲人不倦 – 'instructing with tireless zeal' – in your thank-you cards. This phrase would be especially well received, since it dates back thousands of years to Confucius's Analects. In other words, the Chinese have been respecting teachers with special idioms for millennia. And while Michaela pupils haven't yet started to devise idioms to praise their teachers, I am still struck by how most of my pupils take the time to thank me earnestly for the lesson, whilst they rush off to their next lesson. When they leave Michaela, their impression of the teaching profession will be drenched in gratitude. They will be filled with respect for teachers.

Relatedly, the lack of respect for the teaching profession is particularly strange considering how enjoyable the job can be. Teaching is purposeful, meaningful and beneficial to those we work with. In almost every single hour of our job, we make a tangible difference to the human beings in front of us. How many careers can offer that? Teaching is also engaging and challenging on numerous levels, combining aspects of acting, coaching, sales, parenting, academia, research, leadership, not to mention others. We're also given a huge amount of autonomy to do the job how we see fit. As a result, teaching is rarely boring. Indeed, most days on the job I find myself in a state of flow or being in the zone; time sweeps me along as I'm fully engaged in what I'm doing. Flow, autonomy, purpose and challenge are proven to be several of the key indicators of a satisfying job. Of course, teachers face significant challenges with workload and behaviour, but if you can get through those, it is a great job. On top of all this, teaching is not poorly compensated: an NQT starts off at just below the UK median salary, and after five years of pay progression, a teacher earns more than 80% of all workers in the UK. Given all these characteristics of teaching as a job, we share many similarities with doctors. Notably, the 2013 Global Teacher Status Index showed the Chinese respect teachers on the same level as doctors. Yet teachers are nowhere close to doctors' level of respect here in the UK.

I'm also struck by the pupils of my first school's aforementioned incredulity at the attractiveness of a career in teaching. They attended a school that delivered excellent results. That school is full of good and often inspiring teachers, with whom the pupils interact, day after day, during their formative years. Given their experiences, there seems to be no ground for anything other than respect for teachers. Yet for all this, they nonetheless cannot fathom how someone could get a good degree, 'only' to become a teacher. Contrast their responses with my experiences living in China: upon discovering I was to become a teacher, peers – and even superiors – would look upon me with admiration, often verging on reverence.

Perhaps the quickest way to see our society's lack of respect toward teachers is to read any internet article or discussion that concerns us. There will inevitably be a comment mentioning at least one of: how we swan in to work at 9 and leave at 3; how we work barely half the year; how we're overpaid. Sometimes even searching for such articles is enough to prove it. Take a look at how Google completes this sentence, based on previous searches:

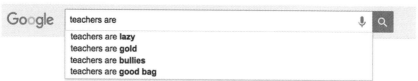

Whether in comparison with attitudes elsewhere, or just on our own terms, I think the picture's fairly clear: teaching in the UK isn't as respected as it ought to be – either in schools, or in society. Indeed, if teachers do not expect respect from their pupils, disrespect for teachers across society can do nothing else but continue.

Finally, why get so worked up over respect in the first place? We normally associate a focus on respect with gangsters and prisons – isn't this all a bit unhealthy? There are three major reasons for making it a priority. Firstly, a respected profession is one that attracts and retains high-quality applicants. Teaching in the UK is in the midst of a well-publicised recruitment and retention crisis. The National Audit Office's 2016 report 'Training New Teachers' revealed that the Department for Education's (DfE) teacher recruitment targets were last met four years ago: from 2011 to 2014, the recorded rate of vacancies and temporarily filled positions in state schools has more than doubled; in that same time period, there has been an 11% rise in the number of teachers leaving the profession. Over and over again, poor pupil behaviour – i.e. disrespect – is cited as a reason for leaving the profession. We need teachers to be respected in their own classrooms so that schools are fully staffed with high-quality teachers.

Secondly, and relatedly, recent studies are showing that teachers in the UK are demotivated. While the causes are many, a sense of greater respect both inside and outside the classroom would undoubtedly make a difference to many teachers. Thirdly, and perhaps most importantly, respect for others is the foundation of a civil society. Recent political and public discourse makes it abundantly clear how deeply we lack this foundation. Yet overly tolerant behaviour management techniques, championed by many, fail to build this foundation with our pupils. If we don't expect teachers to be respected, we allow pupils to talk back, challenge, lie to our faces, and follow instructions in their own sweet time. They learn that respect isn't important. They learn that they can get away with disrespect. And so our society suffers as a result.

There is another way. At Michaela, we expect pupils to listen to teachers instantly, to follow our instructions, and we back that expectation up with consequences. That's emphatically not to say that we should revert to bullying or tyrannical forms of behaviour management. At Michaela, sanctions are given calmly, always accompanied by clear explanations why disrespect is not appropriate towards teachers. We show them how we treat all pupils with respect and how unfair it is not to return it. We make it abundantly clear to pupils how lucky they are to receive a free education from dedicated teachers, and how disrespect is completely inappropriate. We talk about how important respect is throughout adult life, how it shows maturity and kindness, and how it smooths interactions. We underline, again and again, why we do not tolerate disrespect. The result of all this is that Michaela is filled with pupils who are an absolute joy to teach. Perhaps more importantly, our pupils are filled with joyful gratitude, amazing our many visitors and members of the public. Our pupils are primed to enter the world armed with kindness and respect. Hopefully, some of them might even dream of becoming teachers.

Kindness

Brett Williams-Yale

One of the things that may strike you when visiting Michaela is how happy the children are. Pupils with twinkling eyes, brimming with enthusiasm, greet you as you make your way around the school throughout the day. There are warm greetings in corridors, happy laughter in lessons, friendly chats over lunch, spirited energy in break times and cheerful smiles everywhere. Talk to the pupils, and they'll tell you: 'I love it here!' Often they go on to say: 'I was really quiet in primary school, but now I feel so much more happy and confident.' Why is the school such a happy place?

Our motto at Michaela is 'work hard, be kind.' Hard work pervades lessons, and what pervades the atmosphere of the school in classrooms, corridors, breaks, lunch, lunch breaks, and even outside of school into family homes, is kindness. Compared to all the other state schools and private schools that I've taught in and visited over all the years of my teaching career, kindness is one of the things that makes Michaela most different.

Being kind and considerate is less often associated with teenagers than being surly or grouchy, but all around Michaela you see surprising things. A pupil holds open the door for his form as they stream through, and without fail every one of them says thank you. Pupils walking purposefully to their lesson in single file stream see two adults they have never met, and bright-eyed and bushy-tailed, they call out one-by-one as they pass, 'morning, Sir! Good morning, Miss!' I heard an astonished cleaning lady on her first day at the school exclaim to herself, out loud in disbelief, 'I've never known children to be so polite!'

On my second day, I saw a pupil who tripped up and spilt their workpack and books on the floor. Just as I steeled myself to reprimand those pointing and laughing, I was instead surprised to see four other pupils silently crouch down, picking up the books and helping her to repack. On another day, at lunch, a plate crashed loudly to the ground, curry spewing out all over the floor. I've seen this scene countless times in many school canteens, and then usually I've had to silence the chorus of jeers. There's no need for that at Michaela. Instead, several pupils leapt up, completely unprompted by any teacher, to lend a helping hand; they were all happy to get their hands dirty. I can think of many schools I've been to where that may have escalated into a scuffle or at least unsettled the canteen and caused a ripple of laughs. Occasionally in lessons, a pupil will have a leaking pen and several pupils immediately and unhesitatingly offer to lend a spare. It's a special classroom where one pupil is happy to lend or even give away their stationery, but to have three or four pupils who without fuss all offer their spares is rare. What's more, you don't see pens flying across the classroom disturbing the lesson; instead, it's a quick pass over.

Outside of school our pupils regularly help old ladies with their shopping. Over and over, I have seen pupils say 'thank you' to astonished bus drivers. On trips, members of the public are astounded that Michaela pupils read quietly on the tube and politely offer their seats to adults. Following our most recent trip, one gentleman wrote in to the school: 'Never in my 20 years of commuting have I experienced the politeness and generosity that I saw from your students this morning.' Parents write in to say that their children are becoming more thoughtful at home, making their mums' breakfast in bed on a Sunday. They have stopped taunting their brothers and sisters and, instead, are now helping their younger siblings with their homework in the evenings. I think one of the reasons why pupils are happy at Michaela is because they are kind to others and because others are kind to them. It is a culture of kindness that creates this climate of happiness.

Impeding unkindness

When I ask pupils around a Family Lunch table what they most like about Michaela, a frequent favourite is 'there's no bullying here.' I push at this response to find out if it's the truth: 'what, none at all?' 'None at all,' they say. 'And what about at your primary schools?' I ask, with some trepidation. Almost all of our kids say there was constant bullying: 'people would be bullied because of their skin colour, their weight, their appearance and some were in tears and wanted to leave the school.' Some of our pupils have been badly bullied in primary school. I ask them what it was like. 'It makes you feel worthless,' one pupil said. 'I felt scared to come into school, so I pretended to be sick and stayed at home.' At Michaela, our pupils feel safe all of the time.

Zero bullying

At Michaela, the culture of kindness starts with preventing bullying. From the very first week of year 7, we spend a dedicated bootcamp lesson reading about and discussing bullying. We share stories of the tragic consequences of bullied children who committed suicide and how devastated their family, teachers and schoolmates feel, forever. In assembly and in that lesson, we explain that we are a zero-bullying school. We teach pupils what we must all do to prevent bullying: everyone must commit to standing up against bullying and preventing cruelty and fear. Pupils are clear that they must let a teacher know if they experience or see any bullying. Bystanders must stand up, speak out and most importantly, let a teacher know, so that we can fix it. 'There's no such thing as snitching at Michaela,' we tell them, again and again. This message goes against the grain of wider popular culture and ingrained prejudices from years of aggressive bullying of those branded 'snitches' in primary school. It is all the more important that we encourage pupils to have the courage to do the right thing and let us know as soon as they see unkindness, so we can help all pupils realise that being unkind isn't who we are or what we do.

Encouraging empathy

Creating a kind school is also about reducing unkindness. Mockery is not often deliberately cruel – it is often unintentional. Much of the unkindness in schools is thoughtless. For instance, in the first week this year at Michaela I heard a confident boy teasing a shy, tall girl because of her unusual height, laughing and calling her a 'giant' in front of others in the playground. This is not intentionally malicious; instead, the mocker was probably unaware that this girl might be self-conscious or awkward about her height. Even so, part of being kind is learning empathy. I wanted this boy to understand what it might be like from her viewpoint. I asked him to consider what she might have felt about the joke. I told him I knew he didn't intend to be horrible, but that choosing to joke about someone's appearance or something they can't change like their height, could end up with them feeling hurt or insecure. Once I made him aware of these unintentional consequences, he'd be more thoughtful and considerate in the future. I am not alone in having these kinds of conversations with our pupils; every teacher does so and every teacher takes the time to expand our pupils' empathy. These little chats contribute to our pupils learning to be more and more kind and considerate as they grow up. But what surprises me most about these conversations is how our pupils listen carefully to the advice; they're not surly, nor are they defensive or dismissive. They genuinely accept what we have to say and, often, even go on to thank us.

Unkindness to adults

Often in schools, children take for granted everything the adults are doing to provide for them. Dinner ladies, cleaners and office staff end up being treated scornfully, and there is a terrible gulf in how pupils treat the Headteacher, with deference because they know the Head tops the hierarchy, and how they treat supply teachers, new teachers and support staff, often with disdain and derision. In many schools I've taught in, pupils bring in sweets, crisps and drinks and consume them secretly in lessons, leaving sweet wrappers, crisp packets and drink cans littered around the classroom floor along with scrawled notes, paper scraps and other mess at the end of lessons, for the teachers or cleaners to clean up after them. Again, this is not consciously malicious, just inconsiderate. Even so, it is ungrateful. Teachers often spend many hours on evenings and weekends preparing activities, card sorts, games, group work tasks, slides, photocopying and worksheets for their classes, but it feels draining and thankless if children are careless and dismissive of these efforts, leaving paper and litter thoughtlessly strewn about the class as they leave. The trouble with being unappreciative is that it makes others feel resentful and less giving. Being ungrateful tends to lead to feeling unhappy.

It's great to be grateful!

Michaela reduces thoughtless inconsideration towards adults by reminding pupils not to take their teachers' efforts for granted, and to be grateful and appreciative instead. One of our mantras is 'it's great to be grateful!' Many of our pupils habitually say, 'thank you sir!' and 'thank you miss!' at the end of their lessons. It's quite surprising how enthusing this is! It gives you as a teacher a healthy boost of energy and optimism. It creates an upward spiral of reciprocal positivity; you feel more excited and enthusiastic to teach your classes because your hard work feels appreciated and not thankless and your pupils feel more positive about your lessons because you bring more energy and positivity into them.

Contrast that with other schools I have taught in, where the draining rudeness, interruptions and ingratitude drag you down into a downward spiral of frustration and irritation where pupils feel negative and hostile in your lessons. In my second week at Michaela, I explained to one of my classes that I had spent my Saturday preparing resources for them. I didn't expect anyone to acknowledge my efforts, but I did want my class to hear about the behind the scenes aspect of my work. I've preached like this many times in the past, and I can't recall ever being thanked afterward; in fact, I'm far more used to someone chipping in and saying 'but isn't that your job?' At Michaela, no fewer than seven pupils separately came up to me and thanked me for the time I had spent making the worksheets. At other schools, both private and state, I have either been thanked by parents at the end of term or by pupils who typically want to forge friendlier relationships with their teachers because they can't do this with their peers. At Michaela every child says thank you; there aren't any exceptions. Michaela pupils notice things the teachers do for them. They see things that in other schools, pupils take entirely for granted. They thank their teachers for innumerable efforts that go completely unnoticed elsewhere such as: creating online Maths logins for them, writing knowledge organisers, writing and printing booklets full of examples and exercises, setting up extra table tennis tables outside, organising sport and booking pitches for them, covering a lesson if a teacher is away so they don't have to have a chaotic supply lesson, helping them solve a difficult problem, running an after-school club, giving them challenging work, reading with great energy and expression in form-time and even for giving them a detention and teaching them self-discipline! The list is endless. Why are they so thankful? How come they notice and see so many things that teenagers so often take for granted?

Gratitude at Michaela is an everyday practice that everyone is called on to be a part of. We remind each other that being ungrateful leaves us feeling resentful and unhappy, whereas being grateful makes us feel glad. We remind pupils not to take their families, parents, siblings, kitchen staff, cleaners, tutors and teachers for granted. One ritual that we have for this is appreciations. Every day, we encourage every pupil over lunch to think of someone they feel appreciative towards, and share why. It reminds us all to ask: 'what are we taking for granted at the moment?'; 'who should we feel grateful to, and express our thanks to?' Our teachers and pupils see it as an incredibly affirming time of the day.

Another gratitude mechanism that helps us go beyond self-centredness is thank-you notes. Every half-term, we encourage pupils to write a postcard to someone they'd like to thank. Some of the most heart-warming times in teaching are when a child takes the time to thank you for making a small difference to them. The postcards are thoughtful, and it is clear that the pupils take their time to properly explain their appreciation; they're sincere. Similarly, taking the time to write a postcard at least once a day to thank a pupil for their efforts makes both teachers and pupils feel happy, showing them and their parents how much we care about them, and giving their parents opportunities to praise and encourage their child at home. Some examples are below.

In a school where pupils are kind to each other, and where they are encouraged to notice and feel grateful for the opportunities they are being given, they can overcome difficult home lives and troubling pasts. I see our pupils becoming happier and happier at school in a virtuous cycle of kindness, consideration, empathy, gratitude, generosity and, ultimately, long-term happiness in their lives.

NAME: Mr Porter

TUTOR GROUP:

Thank you for being such a kind and wonderful teacher. Your debating lessons are the highlight of my week and you never cease to make me smile.

Best wishes,

NAME: Mrs. Ashford.

TUTOR GROUP: Thank you Mrs. Ashfor because lately I've been feeling down, but because of you and Mr. Kirby I feel so much better and nothing can get to me.

NAME: Ms Marttin

TUTOR GROUP: 7D

I would like to give you a post card because you always have a smile on your face and your always in a happy mood - and that made me feel happy and makes me smile so ~~that~~ thank you for being our form tutor. it was great. From: ▓▓▓▓

NAME: Miss Rizvi

$a^2 + 6a + 9$

$+$

$(a+1)(a+2)$

$a/3$

$\times 2/7$

algebra

TUTOR GROUP:

Thank you for teaching us maths this term. I now know some more about algebra ☺. You have encouraged us to be kind and good people by making us give to the people who will have a hard time this christmas. You are sooooooo sososo kind and loving towards Athena and that makes me feel very happy ☺. Also, thank you for showing us your university certificate because it has encouraged me to aim high in life and be successful and kind like you ☺

Happy Holidays,

▓▓▓▓

NAME: Mr Porter

TUTOR GROUP:

Dear Mr Porter, I would like to apreciate the amount of work you have put in to organise the Year 8 winter trip and the booklets and in general because whenever someone is sad you make them happy and you are always enthusiastic.

From:

NAME: Mr Ihirby

TUTOR GROUP: Thank you so much for helping throughout the year with my anger and my self-control from year 7 to year 8. I believe you have made me a better person than I was a year ago. Thank you so much,

From

I would like to thank you for teaching me about humility, gratitude, integrity and taking responsibility for my actions. At the start of the year I was complacent and you gave a sharp and blunt talk which has helped me to improve.

TUTOR GROUP: 8 Zeus

Thank you for always being enthusiastic and encouraging me to come to school everyday. I would also like to appreciate the time and effort you took out of your day to the aid my issues as well as gwing me many ideas to help stay calm, stoical and tranquil.

yours sincerely,

Dear Ms Birbalsingh,

I would like to thank you for making a great school, here in Wembley. If Michaela Community school never existed, we wouldn't be kind to other people and also if we didn't learn a lot of subjects we wouldn't pass our GCSE in future.

Your Sincerely,

Family Lunch

Michael Taylor

'One of the very nicest things about life is the way we must regularly stop whatever it is we are doing and devote our attention to eating.'
– Luciano Pavarotti

Since time immemorial, humans have ritualised the process of eating food. A routine that began as a functional procedure has evolved to become hugely symbolic. Tragically, this process is being reversed, with unfortunate consequences.

'Family Lunch' at Michaela is special. Every day, pupils and teachers eat together in a communal dining room, share conversation, serve each other and appreciate acts of kindness.

The role of good nutrition in boosting educational achievement has been well documented. Rather than outline why healthy eating is beneficial though, this chapter is intended to outline what makes our dining experience unique for both pupils and staff.

My first visit to Michaela was as a guest. During my introduction to the school, I was politely informed that I would be eating lunch with the pupils. After a tour of the school and some lesson observations, my young tour guides dutifully deposited me in the main dining hall, where the children were being addressed by a teacher. I was informed that I was to take a seat on a table with some pupils. Alarm bells started ringing in my head.

I was looking forward to my packed lunch and chatting to staff at the school to learn more about their systems. Never mind, I thought. Slightly bemused, and with some trepidation, I sat down at a table of six pupils and awaited further instruction, whilst at the same time conducting a quick visual reconnaissance of ambush positions and suitable tactical escape routes.

'Roles one and two... GO!' I was jolted out of my Special Forces mindset. The sudden movement gave me a shock. I made to duck, an image of meatballs in a rich Bolognese sauce on a ballistic trajectory flashed through my mind. However, I quickly managed to regain my composure. I needn't have worried. The whole room was alive with activity. The food arrived at the table and the pupils on my table began to serve portions to each other, starting with me. I immediately felt awkward. I could not put my finger on what was wrong. The penny dropped. The pupils had better table manners than I had.

The pupils readily engaged in conversation and I remember it vividly. One explained: 'Sir, every day we are given something to talk about whilst we are eating.' I enquired as to the conversation topic for that day. The pupils were to discuss the most inspirational person they had read about in History.

The pupil to my left kicked things off: 'In my opinion, the most inspirational person was Rosa Parks because she was the trigger for the civil rights movement in America.' A second pupil politely interjected: 'I really like Alexander Fleming. He invented penicillin.'

I pressed him further, to see if he knew any more. He continued: 'He invented penicillin in 1928 at Paddington Hospital. He really changed medicine and we all benefit from that today.' I continued to press the pupil, asking him why this was so significant. 'Well sir, I suppose we would all be living much shorter lives without him, so that's a really big thing.'

The first thing that struck me as a visitor was the astounding level of knowledge that these 12-year-old pupils were able to deploy. However, I was more impressed by the atmosphere of polite intellectual discourse that was so evidently a daily routine.

This is Family Lunch at Michaela.

Guests are astounded by the level of politeness and camaraderie that pervades the atmosphere. How is this achieved? Firstly, pupils are sat in a random seating plan to encourage them to mix with other children from their year who might not otherwise be in their immediate friendship circle. Within a short space of time, this has led to an incredible community ethic among the pupils. There are no groups who feel ostracised and no individual pupils who feel lonely. Lunch can be a difficult time for many children, particularly the younger or more vulnerable ones. Family Lunch ensures that they will always have a friendly, safe and convivial atmosphere in which to enjoy their food.

Each pupil has a role to play. One pupil serves the lunch and another pours the water. The third pupil clears the plates and the fourth collects and serves the dessert. Finally, two pupils clear and clean the table. Practically speaking, this is an incredibly efficient way of doing things. Fundamentally, however, these pupils are learning how to help one another. They are learning how to serve each other, not just literally but in a figurative sense too. Family Lunch is designed so that the act of giving is given equal weight to the act of receiving.

Each table seats six pupils and one adult. We always eat with our pupils. This is the most valuable opportunity we have to teach the children good habits. Guests are always served first, and teachers are insistent that pupils use the correct table manners. Often the children arrive at Michaela unable to correctly use a knife and fork. The food itself is always vegetarian, to enable all pupils from every ethnic, religious and cultural tradition to eat the same food together. Teachers lead pupils in a conversation topic, which is explained in the dining hall each day by the member of staff leading lunch. Conversations are wide ranging and previous topics have included morals, culture, history, current affairs and the joys of reading. It provides us with an ideal opportunity to embed our values and to narrate the school's ethos every day.

After the meal, we set aside five minutes in which the children are able to offer 'appreciations' to the rest of the cohort. They say a few words to thank somebody for an act of kindness. Two claps follow the address to appreciate the person in question.

Why do we do this? Think of your average school lunch hall. The noise would probably be the first thing you would think about. A clamouring of hands straining for food, surging and barging to get through. A din of loud conversations, if they can be called as such, accompanied by the not-so-dulcet tones of children shouting across the table and clanging cutlery on their plates. Younger pupils are pushed and shoved in the queue and more vulnerable children are left isolated. Dinner ladies shout frantically to restore order, and the children often respond in the same way they would treat a supply teacher.

The sense of dread that overcomes many teachers prior to their weekly lunch duty is a common theme. We all remember the cheers and jeers every time somebody dropped a tray of food. We remember the overworked and undervalued dinner ladies who would frantically clear up the mess, without any contribution from the offending pupil. We remember the fights that broke out and the surreptitious creation of edible projectile missiles that were flung across the room. Those who say this is a normal part of school life should evaluate what exactly this is teaching the children. More importantly, there will always be somebody who has to clear the mess up at the end. It is safe to assume that in many schools where this occurs, the children themselves are not those taking responsibility.

This is not the case in every dinner hall, but there is no denying the existence of one or many of these facts in most English secondary schools. Family Lunch avoids all of this, thus creating a happy, purposeful and caring environment in which to eat.

Instead of a canteen culture where pupils can leave their trays behind, expecting an anonymous cleaner to clean up after them, at Michaela, pupils not only clean up after themselves, they clean up after each other. They demonstrate kindness and a sense of responsibility. Family Lunch embodies the wider values of the school. We believe that in the same way we teach academic subjects, we must also explicitly teach soft skills and values such as empathy, responsibility, gratitude and kindness. Every single day we model these values at lunch, and provide opportunities for pupils to display the attributes which will enable them to live fulfilling lives.

> 'A good wine should always be accompanied by a good topic, and the topic should be pursued around the table with the wine.'
> – Roger Scruton

Substitute wine for a healthy and nutritious lunch, and this comes close to the underlying philosophy behind Family Lunch at Michaela. Many children do not have the chance to sit down at a dinner table at home. Through such a simple routine, we give the pupils this opportunity. Studies have shown that eating at a table with others increases children's confidence and boosts their concentration. According to Snow and Beals in *Mealtime Talk that Supports Literacy Development*, children who eat at a formal dinner table have also been shown to dramatically improve their vocabulary when compared to those that do not eat at a formal dinner table with an adult.

Ultimately, what we do every day builds the pupils' cultural literacy, enabling them to access the mannerisms and habits of their wealthier peers. It is perfectly reasonable to assume that many of our pupils will be able to achieve great things academically. There is also no doubt that many of our frontier cohort will attend prestigious Russell Group universities. What is less clear, however, is how well hard-working and academic high achievers will do in environments where their peers are from far wealthier backgrounds. It is true that many students who attend prestigious ancient universities from working-class backgrounds can often feel intimidated by their peers. To some extent, this is even true of relatively middle-class students who often find it difficult to hold their own against classmates who have had a radically different upbringing. At Family Lunch, we teach pupils the soft skills of conversation. An 11-year-old who is able to hold a conversation with an adult over dinner, whilst exhibiting exemplary manners, is just beginning that process which will enable them to survive and thrive in any environment.

Family Lunch is one of the many ways in which we aim to create well-rounded citizens, enabling them to engage with people from all walks of life. This manifests itself during the five minutes set aside for appreciations. Pupils are required to project to a room of over 150 pupils, teachers and visitors. They often thank their teachers, classmates and those who work behind the scenes to make their school experience so unique. The children are always looking out for opportunities to thank people. I remember, during my second visit to Michaela, being both touched and pleasantly surprised when a pupil stood up and thanked me for the lesson I had taught for my interview earlier that morning. Pupils are prompted by teachers to be grateful and kind to others and Family Lunch provides the perfect opportunity to model this. It is clear from the beaming smiles and words of thanks at the end of each lesson that gratitude has become a heart-warming characteristic of Michaela pupils.

In addition to embedding gratitude in their daily life, giving appreciations offers them a superb opportunity for public speaking. Family Lunch provides them with an inner-confidence that is so often only the preserve of the elite public schools of England.

We insist all pupils take part in Family Lunch. The ethos of Family Lunch is so central to the underlying philosophy of what we do; it is absolutely critical that every pupil partakes in this wonderful tradition. Crucially, it also means that no child is ever allowed to go hungry at Michaela. At too many schools, children may never get a healthy and nutritious meal at school. If a child's lunch money is stolen at another school, that pupil may not eat that day. If a child's parents do not give them lunch money, that child will go hungry. This would never happen at Michaela.

At Michaela, we believe in developing children's habits in addition to their knowledge. Our mantra is 'work hard, be kind.' Lunch is the perfect time to teach our children how to be kind and helpful towards each other. We are teaching our pupils valuable lifelong lessons: the art of fine dining and conversation needs to be taught as explicitly as Mathematics, History or Science. We hope that the prospect of a middle-class dinner party, or a formal meal at an Oxbridge college would never daunt a Michaela pupil who has experienced five or more years of Family Lunch.

What we do transforms our pupils' lives. The utter delight of enjoying a good meal, and discussing wonderful topics of great weight is something that is fast disappearing in today's 'grab and go' society. In the culturally impoverished and technologically saturated world of the contemporary teenager, Family Lunch at Michaela provides a beacon of civility.

Labels Damage Children

Katie Ashford

Cast into the bottom sets, surrounded by anarchic misbehaviour, entered only for foundation papers, subjected to low expectations, taught by the least experienced teachers: for the least able pupils, this was once the norm. Over the last ten years, much has been done to provide better support and resources for pupils with the greatest need, yet results for these pupils – particularly those with a statement of Special Educational Needs – have remained stagnant.

In England and Wales, around 1.5 million children are labelled as having a 'Special Educational Need' of some variety, meaning that around a fifth of school-age children are diagnosed with having cognitive or behavioural barriers that make it more difficult for them to learn. Whilst it will always be the case that some children will require more support than others, we must stop to ask whether it is reasonable that a fifth of the children in this country are afflicted with an issue so profound that it prevents them from learning as easily as their peers.

Of course, some kids do struggle more than other kids. Whilst it may indeed be the case that they have particular needs that require attention, their difficulties could exist for any number of reasons. Perhaps they have missed a lot of school. Perhaps there have been issues at home. Perhaps the kid is less motivated than they ought to be, and a few reminders will be enough to get her back on the right track. The common assumption when dealing with a child who finds learning more challenging than her peers ought not to be that there is something profoundly wrong with her. Desperate for answers and an explanation as to why some children underachieve, it is tempting to look to labels for answers. Janelle's struggling to decode? She must be dyslexic. Brandon's incapable of sitting still in lessons? He must have ADHD.

At Michaela, we stand firm with a growing number of educators who refuse to let labels damage a child's education. We refuse to allow a misdiagnosed label set the expectations for each child or to become an excuse that will hang like a millstone around the child's neck for the rest of their life. We want all our pupils to be liberated from labels, rather than be shaped and defined by them. For too many children, the unfounded assumption that underachievement is a result of something irreparably wrong with them has led to a catastrophic reduction of expectations. For a child to be convinced of some fundamental inability to achieve at such a young and impressionable age is tragic. No child should ever feel that, due to a supposed medical issue that is not within their control, they are incapable of reaching excellence.

We must open our eyes to the damaging effect of labelling. Any diagnosis given to a child affects the perception they have of themselves and their ability to learn and achieve. To impose a label on a child is to remove her agency and make her dependent upon support mechanisms that will not be there to prop her up once she enters the real world. She learns to be helpless, not independent. She learns to feel hopeless, not hopeful. She learns disenfranchisement and disengagement right from the start of her life, before she has even had the opportunity to grow and experience everything the world has to offer. The reduction of expectations narrows a child's horizons and future prospects, imprisoning her in the world she was born into, rather than raising her out of it.

As the tides change, more schools are moving away from this damaging paradigm towards a way of thinking that will allow all children to make as much progress as possible. At Michaela, we refuse to believe that any child's future should be restricted by a label. Unshackling pupils from the tyranny of labelling is the first step to ensuring that every child, regardless of starting point, achieves their very best.

The Label-Free School

Quite simply, the weakest pupils need more rigour, more focus and more practice. And at Michaela, we make it our mission to ensure this happens every single lesson, every single day.

When the disengaged reign supreme in the classroom, chaos ensues. Rather than allowing precious minutes to melt away, we maintain a razor-sharp focus on ensuring that every child is held – and indeed, holds themselves – to extraordinarily high standards of behaviour. I frequently remind myself that every time I allow the slightest transgression to slip, I'm allowing the child to get into bad habits, the cumulative effect of which will dramatically inhibit their learning in the long term. The occasional daydream drift-away moment may seem innocuous, but those seconds gradually amount to minutes and hours of learning time lost. I don't want any child to miss learning time, because I don't want any child to learn less than the rest of the class, who are listening carefully. And if I know the child's label – perhaps they have a history of not focusing well in lessons and are suspected of having a cognitive issue – then I have even more reason not to allow the child to fall deeper into bad habits. Like trudging through boggy marshland, once one is in the mindset of not paying attention in lessons, it's hard to climb back out. So instead of allowing this to happen, I calmly remind the absent-minded pupil to listen, helping her to get back on track and keep on learning.

When pupils find extended reading and writing difficult because of literacy difficulties such as dyslexia, there is a temptation to reduce the rigour in the content and tasks they are asked to do. It's tough to give a kid with a reading age of 7 a full page of text to wade through, but surely it is better for them to struggle and come out the other side than to never even attempt such tasks. Again, we feel like it might be cruel to expect pupils who have been labelled in this way to sit and read a challenging text for an hour, but isn't it crueller to never give them the chance? Reading texts in lessons with weak pupils is tough, but it isn't impossible. If they get into the habit of doing it every lesson across subjects, they improve and feel successful. At Michaela, we embrace this philosophy wholeheartedly, insisting on high levels of focus on demanding content every single lesson, every single day.

If a child with developmental delay arrives in year 7 with a limited vocabulary and little grasp of basic spelling, she needs to spend the bulk of her time in lessons reading and writing. Pupils in this predicament are literally years behind where they should be, and we simply do not have a moment to spare. Every planning decision we make gives us a choice: spend time doing things they can already do easily (such as drawing a story board), or spend time developing subject skills they desperately need to master if they are going to stand a chance of being successful in the future.

We must also remember that pupils only spend around 25 hours per week in lessons. This time is so precious. With such limited exposure to teachers and their expertise, we should strive to make the most of every second they have. They can watch films, make posters, do a bit of drawing and chat to their mates at home or at break time. They can't work out how to solve quadratic equations or read and understand a Dickens novel without the support of a subject expert. We've got to make the most of every second we have with them. Again, this is central to the Michaela ethos. Our refusal to allow prescribed labels to determine how and what we teach liberates our pupils from the manacles of mediocrity. Rather than reducing the bar to their level, we push them to rise up and reach what may at first appear to be an insurmountable goal.

We believe that every child can do it if they are given the right opportunities to practise. Our intake is challenging, as Joe Kirby has outlined in his chapter on bootcamp. Some of our pupils arrive unable to read the simplest words, or add 1 to a number. Some of our pupils have profound cognitive needs that make learning a far more arduous process than it is for most. Some of our pupils really struggle to sit still and listen to their teachers when they arrive at the beginning of year 7. And yet time and time again, we see enormous transformations and turnarounds. Later in this book, we share some of these case studies with you, demonstrating further how our refusal to allow labels to damage children enables their success.

For some children, there is an enormous mountain to climb. It takes years of restless urgency and unrelenting ambition to reach the peak, and whilst some may never get there, we should at least give them the chance. As educators, it is incumbent upon us to do everything in our power to give every single child the best possible chance in life. At Michaela, we refuse to allow our children to be dragged down by the label-obsessed status quo, instead doing everything in our power to reduce the impact of any barriers they may face.

Our methods are controversially simple: enforce strict behaviour systems and routines, offer an immensely challenging curriculum, provide plenty of time to practise reading, writing, speaking and arithmetic, and never give up. Treat every child as if they are aiming for Oxbridge, regardless of starting point or supposed 'need.' And make no excuses, for excuses do nothing to teach children about having true agency and a sense of personal responsibility.

At Michaela, we are very clear that we have the same expectations for every child, regardless of label. If Jimmy doesn't do his homework, it is not a result of his ADHD, but a failure to make the right choice. If Holly stares out the window and writes nothing during the lesson, it is not a result of her dyslexia, but her choice not to focus. To say that a child's inability or lack of motivation to work is a result of anything other than their own choice is to condemn them to continue to make that same weak choice. To say that the problem is beyond their control is to remove any ability they might have to change it. Telling the child that they need to work harder may jar and feel harsher than making an excuse in the short term, but it is by far the more caring route to take in the long term. If we are to instil true responsibility and empowerment in every child, we must force them to make the tougher, better choice.

Ultimately, because we believe that all children are capable of achieving, we will never allow them to make an excuse or refuse to take responsibility. Michaela teachers believe in every pupil's ability to excel. We do not believe that an SEN label removes one's ability to work hard. On the contrary, we believe that the more 'issues' they have, the harder they must work and the more they need to be pushed by their teachers.

Later in this book, I outline the impact of our methods. If you don't believe that what I've said here will work for SEN children, take a look at the chapter written by my colleague Joe Allan, where the Michaela pupils get an opportunity to share their stories and work. Even better, come and visit the school and ask the children yourself.

This is why we do things the way we do them. Our irrepressible desire to get the very best out of every child drives us to reject labels and increase the discipline and rigour. It's why we never let a misspelling slip or a mispronounced word go by. It's why we will never reduce the challenge in the curriculum, ask fewer questions, or expect less writing at the end of the lesson. It's why we will never, ever reduce our standards. Most importantly, it's why we will never lose sight of the unshakeable faith we have in the belief that every child can succeed.

Competition is Crucial

Dani Quinn

'Cursed is he who enters without an offering to the bell curve god.'

So reads a sign, held up by a grinning plastic skeleton, outside the examination hall of a Singaporean university. Beneath is a shrine overflowing with 'food offerings,' albeit in the form of typical undergraduate fare: Nutella, noodles and Oreos.

Devotion to competition and the harsh mechanism of bell curves to award grades, even in small cohorts, is a normal part of school and university life in many parts of South-East Asia. The most intense elements of this culture are reflected through tongue-in-cheek devotions to gods, but also in linguistic changes: the Hokkien terms *'Kiasu'* (afraid to lose out) and *'Kiasi'* (afraid to die) have come to be used interchangeably.

State of Play: competition in British schools

This is a far cry from the culture in Britain and the United States. Dubbed the 'prizes for all' culture, this difference has its roots in two phenomena. The first is in values and mindset: the self-esteem movement of the latter half of the 20th century emphasised building up children's confidence and shielding them from failure or overt criticism. The second is a two-part mechanical change. Over the course of the 20th century, there was a proliferation in the number and type of activities that could be considered competitive, from Octopush (the pleasing name for underwater hockey) to national Monopoly championships. This increase in the number of ways that committed nerds can happily while away the hours together is not harmful (as a nerd, I celebrate it), and increases the number of opportunities to win awards and titles. Additionally, both long-standing and newer events have fragmented into increasingly smaller categories based on regionalisation and age grouping (Devon Football Association offers 11 age-bands for under 18 players). These are typically sensible moves: categorisations by weight or age in contact sports act as a basic safety mechanism; the junior version of *The Great British Bake Off* allows the competition to tailor itself to a very different audience and pool of participants. However, the inevitable result is an increased number of opportunities to win prizes (or, as the journalist Hilary Levey Friedman describes it, 'the carving up of honour').

In British schools, results for work are typically given privately (although the best results, or most-improved ones, may be commented upon and celebrated).

Pupils are rarely ranked and, where it does happen, it is unusual to share this with the group. Most pupils don't participate in external competitions of any kind and there is little opportunity for authentic competition within schools. Sports days are gradually returning, but most pupils don't participate in any sport outside of PE. Anecdotally, the landscape is different in more traditional private schools, and academies who seek to replicate elements of their ethos. In these cases, house competitions and published lists of academic results are more common. That said, Oxford ceased publishing individual exam results in 2009, with Cambridge currently under pressure to follow suit – even in Britain's most traditional academic institutions, the trend seems to be away from the publication of individual's scores.

Competition at Michaela

The approach in Michaela is different; we believe that competition is crucial and that all children benefit from knowing where they stand relative to their peers. This takes many forms:

- Daily rankings of their performance in IXL (online Maths homework). By year group, this shows the number of questions pupils completed correctly on a prescribed topic.
- Publicly available rankings on their performance in Times Table Rock Stars, showing both their speed (i.e. the number of times-tables they can complete correctly in one minute) and their effort (measured in 'wealth', whereby each minute of practice earns a coin).
- Daily quizzes in lessons, with a quiz per subject per week (e.g. a Maths quiz on Monday, an English quiz on Tuesday, and so on). This is usually designed to test the quality of their self-quizzing (homework), although in some subjects it also includes longer responses (e.g. in Maths the quizzes are a mixture of knowledge and problem solving). The results are shown and narrated to the whole class, and pupils are occasionally shown how they've fared compared to peers in other classes.
- Participation in external competitions and exams, such as the UKMT national mathematics competition, football tournaments and so on.
- Merits and demerits are displayed to the whole form on a near-daily basis, with the form tutor narrating improvements, regressions and particularly good or poor performance.
- Weekly competition to qualify for 'Friday Football': the 15 pupils in each year group with the highest merit balance (the number of demerits subtracted from merits) play football after school with peers and staff in an enjoyable, relaxed session.

All of these take place within a highly consistent and heavily-narrated culture that is driven by values and a firm belief that all pupils are capable of growth and improvement. The school motto of 'work hard, be kind' underpins how staff narrate preparation for, participation in, and the results of the activities listed above.

Treat those two imposters just the same

As a result of explicit competition, the results of assessments and other academic work are publicly known, at least within forms. Teachers at Michaela aim to explicitly narrate both success and failure (and the myriad outcomes that sit somewhere between the two), linking them to factors that are within a child's control and turning outcomes into teachable moments.

A pupil has done well in a test? Great: explain to the class the actions they took that led to that outcome (their focus in lessons, the quality of their homework or self-quizzing, the insightful questions they asked, the way they made use of advice to improve their writing or methods). Make sure the pupil knows how they got to where they are and that their peers can see how to follow that path too. At Michaela, we narrate improvement to the whole class: 'I'm so impressed with Tamanna's improvement. Her focus in class has been really good, I can see her paying more careful attention and pushing herself to answer every question, even when she's not confident. Her notes on the practice quiz were excellent and showed she was really thinking about how to understand her mistakes. It shows how smart you can become when you work hard.'

A pupil has done badly? It's disappointing, but can be learned from: explain to the class that it's disappointing (anything else suggests embarrassment in the face of or, even worse, acceptance of, poor performance). Build the narrative of *why* it happened, tempering the instinct for kindness or soft words with the need for honesty: poor behaviour or focus, poor attendance, lack of time revising, not asking for help or clarification, not taking responsibility to get help after school, ineffective revision strategies, lack of effort. Make sure the pupil knows how their choices and actions influenced the outcome, and what could have been done differently. There may be scope for an additional private conversation, but have the public one too. Let their peers learn from it and see how choices lead to consequences, and how much those choices are within their control. A Michaela teacher might be heard narrating to the class in this way: 'I'm really disappointed with Corey's result this week. We all know that Corey is able to do really well, and in lessons this week I had no worries about him, as his answers were of a good quality and he got through the practice well. Maybe it made you complacent. Did you practise over the weekend, before the quiz? *[Embarrassed look]* That explains it! It's not enough to be able to do it in lessons, or understand it while I'm explaining it – you have to remember it! That means practice at home, explaining it to yourself and not going easy on yourself. I wouldn't say this if I thought you couldn't do well at Maths, I'm saying it because I believe you can do better and you need to know the truth.'

Furthermore, by taking control of the narrative around setbacks, the teacher reduces the scope for nastiness outside of the lesson, or snide whispering. By making clear why it has happened, there is little scope for cruel comments or speculation that someone is 'just stupid.' Even without shared results, children rank each other and form opinions. By making the implicit explicit, and controlling the narrative, teachers can empower underachievers to deal with a nasty remark (and their private doubts). The response is already established: 'I'm not stupid, I just didn't work hard enough that time. If I work harder, I'll do well.'

Rankings as information

A natural reaction is to leap to thinking of the experience of each individual. They must feel vulnerable and embarrassed when results are called out! Doesn't it entrench bad reputations if the whole form knows who is where when it comes to merits? Doesn't this crush self-esteem?

This reaction is normal. Our instinct in many situations is to think of our own emotions, or those of the person affected. However, children can only mature if they learn to move beyond their immediate emotional response and if we have the resolve not to allow them to indulge in those responses. Often our resistance to telling a pupil the truth of how they are doing is due to the fact that we, the messengers, can't bear how it makes us feel to see their reaction. But this is to discount the child's needs. Showing a child the facts of their performance can be done kindly, but must be done firmly and with a clear rationale. Here are some examples of the information a pupil (or anyone, for that matter) can gain from competition and 'public' results:

- An individual's position in a group of peers, or position within a bell curve.
- How a pupil is doing compared to their previous self (e.g. comparing their homework scores from when they used to put in lots of effort, to when they did the bare minimum).
- How efforts are paying off (e.g. if a revision technique, or extra help after school, is improving how they are doing compared to the class).
- Who in the class is doing well, not just appearing to do well.
- Who in the class is doing badly, not just appearing to do badly.

· Who in the class is improving, or regressing.

This raises the criticism: 'Couldn't you give them information on how they're doing without making it public?' Yes, that's possible, but not as valuable. This is for two reasons, one technical and one social.

On a technical level, comparative results are more useful because they bypass problems around a test being relatively easy or difficult. If a teacher designed a test that is more difficult than they intended, or the class has consistently done badly on a specific element (suggesting the teacher needs to reteach it and improve their explanation of it), then results without a position would be gloomy for all the pupils. Similarly, if a test or task is easier than intended, then pupils can have a false sense of improvement. By showing positions within a group, teachers can help pupils to more meaningfully understand how they are doing ('Your score is lower than last week, but we can see from the averages that this test is harder. In fact, I think you've improved; your score is above the class average this week' or 'I'm sure most of you are feeling pleased with your score. Be cautious before being too confident: we can see from the list of results that everyone got over 80%. Considering this, I would say that, for this test, 80% is a disappointing result, and means you'll fall behind the rest of the class if you don't improve on and practise the parts you got wrong').

Comparative results don't mean that there must be losers; teachers' professional judgement means they will interpret the results to build the narrative. There isn't a set script, and there doesn't have to be chastisement or encouragement every week. A teacher who knows their class will judge if the vast majority have done well, and praise them appropriately, or vice-versa. The key is not to fixate on position alone, but distance from the average (in the case of under-performance), movement (in the case of improvement), outliers (to narrate how their actions were different and how this caused their results to be different) and absolute scores (when pupils have either 100% or an exceptionally low score).

There is also the social benefit of comparative scores. As listed above, comparative scores give the whole class information on how their peers are performing. Knowing this allows children to see how actions and choices lead to consequences. Those with poor attendance will typically have poor results. Those who have been sent out of a lesson, or who don't complete their self-quizzing, will typically have poor scores. Pupils who participate actively in lessons, answering questions even when under-confident, or asking thoughtful questions to clarify or probe, will typically do well. In any case, if children don't know the results, they'll decide what they think they are (we've all overheard pupils say 'I bet *so-and-so got such-and-such*' and then see it become gospel).

Giving results makes the implicit explicit, and prevents result-swapping being a source of playground gossip. This is especially important if pupils are to be marshalled in supporting each other to improve. If a struggling pupil is keeping their struggles secret, friends and peers can't lend a hand. If a naughty pupil is keeping their results secret, their friends don't have the important 'carrot' of improved performance to encourage them to work harder and behave well. Pupils are people: they are building narratives in their minds all the time. It is better that they do so with accurate information, mediated by a caring, yet demanding, adult.

Of course, people can respond to this information in a number of different ways, depending on maturity, temperament, how they've been prepared to respond (the school's and parents' narration around results) and the result itself. An important element is that it needs to be completely normal to get this sort of information all the time to reduce the scope for it to feel high-stakes or emotionally charged. Additionally, there needs to be consistency from adults on how they help pupils to interpret the information. Discussions should be focused on honesty (there is no value in pretending that a result is good if it is not, and there is no value in a pupil lying to themselves about whether it represents their best effort), the actions that led to the result and how to improve (or avoid complacency). Having these conversations with the whole class allows pupils to pick up on this language and reinforce positive responses.

We don't need no competition

At an instrumental level, public results and information are excellent preparation for life beyond school. This may sound odd – shouldn't an aspirant musician, or environmental activist, be thinking about creativity, or cultivating leadership skills, not their ranking in tests? Perhaps, but this is not enough. Contrary to our romantic image of the creative or caring professions, they are exceptionally cut-throat. The arts and sport may produce some of the best pieces and performances that humanity has to offer, but they leave many crushed in their wake. Would-be writers enter a harsh world of blunt rejection from publishers, editors and the public. The number of aspirant athletes far outweighs the number who ever get even semi-professional funding, let alone enough to make a modest living. Even roles requiring professional qualifications are cruel worlds: architects' projects are funded in light of highly competitive bids, only 3.5% of PhD holders go on to academic positions and applications for paid roles in the charity and creative sectors are numerous and the best applicants are of exceptional calibre.

Should the world be so competitive? It can seem cruel or, at least, reductive. Within the world of meme-able social media, there is the ebb and flow of 'inspirational' letters from teachers letting their pupils know that their results don't matter, it's their character that matters. This is naïve at best; irresponsible at worst. For one thing, good traits and character aid competition: a person who collaborates, reciprocates and works well with others will be popular and get ahead on professional metrics anyway. A person who has a mindset of gratitude and altruism will have a happier and better life, all things being equal. Competition isn't needed to grow and improve in these traits. Furthermore, they are not zero-sum in the way that, say, paid roles at the National Gallery or Oxfam are. Like it or not, when it comes to performance, it is important to know who is the best and if we are moving towards being the best. When it comes to medical care, we are much more interested in our surgeon's technical knowledge and skill than in their kindness. The overriding concern when flying is that the pilots were held to rigorous standards and had to compete for their role, not if they are loving parents.

Acknowledging that the world is competitive doesn't mean that everything has to be a competition. For questions of character and personality we might have lines in the sand – be honest, show integrity, be considerate of others – but the complexity of these actions and the underlying motivations makes them more suited to individual responses than to simplistic comparison (although we might still publicly celebrate good traits, or point to role models). In contrast, the results of a Maths test are simple and are the result of relatively simple decisions and choices, so are appropriate for comparison and competition. So too are the daily 'results' of a form's merits and demerits; simple misbehaviours (speaking out of turn in lesson) lead to a simple consequence (a demerit), so are suitable for comparison. No sensible form tutor would try to distil complex behaviours into simplistic comparisons.

Self-esteem: who are you really trying to protect?

It is normal to want to shield pupils (and ourselves) from competition, in a bid to protect self-esteem. However, avoiding challenge and rejection isn't a route to self-esteem. It is a route to mediocrity and wasted potential. Those who don't challenge themselves know this to be true, even if they don't like to admit it aloud. Challenges entail the risk of failing in comparison to peers; this is why improvement and success feel like such accomplishments.

Be honest with yourself: how often have you told a 'white lie' to a child about how they did because you couldn't bear to see them upset, or to disappoint them? It's incredibly tempting. Ask a more difficult question: what was the real reason for telling a lie that seemed so inconsequential? Often it is our own self-image that we are trying to protect. We don't want to be the bearer of bad news. We don't want to risk any harm to the nice relationship we have with that child. We don't want to answer difficult questions about how they can improve, because it is often hard to say. So we tell a white lie for selfish reasons. It's not really helping the child to do so: they will look like a fool if they wander out in the world thinking they are doing well as they are. They will also be made to feel like a fool by indifferent strangers who don't share our qualms about feelings and self-esteem. It is far better for the child's self-esteem to be told a difficult truth, about the performance of their comparative position, when they are young and are in an environment where they can be helped to improve, than when they are being rejected for a place at university, or a job they hoped to secure.

True self-esteem doesn't grow from never being tested, and never knowing where you stand. Allowing a pupil to spend years oblivious to how badly they are doing is setting them up for a much more terrible fall. Not only will they be offered few opportunities, they will have not learned how to deal with such a setback. The real world is intensely competitive and, crucially, unmediated and uncaring in how it tells the message. True self-esteem comes from being able to face the challenges and setbacks of the world outside the school gates, knowing that you have the resilience to cope with it, knowing from experience that working harder and acting on advice is an essential response to achieve success. It is far better to learn that lesson in school, where adults care and take time to help children navigate a competitive world, and where the stakes are lower.

Troublesome outliers

Of course, there are two outliers that remain troublesome: the pupil who works hard and rarely succeeds, and the pupil who visibly coasts yet excels in tests. Both are rare, but familiar: most teachers have a small number of pupils like that each year.

Shanice

Shanice works hard in Maths lessons. She finds Maths difficult and struggles to make connections between ideas, even when they are spelled out and carefully scaffolded. She is focused and diligent, visibly annoyed if anything interrupts the lesson and clearly disapproves of anyone who doesn't do their homework or who isn't getting on with their work. She works slowly, but is willing to give everything a go. She asks questions and participates enthusiastically when she thinks she knows the answer (about 50% of the time). Her homework is always complete, and her parents are paying for her to work with a tutor once a week. She sometimes stays behind to get help from her teacher.

In her weekly tests, she typically scores around 60%, and is usually in the bottom third of the class. She never gets the worst scores – those are typically pupils who have been absent, or who have failed to revise. But she never gets the best scores, despite consistent effort and positivity. It is obvious how dispirited she is by this.

Other pupils in the class might get the same score, when her teacher knows they could have done much better with only a little more effort. Surely the public ranking hamstrings the teacher's ability to narrate to the class?

It doesn't hamstring them, but it does require subtlety and professional judgement. Teachers must explain frequently to the class about how improvement looks in practice: plateaus followed by spikes of 'ohhhh, *now* I get it' where the ideas suddenly fall into place. Some pupils alternate between plateau and spike in a single lesson, some week-by-week and some take much longer. Shanice is in the final group. However, the plateau and spike aren't inevitable: without hard work, the plateau becomes a dip and the spike won't happen. A plateau, in the context of learning new content, still represents progress: Shanice is still remembering and applying around 60% of what she learns each week. This is far better than what would happen if she gave up. Encouragement, and a consistently repeated message of 'I know you find Maths hard, but I know you can do really well in it, I've seen you give great answers and make really interesting connections' are required, coupled with interrogation of her methods for revising. She might be working hard, but she might not be working smart. The weekly feedback might feel crushing but, without it, she would never know that she still has a long way to go. It does a disservice to pupils to let them think that hard work alone is enough for success. They need to work hard using methods that work, and they need to know how they're doing compared to what's 'normal' (for their group) to get an honest picture.

Of course Shanice is capable of improvement, of working harder and of working smarter. She does better the weeks that she stays behind to get extra help from her teacher. She does better when she asks her parents to quiz her, in addition to self-quizzing. She does better when she annotates her work and uses that in practice quizzes at home. That is an awful lot of work, compared to what some pupils might need to do, and that might not seem fair. It would be much more unfair to allow her to be deluded about how she's doing and not know she needs to make a difficult choice between doing what's expected (yet thus fall short of expectations), and going above and beyond in order to achieve what she is capable of.

Behar

Behar is exceptionally capable, characterised by how effortlessly he achieves academic success. Being present in lessons and hearing what is said, and doing the more difficult questions, seem to be enough to make concepts stick in his mind. He makes connections with ease and, when he participates, his answers are insightful and his questions interesting and challenging. His behaviour in lessons is arrogant, often distracting others or trying to draw attention to himself, even though this costs others the time and focus they need to keep up. His homework is the bare minimum to avoid detention, and his peers know it. This can seem like a nightmare situation for a teacher; how can they push a narrative of 'work hard and smart, and you will succeed' when Behar so clearly contradicts this?

As before, this is where professional judgement and careful investment in relationships, trust and challenge come in. Yes, Behar is doing well, compared to others in his class (although he may do well to bear in mind the children excelling in other schools around the country with whom he will compete for university places and jobs later). But he is not doing well compared to what he is capable of. The narrative isn't a simple one of 'Well done for being in the top three' but one of 'Considering how easy you said you found the work in lessons this week, it is disappointing to see you didn't get 100%. It looks to me like you just relied on what you did in lessons and didn't do anything more. If you want to be really brilliant at Maths, you need to be pushing yourself to 100%, just like [other pupils] push themselves every week.' Thanks to Carol Dweck et al we know that intelligence is malleable and that all neuro-typical children can succeed, but it would be a strange lie to pretend to pupils that there aren't big differences in how easy they find it to learn new content.

The subtle challenge is making sure that, in pushing the capable-yet-complacent, we don't imply we have different standards. Hence, qualifiers like 'I'm really impressed with Shanice; she struggled really hard with the work this week and did extra at home and has improved from 55% last week to 75% this week. That's a big jump. If you keep going like this, Shanice, you'll be really successful and have great habits for when the Maths gets even tougher' and 'Behar's score is good; lots of his answers were really clearly worked out and well-explained. But I'm disappointed that he didn't get 100%. This isn't because he's smarter than anyone else but because, in this topic, it doesn't take him as much effort to get 100%. If you don't get into a habit of working hard, you won't have the self-discipline you need when we do get to a topic you find difficult.' Of course, this is done within a context of a safe and challenging classroom environment, once the teacher has begun to have a sense of the pupils' personalities and how to push them. And, unsurprisingly, Behar has gone from being someone who does well every week to someone who unfailingly gets 100%, asks for more and harder questions to work on while the others finish, and willingly shares his revision strategies with the class.

Shanice, Behar and everyone in between

All pupils can benefit from explicit ranking and competition in areas where effort and self-discipline are the determinants of success. Some of the weakest pupils in Michaela routinely out-perform their apparently 'smarter' peers in daily homework rankings – and take visible pride in being lauded for this – and many of our 'turnaround' pupils point to their merit balance as the concrete evidence of their changes. Consistent and relentless use of hard evidence forces pupils, and teachers, to be honest with themselves, and making it public makes excuses impossible. Outliers and pupils such as Shanice and Behar provide a challenge, but also allow us to show to the children, and ourselves, what we really mean when we say that we believe that all pupils are capable of becoming better than they have ever been.

The Devil is in the Detail

Sarah Cullen

'I would like to give an appreciation to my friend, who went to get a haircut this weekend. The hairdresser asked him what cut he would like to impress his friends, but he told the hairdresser that he would prefer a haircut that was professional, and that he only wanted friends who like him for who he is.'

The lunch hall responded to this articulate anecdote with two sharp, resounding claps and earnest smiles, whilst I twisted around in my seat, seeking out the hidden cameras in what I had begun to suspect must be some sort of reality TV set up. Before I had visited the Michaela Community School for an interview day I had done my research. I thought I knew what to expect – strict rules governing every aspect of school life; which side of the corridors to walk on and how to sit properly. A school full of pupils blindly and perhaps fearfully following orders.

I was half right. But half very, very wrong.

When I saw Michaela pupils in action, I saw them go about their lessons and transitions in perfect order; I saw incredibly happy pupils with a sense of purpose, taking real joy in everything about their school.

But still I didn't quite get it. I marvelled at how silent classrooms could result in happy, courteous children. I thought how lucky I was to be seated with such 'good kids' at Family Lunch. Michaela was such a well-oiled machine, it seemed: populated by well-behaved pupils who knew instinctively how to act, and run by teachers who knew instinctively how to orchestrate such mythical events as a quiet, orderly game of basketball amongst over a hundred inner-city teens.

Once I had established that the school was actually real, I jumped at the chance to teach there and continued to be astonished as term began. I had seen the impact a week of bootcamp with year 7 had had, but years 8 and 9 were another matter. Children materialise outside my classroom before the bell has even sounded, knocking quietly on the door and announcing politely that they have arrived.

It's hard to appreciate that there was a time when these pupils weren't like this. It's equally hard, and extremely important, to remember that achieving this is down to meticulous planning and to a dedicated staff that know exactly how to 'row together.' Michaela runs so smoothly that it is extremely easy to forget or overlook just how complex and impressive an achievement that is.

I was of course being extremely naïve in underestimating what goes into making Michaela work the way it does. Nothing that I saw at Michaela on my visit 'just happened.' Nor was it wholly due to just having strict rules. Similarly, Michaela children are no different from any other children in the country... until they attend Michaela. What is different about Michaela is the extraordinary attention to detail that pervades every aspect of the school, leaving nothing to chance; every second of the school day is used to its full potential. When I joined Michaela as a teacher I was able to see the sheer volume of details that are accounted for 'backstage.' For example, a complex and detailed duty rota for staff ensures that every aspect of school life is attended to – teachers greet pupils as they line up outside the gate, teachers usher pupils home from the local bus stop at the end of the day, teachers ensure lines for the toilets are orderly and efficient. Teachers work together to ensure classes have the same routines and that curricula complement one another. The pupils are taken seriously and so is the teacher's profession – as a result, both flourish.

Attention to detail

My early comparison of the school to a well-oiled machine was misguided and insufficient. A well-oiled machine is impersonal, boring; the cogs that make it work are anonymous and invisible, with no comprehension of the significance or insignificance of the role they play. A far better analogy is a Heath Robinson machine – one of those compelling arrangements of chain reactions that achieve an end goal. A marble might roll down a series of small pipes until it flicks a switch on a kettle, which produces steam to lift a tiny balloon, which in turn nudges a shelf of dominos which begin their crescendo. Every component of the 'machine' has a seemingly incongruous role to play, but each component relies on the next. Above all, the sequence of events is deeply satisfying to watch. A Heath Robinson machine is still a flawed analogy for Michaela though – the end result of those machines is invariably a mundane action such as turning on a light switch or pouring a cup of tea. In contrast, of course, the collective completion of a thousand interleaving details at Michaela do not achieve something mundane or simplistic, but something truly extraordinary.

From the moment I accepted a job at Michaela, I have been surrounded by details, but not in a draining, bureaucratic way. In so many schools, teachers are drowning under endless forms that need to be filled and boxes that need to be ticked, sapped of any will or energy to teach. To add insult to injury, these details are so often unnecessary or some sort of surface attempt to appease Ofsted. Teaching, in my experience, was often reduced to the crushing minutiae of data and audits all tied up with pretty buzzwords to give a veneer of efficiency. In the past, I would find myself exhausted by long evenings of data input after the school day had ended, but unable to articulate what I had actually done with that time. Nothing had really been achieved. In stark contrast, the details at Michaela are ones that improve my ability to do my job. All of the detailed planning in my day means that my job has boiled down to what I really love – my subject.

I was urged to learn the name of every pupil by heart before I arrived, and this was made easy and even enjoyable with the use of a clever phone app that had been prepared for new and existing staff. I even had access to every lesson they had been taught prior to having me as their teacher. Having this level of preparation dealt with before I even arrived at the first inset day made my transition to the Michaela way of teaching immeasurably easier, and helped to cement my pupils' suspicions that all teachers are omniscient.

Every decision for both staff and pupils has been made whilst considering both its impact and ease of implementation. Which stairway would be used by which year group, as well as which exit year 7 pupils would be directed towards, was discussed in a whole-staff meeting one afternoon. The pros and cons of a variety of options were weighed up. Suggestions were considered and conflicted ideas were adapted to take each other into account. Over which staircase to use. I kept waiting to hear someone in SLT say 'You know what? Let's just leave it. It's getting too complicated and it'll work itself out,' a veritable mantra at other schools I have experienced. Then I remembered – I am at Michaela now. 'Good enough' was not going to be accepted and details were certainly not going to be left to chance. The problem was sorted through meticulously because that is how the school works – planned and accommodated down to the last detail.

At Michaela, pupils complete every action in an exact way, following precise instructions from teachers in a set amount of time, which is counted out loud as the process is being cheerfully completed. They are cheerful because they want to succeed and enjoy doing well. They complete their roles, even one as small as passing an exercise book down a row or thanking a teacher for giving them a detention, with full knowledge of how important that role is. They have had the bigger picture painted for them in bright technicolour – a future filled with choice and autonomy because they have learned traits like kindness and integrity. When I first heard a teacher count down to the moment all pupils would stand at the same time, on the right hand side of their chair, I stifled a laugh. Really? We were to tell them which side of the chair they were permitted to walk around? The teacher I was observing continued: if we do this, all pupils are able to get out of the classroom quickly and without getting in each other's way or hurting one another. Of course. I felt foolish for not having understood the simple elegance of this rule immediately. No chairs clanging against one another, no innocent knock of a bag misconstrued as a malicious act, escalating into a full-blown fight. Pupils had their small job; they knew why they had their job and what they were contributing to. They walked around their chairs from the right-hand side without event and everyone was able to get to lessons quickly.

The notion of paying attention to small details in order to combat larger issues is not new. The 'broken windows' theory adopted by police in 1980s New York has leaked out into business management and schools in America. The idea that small, seemingly inconsequential features of poor standards can generate and sustain poor standards across a school means that when a school focuses on details like whether or not a child has tucked their shirt in, they take similar pride and care in their work and their general conduct. Similarly, teachers must 'sweat the small stuff' in their day-to-day routines – correcting how a child holds eye contact first thing in the morning and their cutlery at lunch. The differences with how Michaela employs such an approach are small but mighty. We don't sweat the small stuff so much as we love the small stuff – pupils and staff alike relish the small details that go into every interaction at Michaela because we tackle them as thousands of tiny opportunities to question the status quo and possibly do things better. When every last detail is thought of, nothing but teaching and learning in its purest form is left. As a result, the school culture is fiercely and lovingly protected. For new teachers, constructive feedback is given for almost every lesson, concerning details as fine as the amount of time given in a countdown for books to be handed out. Erosion of the school's culture on any level – by pupils or staff – is addressed swiftly and succinctly, always with a clear focus on just what is at stake if standards fall, or any small detail is ignored.

It is also important to note that beyond the Herculean task of closing the achievement gap, the school is also shaping these kids into individuals with kindness and integrity through explicit character training that is evident in every one of the interactions we have with pupils. It is not simply a case of telling pupils to play nice – it is, as with every aspect of the school, a matter of breaking down sometimes abstract concepts, such as building trust, altruism or earning respect, into achievable and measurable goals that are reinforced by every member of staff, every moment of every day. They are taught how to maintain eye contact, how to project their voices across a packed room and give eloquent, concise appreciation for everyone from teachers to kitchen staff to classmates. They are taught which questions are appropriate to ask a guest when making conversation. They are taught to listen carefully and contribute readily and to be very, very grateful for what they have. They are continually reminded of how to sit up straight and how to shake hands; how to articulate responses in class and, yes, even which side of a chair to walk around after standing up.

Of course, the achievement of this intense character-building necessitates a constant teacher presence: in the corridors, at the gates outside school, even at the bus stop, teachers are there to talk with the children and show them how to behave. Far from being Orwellian, this level of surveillance is a constant reassuring presence. Teachers are looking to congratulate and reward more than catch wrongdoing. There is consistently a ratio of around four merits to every demerit given in a lesson. Instruction is detailed and explicit, which gives pupils a clear choice – do the right thing and flourish, or reject it and likely struggle in the highly competitive job market. Rather than being stifling, these myriad details actually make the pupils *freer* than so many of their contemporaries by giving them a clear choice. Thousands of times a day, Michaela pupils choose to do the right thing. They understand what the choices are and the likely outcomes of those choices. It is hugely empowering; they are utterly in control of their actions and subsequently their futures.

The better angels

The devil, as we have all heard, is in the detail; lurking amongst the small print of life, waiting to derail carefully laid plans. And we all know what happens to the best laid plans of mice and men. I am fond of idioms, but the devil being linked with details irks me somewhat. I understand of course that the phrase is intended to convey the importance of small details – that they must be dealt with thoroughly in order to avoid things going awry. No one can argue that it is all too often the seemingly small, incongruous details that can wreak the most havoc. I am sad enough to have had nightmares on this theme; having forgotten to wash my outfit the night before, I am forced to wear a sparkly cocktail dress to work; having not bought my morning coffee, I fall asleep on the train and miss my stop. I have these dreams because I am a fairly meticulous person (isn't it telling that this trait is largely considered negative?) and so details were a cause for concern. Details, I thought, presented chances for things to go wrong.

But since working at Michaela, I have begun to see that angels, too, lurk in the details. This is the theme of Michaela, it seems – taking something ostensibly negative like details, demerits or detentions, and proving that in fact the opposite is true. Details, I now see, are thousands of tiny opportunities for our children to make the right choice and thus take another step towards achieving the best.

No Nonsense; No Burnout

Jess Lund

'What upsets me about the job? Erm, wasted talent.' – David Brent

Have you ever felt like you're working harder than your pupils? Have you ever thought that you're not getting enough out of the pupils for the effort you're putting in? Have you spent evenings and weekends marking, or preparing resources, or planning activities for your lessons? Do you sometimes resent the amount of work you have to do just in order to stay afloat?

In the year to November 2014, 1 in 10 teachers left the state sector. The DfE also estimates that around 100,000 teachers who have completed their teacher training have never actually taught since. There are many contributing factors: poor pupil behaviour, poor management, poor salary (compared to other professions or independent or overseas schools), excessive teaching or administration workload, and perhaps many more possible factors and explanations besides.

Are you one of the 43% of teachers who is planning to leave the profession, or the 74% who have seriously considered it? Perhaps we shouldn't take the findings of the NUT, NASUWT or *Guardian* as gospel. Perhaps far fewer teachers are actually planning to leave, or are thinking seriously about it, or want to leave. Perhaps those surveys targeted those union members who had a real grievance about their working conditions.

Some things are clear though: there is significant 'wastage' in the system – trained, talented, dedicated teachers who are being driven from the profession by their lack of work-life balance, among other things. We cannot rely on the hiring of endless new teachers to plug the gaps in staffing, as recruitment targets indicate that this is not happening. And the spending of £1.3 billion of taxpayers' money on agency staff (and, more pertinently, agency fees) demonstrates the immensity of the problem.

So, what do we do? We cut out the nonsense. Poor pupil behaviour? We manage it properly, with a 'no excuses' approach as argued for by Jonathan Porter. Too much marking? We find more effective, more sustainable ways, as laid out by Jo Facer. Perverse incentives to teach in onerous ways that will move you up the pay scale? Get rid of performance-related pay and the ridiculous cycle of high-stakes observations, says Katharine Birbalsingh. And what about teaching skills and using group work? Well, Olivia Dyer has explained the inimitable virtues of simplicity and drilling knowledge as a means of getting pupils to actually learn things.

But there is more to that last part than meets the eye. And it is just that – what goes into planning, and what goes on in the classroom – that I want to focus on. I want to focus on it because the preponderance of nonsense in the day-to-day act of just teaching was almost enough to force me out of the profession. I have only been teaching for three years, and I love teaching with all my heart, and yet 18 months ago, I worried daily: I just can't hack it, it's too hard, there's too much. I became sick with anxiety – about appraisals, about pupil behaviour, about passing my NQT year and trying to run and resource a department at the same time.

What impacted on me most, on a daily basis, was the effort that I was making to deliver lessons that, in the final analysis, had precious little impact on what the kids knew or could do. On the one hand, I wasn't very good at it; on the other, this was how I'd been trained, and what I'd been told consistently was 'good practice.' The 'gamification' of learning (I'm a languages teacher, but I know that this goes on in most subjects) meant that I was putting more thought into how to motivate the kids to stay on task than I was thinking about the content they were actually assimilating, and what they would be able to do as a result.

Coming to Michaela has changed everything. Now, I try to think of every activity I undertake to plan a lesson or a part of the curriculum as a response to the following question: what is the learning return (the amount, quality and durability of learned content) on the time (and resources, and effort) invested? What we do at Michaela is completely divorced from how I was taught to teach, and I'm much happier for it. Even better, my pupils make the kind of progress, and speak the kind of French that I could never have even imagined before joining Michaela.

If I could go back three years and strip away just a few elements of my teaching practice – time-consuming, low-leverage components that led to boredom and frustration on the part of my pupils and myself – some of the biggest would be games, technology, display and lesson plans, none of which we do at Michaela.

Gamification

I attended around 30 CPD sessions during my training year, and another ten or so during my NQT year. Three in every four of these were MFL-specific, and the theme that ran through all of them was 'activities.' Only once or twice was I invited to consider exactly how pupils assimilate language, and how they might best be encouraged to commit it to memory. Everything was games – individual, nugatory activities designed to 'practise' a particular set of words, phrases or a grammar rule. These games and activities were not rooted in research or cognitive science: they were how my trainers had been trained, and what was considered 'good practice' in the pedagogical orthodoxy. So if sound, evidence-based educational practice was not the bedrock of these activities, what was?

Engagement. That was what we were all aiming for. Encourage our pupils to love the subject by engaging them through the activities that you set them, where they feel a sense of achievement and also have fun. Where does that fun come from? From the activities themselves. All of these treasure hunts, running dictations, pair discussions, word searches, *realia*: they were the ticket to engagement, and thence (by some miracle on a par with turning water into wine) to mastery of the subject. And did the kids enjoy them? Sure. Except the kids didn't *actually* enjoy the activities per se, they enjoyed the opportunity to do minimal work and have everything handed to them on a fun plate. Did even the brightest and hardest-working pupils get a lot out of it? No – they would have loved the chance to sit quietly and get on with something challenging. And the worst part? Every other kid would have loved that too, and I never gave them the chance.

The problem was this: I was encouraged, at every turn, to engage pupils not through an appreciation of the subject I was teaching – the language – but by the way in which the language was presented to them. Engagement was achieved through games: there was no indication that you could sit the pupils down, present them with some French, practise it, repeat it, talk about it, manipulate it and recall it, and they would enjoy the lesson. We were encouraged towards variety of activities, not adhering to processes that would actually get pupils to learn and remember what they have learned. Even worse, my pupils were bored: an activity-based approach left the confident ones unchallenged and the strugglers free to not apply themselves and not improve. I wasn't aware of this at the time – I can see it only with the benefit of hindsight – but nobody around me pointed out that the pupils' learning was inadequate; indeed, they often said the exact opposite. Nobody knew that it was inadequate, because nobody knew any different.

All of these games and activities took a lot of time: finding or making, adapting, printing, strimming, copying, putting into envelopes... I had a light timetable as a trainee, and could therefore dedicate myself to interactive PowerPoints and hunting down the 'Snakes and Ladders' boards in the MFL cupboard. Even then I still didn't manage to adhere fully to the school's marking policy, and can only imagine what would have happened to my sanity had I had anything approaching a full timetable.

The most damaging thing about this approach was the impact it had on my professional development. Time that could have been spent thinking about how best to impart real, useful knowledge was wasted instead on the construction of games. I became convinced that the love of the subject itself wasn't enough, and that in order to encourage pupils to see French how I saw it I would have to impart it as small, sugar-coated pills with precious little reference to the joy of understanding, decoding and mastering the language itself. Finally, it inculcated in pupils the expectation that learning had to be *made* enjoyable; it couldn't just be enjoyable. Teaching using games, even for a few weeks, degraded the value of the subject for its own sake, and allowed pupils to believe that learning was a low-effort activity.

This is particularly problematic for languages. The continuous drop in pupils taking the subject to A-level and beyond cannot simply be ascribed to the 2004 government decision to make languages optional at GCSE where they had previously been compulsory. The increased emphasis on engagement has stripped the MFL classroom of the integrity and intrinsic enjoyment of the patterns of language learning. There has been no call for, and no incentive to encourage, mastery and automaticity. Hundreds, if not thousands, of new MFL teachers have been instructed that in order to make language-learning acceptable to young people, you have to teach it through the medium of games. We can all see where that has left us.

What's the alternative? What have I learned to do since arriving at Michaela? I learned to think back to how I learned languages, and what made them enjoyable. The answer was always the sense of fulfilment I gained in learning to understand something new, particularly when it was presented as something challenging (the opposite of the way in which language is presented through games). I thought about the repetition, manipulation and mnemonic devices I used to remember the language well, and started to invest time in developing those instead of working out activities that would allow the pupils to work towards understanding it themselves. In essence, I just started to teach, rather than facilitate 'learning'.

I read a comment recently that NQTs tend to view lessons as chunks of time, rather than chunks of learning; that they would begin their teaching career devising activities to fill certain portions of the lesson, and as they come to better understand the learning process, they would then devise and sequence these activities in order to actually impart knowledge. I think this is true, and this is exactly what I did as an NQT, but it is also what I've seen a lot of seasoned practitioners do. The most productive, efficient and effective end-point of this development is to stop devising individual activities – and certainly eschew all games – in favour of introducing and practising the subject until pupils feel confident. That can be incredibly simple, and incredibly effective, and yet the dominant discourse in most subjects is just the opposite. 'Engage them through activities and games', we're told, 'and the understanding and love of the subject will come.' This is simply not true: the love comes from the subject itself, and games are patronising at best, damaging at worst.

The more the pupils practise, the better they'll know it, the more confident they will become and the more they will love the subject. The corollary of that is that the teacher can spend more time focusing on the elements of their practice that will have a real impact on pupils rather than spending time thinking of new ways to make learning 'fun.' The outcome is improved learning and less wasted effort.

Technology

Get rid of iPads, tablets and computer-room lessons. Say no to apps. They add very little to the learning process, and are best used as a helpful supplement for the more motivated pupils. To promote the use of technology in the classroom is, as far I can see, a tacit admission of the fact that technology can do more for learning than the teacher in the room: the person in the room with the degree qualification, the experience and the wisdom is relegated to the role of Apple Genius in the corner. Of course, the teacher is rarely a genius when it comes to troubleshooting the myriad problems that tablet technology can introduce to the classroom, and so much time and energy is devoted to mitigating that disruption rather than, say, teaching the subject in which they *are* well-versed. I know that much stress can be avoided when the teacher relies on a learning tool they can control, namely themselves.

It is very difficult for the ordinary classroom teacher to make good use of technology in the classroom, and nigh-on impossible to achieve better results through the use of technology rather than through simply teaching useful content, or having a meaningful discussion about a topic. If technology is used to make assessment more manageable, that's one thing, but then let's not pretend that we're doing it for the sake of the pupils and what they learn. Personal, and recent, experience indicates that, even when taking into account large classes and lots of them, using pen and paper is much more effective. If technology is used as a method of behaviour management, we have a far bigger problem on our hands.

The drive to get technology into our classrooms robs teachers of their status and of a lot of time that could be better used actually teaching, rather than booting up software. Equally pernicious is the diversion of funding (such as the abortive $1.3 billion plan to introduce iPads into every school in the Los Angeles Unified School District) that could be spent on more effective teacher training, subject knowledge development and shoring up struggling school budgets. Technological solutions may be sold as an immediate panacea, but they appear to make the problem worse in the long run.

Associated with this are the sums spent on 'up-skilling' teachers in edutech, and the money paid to snake-oil salesmen promoting ways to use the latest, quickly dating, trends in the classroom (at the time of writing, this includes the deplorable *Pokémon Go*). There is a thriving market for apps, such as ones where children record themselves speaking French and then can spend the best part of an hour taking pictures of themselves, superimposing their own mouths onto images of potatoes, and creating a funny skit to share with peers and family that, at most, only takes about one to two minutes of actual thought about the language. The quality of these outcomes does not matter: it's the experience and the 'fun' of doing it. There is no argument that can be made for this use of classroom time over that of even mediocre teacher instruction. With technology, far too often, we are focusing on the wrong things. Playing with an app for an hour is not learning, unless the goal is to learn how to use the app (and even then, there's no guarantee!).

Displays and other proxies

As a new teacher, there are a number of pressures upon you to meet a range of standards. There are the teaching standards, which you must meet in order to qualify: I have no real axe to grind there, except that I'm fairly certain nobody really looked at the giant ring-binder of evidence I took hours to compile over the course of the year (there was a joke that you would pass your QTS if the assessor dropped your folder out of the window and it made a satisfying thud on the ground; an acquaintance from another school actively boasted that they had photocopied another teacher's folder in its entirety, changing nothing, and still been granted QTS). I'm also certain that it didn't benefit any of my pupils.

The exigencies of qualification aside, there are numerous things that teachers do which are unquestioned orthodoxy. Classroom display is one. I can't count the number of hours I've wasted putting up backing paper over other tatty backing paper, constructing carefully planned wall displays that were never used or scrutinised by anybody (least of all the kids), and served no purpose other than to prettify the classroom environment. If the work on the walls isn't also readily accessible in pupils' heads, it shouldn't be on the walls (besides, who can read it? It's on the wall, and no teacher I know has ever had ten minutes of 'read the wall' time in a lesson). And, of course, if it's in their heads, it needn't be on the walls. It seems to be an unwritten rule of pleasing the Senior Team in most schools: if your classroom looks like it encourages active learning, then active learning must be going on.

Another pointless expectation is written lesson plans. Teachers around the country are dedicating hours each week to filling lesson plan proformas. As an unqualified teacher, I did it to show I could, although I rarely stuck to them; as an NQT, I did it because I had to, although I rarely stuck to them; and now at Michaela, thank heavens, I don't have to do them. I'm not talking about not planning lessons – of course I still do that, even if sometimes it is simply a few bullet points jotted down on a Post-it. I'm talking about the multi-part, 12-box, granular, 'what have you done about the G&T kids' kind of lesson planning. It serves no purpose other than to reassure those who aren't in the room that something good is going on in the room, even if nine times out of ten it isn't. I can see the point (just) for trainees, but on a real teacher's timetable it is a waste of everybody's time and effort, and the perfect example of the kind of task that tips teachers over the work-life balance edge.

Of course, marking is a third dogma. I can't add anything much to Jo Facer's analysis of the benefits of hardly marking, but it is another thing that teachers do without it having much impact on what pupils learn, largely because they do it as a routine exercise because it's what they've always done or what they have been asked by the school's leaders to do. I remember marking class sets of books, putting comments on each one and drawing out points for improvement for individual pupils, only to be too exhausted at the end to actually put those points into practice, work out how to teach it better next time and integrate that feedback into the following lesson. But hey, at least I passed the book scrutinies!

When thinking about all of the things that I used to do which I no longer have to, I realised that there are numerous commonalities underlying them. The most obvious one is the tired justification that 'this is what we've always done' (or, what has been done in the living memory of the school); teachers are often *required* to do things that don't improve their pupils' outcomes in any measurable or meaningful way. Another is the poor return on time and effort invested: creating displays, marking books and writing lengthy lesson plans are all poor uses of time when a teacher has a full timetable, let alone other responsibilities.

The common feature with which I most identify, and the one that troubles me most, is what I call 'the competence illusion.' Done consistently, these tasks can give the impression that a teacher is a good teacher, or a great teacher, and certainly a better teacher than one who does not go in for displays, marking and exquisitely presented four-page lesson plans. These ultimately meaningless tasks mask the reality: this teacher is nowhere near as good as they should be, given that they spend so much time on low-impact practices that have the side-effect of making them look good. That in turn has an impact on new teachers coming into a school: these superficially competent teachers are held up as examples of good practice, particularly as it may be a very rare occasion that anybody actually goes into their classroom. I know, because I've tried to be one of those teachers and – at one point – was one. The truth of that situation is that the teacher is more worried about how they are perceived by their colleagues and superiors than whether they are doing what's right for their teaching practice and, ultimately, their pupils. When you eschew tasks that contribute to the competence illusion, give up the hope of being the hero teacher, and focus on what you know to be the best thing for you and your pupils, you do the one thing that really matters (even if it's difficult to see): becoming a better teacher.

The Michaela Effect

Michaela is unique in many ways, and one of the ways in which it stands out is what informs decisions about workload. Every decision about what teachers do, and what happens in the school, is weighed up in terms of impact on the pupils against the effort and time put in by teachers to make it happen. It's a simple, but incredibly powerful, feature of the way Michaela runs. When the Senior Team makes a decision, they think about the impact-to-effort ratio. It isn't just the Senior Team, either: the entire staff body bases decisions on that same ratio. It's part of how everybody thinks and makes decisions. We all row together. As a result, we can leave school before 5pm, and take no work home. As a result, we needn't work at weekends or during holidays. Where we choose to do so, this is more a function of being a new school: we are setting up curriculum and infrastructure for the next few decades, and this takes more time than simply reviewing lessons and thinking about practice.

Here are some of the decisions that we at Michaela have taken to reduce the cluttering nonsense that encumbers teachers in many schools:

- No graded or high-stakes observations
- No performance-related pay or divisive bonuses
- No appraisal targets based on pupil data
- No individual lesson plans at all
- No unit plans with 'assessment foci'

- No skills descriptors for assessment
- No expectation of all-singing, all-dancing lessons
- No starters, plenaries, group work, attention grabbers, whizzy or jazzy nonsense
- No cardsorts, discovery activities or flashy interactive whiteboards
- No writing, sharing or copying learning objectives or outcomes
- No extensive photocopying of worksheets
- No shoe-horning of IT into lessons
- No mini-plenaries or checks on progress within a lesson
- No labour-intensive homework collection, marking or chasing up
- No unnecessary manual data input or entry
- No unnecessary paperwork
- No labour-intensive written 'dialogue' marking
- No time-wasting, transient display
- No split timetabling
- No lessons on slides
- No class data sheets or data-driven seating plans
- No tablets
- No computer room lessons
- No long-winded written reports to parents
- No year 7, year 8 or year 9 parents evenings
- No lockers or lost keys
- No class exercise books taken home so none are lost
- No cover work, just self-quizzing
- No work to set for pupils sent out of lessons, detention, isolation or long-term absence; just self-quizzing

And me? At Michaela, I have never felt overwhelmed by work, or been asked to do something without a very clear sense of the impact it would have. More often than not, when I've suggested something that would have been terribly popular in any of my previous schools, I'm told, 'Okay, but what are you trying to achieve?' or 'Is there an easier way to do that?' Most importantly, where previously I had feared that I wouldn't last five years in teaching, I can now see myself teaching for many decades.

If more schools considered the impact-to-effort ratio of school activities, there would be less burnout. If more schools dealt with the illusion of competence, and stripped away pretty but unnecessary elements of teaching practice, focusing instead on the elements of teaching practice that actually make a difference, there would be less burnout. If more schools completely discarded the myth of the hero teacher, and encouraged all teachers to be genuinely collaborative, there would be less burnout. If teacher training focused on getting pupils engaged in the subjects themselves, drawing on their intrinsic interest, rather than devising endless activities and games to capture the attention of Generation Z, there would be less burnout. In short, if more schools thought and taught like Michaela, there would be much less burnout. So, what do you have to lose?

Education, Education, Education

Barry Smith

I started teaching in 1997 and in the nearly 20 years since I've been told some absolute nonsense as to what constitutes effective teaching. I used to be very, very angry about the state of education. I used to rage against the state of our country's classrooms. But lately, I've been a lot calmer. Michaela is a very calming place in which to teach.

You may still find this chapter a bit ranty. You've been warned! Just be grateful you didn't know me when I was really angry. I'm a lot more positive and hopeful about education than I was pre-Michaela. There's a lot to do still. Certainly at Michaela we are learning every day: we're a tiny school and only two-and-a-bit years in. We've no room to be cocky or complacent. We make mistakes. But we are not an island: there are good examples around us. There are headteachers and teachers doing extraordinary things who we can look to for inspiration. That's a nice place to be.

The stuff that really used to rankle, in my angrier, rantier, pre-Michaela days, was the teaching-by-numbers 'good practice' that rose to prominence from the late '90s. The starters, the plenaries, the WALTs, the WILFs and the EBIs. All that tick-box teaching still makes me shudder.

For ten years I taught teachers. I'd travel the country delivering what I hoped was a very different kind of inset. I'd be telling teachers to teach. I'd be quoting Woodhead and, eventually, Wilshaw. I'd tell teachers that 'didactic' wasn't a dirty word, that, actually, kids *are* empty vessels. I challenged the fashion that said 'facilitation' and 'fun' were the way forward. I'd be talking about direct instruction and I'd be exploding pseudo-science myths and telling teachers to trust themselves.

It wasn't always an easy path to follow, but I felt I was doing my bit to fight the good fight. Teachers I met on my travels often felt demoralised by the fads and the fashions that only seemed to make their job impossibly difficult. Rarely a week went by that some teacher didn't sidle up to me at the end of a session to relate their woes and then burst into tears. They'd often say they felt I'd given them permission to teach. How crazy was that? Teachers felt they needed someone's 'permission' to teach. They felt under pressure to talk less, to be less authoritative, to transmit less knowledge. It was like their whole purpose had been removed. To teach, just stand at the front and tell kids stuff; it had become both anachronistic and subversive. Or that's how it felt for many of the teachers

I met. They were panicked. They no longer understood what their role was.

Observations were what the teachers I met feared most. Observation lessons, they insisted, had to be 'interactive.' Light on teacher talk; heavy on fun. At various stages between 2004 and 2014 teacher fears focused upon PLTS, learning styles, visible progress in 20 minutes, independent learning, assessment for learning, raising boys' achievement, marking dialogues, teaching the more able, teaching the less able, technology in the classroom – there was always a new buzzword to be incorporated, a new fashion to be followed, a new dogma to bow down to. So many teachers I met felt as if they were building their lives on shifting sands. They were simply disorientated.

I met lots of tired teachers. There are still lots of tired teachers out there, I don't doubt, but I hope things are changing. The pressure to perform to a set of rules that would assure 'outstanding' status, that's what really seemed to drain the teachers I met. Their SLT would try to second-guess Ofsted; the teachers would then try to second-guess SLT. The observation game was all so draining. And it was all so dishonest. The show lessons, that ticked the fashion boxes but left teachers feeling only a sense of temporary reprieve because they knew that they were only as good as their last observation, made me most furious. Lolly sticks, traffic lights, thumbs up, green pens, Bloom, Kagan. There was always a new panacea *du jour*.

So many teachers I used to meet were great teachers – but they'd teach with flair and charisma and aplomb only when nobody was looking. They'd teach by stealth. In secret they'd do the stuff they knew worked but when observed they'd do the song-and-dance routine. It was schizophrenic. It's hard work pretending to be someone you're not. It's hard work loving what you do but having to hide it because fashionable orthodoxy says it's forbidden. A lot of the teachers I met led a dual and tortured existence. They loved kids, they loved their subject, they loved really teaching it; but they often worked in schools that straitjacketed them.

We've probably all known schools who roll out initiative after initiative, schools where the initiatives were poorly understood and where they were never really given time to embed. I saw a lot of that in my years visiting schools and teaching teachers. Teachers become battle-weary, sceptical, even cynical. I understand that.

We've probably all heard a variant of 'Look after the learning and the behaviour looks after itself.' I came across that a lot in my years training teachers. Of course there were good SLTs out there who recognised that a full timetable and difficult kids was no walk in the park. But there were also the heads who bemoaned any form of prolonged teacher talk. There were schools where teachers were scolded for activities that lasted longer than a prescribed number of minutes. There were schools where the fun quotient had to be kept high at all costs.

I think that the 'Fun at all Costs' concept is on the wane now. That's a good thing. I'm not advocating exam factories; I'm not proposing lifeless lessons of nose-to-the-grindstone drudgery. Anyone who visits Michaela can see that that is not what we do. But there's a general acceptance now that rigour was sometimes lacking, that edutainment was sometimes regarded with too much veneration.

One of the things I love about Michaela is that kids work hard in every lesson. They expect to work hard. They expect to *be worked* hard. They go from lesson to lesson and the demands are relentless. But there is an awful lot of warmth in those lessons, a lot of humour, a lot of teachers being passionate, being themselves. You'll note a lot of consistency across lessons and across routines, but teachers are encouraged to bring their own personalities to the fore too. That was lost for a while in teaching, I feel.

In the days of 'talk-less teaching' and 'guide on the side,' the teacher as subject expert and performer was lost. When I say 'performer' I'm not saying every teacher has to be a stand-up comic, a raconteur or, God forbid, a kiddies' entertainer. But it's nice to work somewhere where you can teach the way you feel is best, where the Headmistress says, 'Don't change a thing when I pop in. If you feel the need to change when I come in you are doing something wrong.'

There's a real sense of belonging, of safety, in a school where you are expected to *really* teach, where you are valued for your ability to transmit subject knowledge succinctly, effectively, unashamedly. The mark of a good Michaela teacher is that their pupils retain knowledge and then go on to make it their own. The mark of a good Michaela teacher isn't your ability to perform like a show pony in sporadic observation lessons or to use strategies aimed at appeasing the God of Inspection.

You might hate me for this, but, in my very humble opinion, they were dark days in education before the arrival of Michael Gove. Was he divisive? Of course! Always right? No. Do I like the EBacc? Don't get me started! But 2010 saw things change for the better. Ofsted too has changed for the better. It's a huge juggernaut and massively unwieldy and there remains lots to do, but we are heading in the right direction.

I started teaching in 1997. I saw 13 years of fashions come and go that really were not to my taste. I saw an excuse culture explode. I saw teachers worn down by one 'latest thing,' then the next, then the next. I saw SLTs running scared from the bogeyman Inspectorate. I saw some very, very dodgy inset messages proliferate. 2016 is a very different place. A better place, I'd venture. There are schools like Michaela: schools that are free on so many levels.

I used to joke that, if I won the lottery, I'd set up my own school and the school motto would be, 'Sit Down, Shut Up, Do as You're Told.' Well, I didn't win the lottery. But we did set up our own school. It's a tiny, little school on the edge of a noisy and very busy rail track, but it's ours.

One of a handful of mottos we use is: 'Us Against the World.' And it's true, there are days when it feels like Michaela is really swimming against the tide and that the world, or at least noisy sections of the Twitterati, are against us. But I can honestly say, hand on heart, in nearly 20 years of teaching, I have never felt so excited or exhilarated. I have never felt that what I am doing was so important or so right. It's a funny old place, Michaela, but I am so very, very glad that I am a part of it.

Rethinking Initial Teacher Training

Jake Plastow-Chason

I used to arrive at my placement school in Manchester at 7:30am every Monday morning, USB in hand, praying that there was a working computer available in the staffroom and that the reprographics room had been unlocked. My word-processed lesson plan documents and PowerPoint presentations were ready to be printed in preparation for the week, so all I needed now was a stroke of technological and janitorial luck. Unfortunately, this was something that was not always afforded to me. Later that day I had a meeting to discuss all of my work, and the stress that I wouldn't be able to deliver the goods had me on the edge of a nervous breakdown. During period one some of my year 8 pupils had decided to engage in a professional-wrestling-style Royal Rumble. During period two a year 9 pupil wandered into the classroom, not wearing uniform, carrying a 'DANGER! SLIPPERY SURFACE' sign. On my way to period three I counted myself lucky for only receiving mild verbal abuse from some passing year 10s. By the time my period four meeting came around it was safe to say that my stress had reached tipping point. I then proceeded to sit through an hour-long meeting only to hear that my planning was not up to scratch and that the 15 hours of work I had put in over the weekend was insufficient. I would like to say that this wasn't a typical Monday morning, but it most definitely was, and it was nothing that my introductory training could have prepared me for.

I resigned from my position at my training school within a year, adamant that I would find myself another profession. The chaos I was confronted with was more than I could bear. Roughly a year later, through complete chance, I met the Headmistress of Michaela Community School and have found a new lease of life as a Science teacher here. Working at Michaela couldn't be further from the experience I had at my placement school: I am enjoying every moment. It's not only because Michaela has better discipline, but also because the training on how to teach is so radically different.

Although there has been a shift in Initial Teacher Training (ITT) towards school-based rather than university-based training, the pedagogy of the universities remains prevalent in UK classrooms. There can be no doubt that Higher Education Institutions (HEIs) play an important role in reinforcing the status quo of the educational establishment. HEIs are the only institutions capable of awarding postgraduate certificates in education (PGCEs) and qualified teacher status (QTS), which necessitates these partnerships, but because of this, HEIs hold an academic and political monopoly over the teaching profession.

Throughout this essay I'll be discussing all ITT routes that contain an HEI component and collectively refer to them as Normal Teacher Training (NTT). I'll discuss Michaela Teacher Training (MTT) and NTT with respect to the pedagogies taught by each and argue that MTT leads to largely *convergent* pedagogical thinking and that NTT leads to largely *divergent* pedagogical thinking. By convergent thinking I mean the concept of finding an optimal way to solve a problem. In contrast, divergent thinking means the active encouragement of a range of possible solutions to a problem, arguing that each is equally worthy of merit (Hajesfandiari et al, 2014; Williams, 2003). The problem I'm highlighting in this essay exists for teachers in every school: how can we get our pupils to learn as much as possible, and thereby maximise their chances of success in the future? Teacher training in the UK is built upon divergent pedagogical thinking. At Michaela we're radically different because we believe that there is – and ought to be – one particular, optimal pedagogy.

The outcomes of the UK's state education system are undeniably poor. Kuczera et al (2016) report for the Organisation for Economic Co-operation and Development (OECD) that 'there are an estimated nine million working aged adults in England (more than a quarter of adults aged 16-65) with low literacy or numeracy skills or both.' It also reports that 'these nine million people struggle with basic quantitative reasoning or have difficulty with simple written information. They might, for example, struggle to estimate how much petrol is left in the petrol tank from a sight of the gauge, or not be able to fully understand instructions on a bottle of aspirin.'

Some of the objectives set out by my teacher training were surprisingly compatible with those of MTT. Firstly, developing one's vision to 'understand the importance of having high expectations and believe all pupils can achieve': Michaela prides itself on high expectations and I, along with all the teachers at Michaela, have always been driven by the desire to allow the pupils we teach to succeed in learning and in life. Secondly, using a pedagogically informed approach to 'make informed decisions about the routines pupils are going to use in their class and be prepared to introduce and embed them effectively': routines are a cornerstone of all classrooms at Michaela and the pupils' learning relies heavily upon them. Thirdly, improving one's subject knowledge to 'understand the impact of subject knowledge on pupils' learning and how to sequence learning within and between lessons': as Joe Kirby explains in his chapter on knowledge, Michaela teaches knowledge-based curricula across all subjects and rejects skills-based learning. This requires the teacher to develop deep subject expertise and to sequence subject knowledge thoughtfully.

So whilst MTT and NTT do indeed have some common values and overarching objectives, the convergent pedagogy of MTT and the divergent pedagogies of NTT mean that their ways of achieving them are markedly different. Moreover, some MTT objectives are categorically different from those of NTT.

Knowledge-based teaching vs. Skills-based teaching

Knowledge-based teaching is paramount at Michaela, and whilst I was given some training to improve my own subject knowledge during NTT, I was offered no training on the pedagogy required to directly pass this knowledge onto the pupils I taught. The pedagogy that was offered instead suggested that I should be a 'facilitator of learning.' A facilitator of learning remains neutral in the classroom, and the term implies that my role was to merely help pupils drive their own learning. I was told that I should limit teacher talk to 20-30% of the lesson. I failed a graded observation because I failed to do so. But the incongruity of the only one with the knowledge being prevented from sharing that knowledge grated on me: why should I facilitate the learning of pupils, when they don't know what they should be learning, or the best way to learn it? That would be unfair on them. As a Science teacher with a Chemistry degree, I've already studied the intricacies of chemical bonding, I've already worked out the simplest method for balancing a chemical equation and I've already practised how to perform a titration correctly, efficiently and safely. Most pupils haven't met any of these topics yet, and it's my job to help them master them. How is setting them up to discover and guess at this alone, allowing many of them up to flounder and fail, helping them?

NTT offered me various skills-based activities to supposedly 'develop' pupils' knowledge. Whether it was an activity in which pupils made paper parachutes to learn about air resistance, or an activity in which pupils pretended to be charges moving around an imaginary circuit to learn about electric current, the teaching and learning was purely skills-based and the pedagogy was largely unsubstantiated.

When I first met the Headmistress of Michaela, she made it clear to me that models like these confuse pupils because their focus is wrong. Creating paper parachutes teaches pupils about how to make paper parachutes, not about air resistance, and walking around a room just distracts from any actual learning taking place. Passing on the core scientific knowledge underpinning these models was, and still is, considered secondary in NTT and this has negatively influenced what is considered best practice in schools across the UK. When the Headmaster at my placement school observed me, I had pupils walking around the laboratory pretending to be atoms in a gaseous state. Did they learn about the structure of an atom? No. Did they learn about gases, liquids and solids? No. What were they actually learning? Spatial awareness. I was lauded for best practice during a staff meeting for simply telling pupils to walk around in random directions. This is nonsensical. It would never happen at Michaela, because teaching core knowledge (rather than engaging activities) is considered the primary focus.

Despite a new Key Stage 3 (KS3) Science National Curriculum (NC) being published in 2013, my university lecturers provided me with its 2007 predecessor and, through the course of a comparative activity, spoke about the benefits of the 2007 document. The 2007 Science curriculum revolves around the key concepts of 'scientific thinking,' 'applications and implications of science,' 'cultural understanding' and 'collaboration' and key processes of 'practical and enquiry skills,' 'critical understanding of evidence' and 'communication' (Qualifications and Curriculum Authority, 2007). Any identifiable content in the 2007 curriculum is far smaller than the details of these concepts and processes, and the majority of the document is devoted to hollow 'attainment targets.' The nebulous set of skills lack any subject-specificity whatsoever, let alone any sequence towards expertise in Science, and provide no assistance in teaching pupils vital scientific knowledge. To say I found it bewildering is an understatement.

My university tutors seemed convinced of the superiority of the 2007 curriculum, which raises serious questions: why would they actively promote such an outdated and woolly document? It was undoubtedly a political statement. The implication was that the coalition government's curriculum was inferior to that of the Labour government's. This action, in effect, imposed ideological views on impressionable trainee teachers searching for guidance and desperate for answers.

The vague and hazy skills-based pedagogies advocated by NTT are harder to grasp for a new teacher than the knowledge-based pedagogy of MTT. Skills are inherently unquantifiable, whereas knowledge is much more tangible: it is clear whether a pupil knows what photosynthesis means, but not whether a pupil is improving at developing their collaboration skills. A reason why divergent pedagogy has become so rife in UK schools is because there is no consensus on how to teach skills-based curricula. Teaching knowledge-based curricula lends itself to convergent learning as knowledge can be easily quantified. One either knows the knowledge, or does not. A class can be easily assessed on their ability to learn knowledge whereas it is very difficult to assess a class's ability to learn the skill of, for example, 'scientific thinking.' MTT requires a teacher be trained to use daily drills and quizzes to make certain that all pupils memorise and remember their subject knowledge.

An opponent to this would question whether memorising knowledge and facts leads to understanding, but in these terms, the notion that skills trump knowledge is false. In *Seven Myths about Education*, Daisy Christodoulou categorically shows that facts do not prevent understanding. Memorising facts actually provides the foundation for understanding because learning depends on memory and those with the best memories learn the most – the pupils that write the best stories have read the most stories. Additionally, skills are simply just a composite of sequential knowledge – all skills can be broken down to irreducible pieces of knowledge. In my experience, NTT teaching skills before knowledge leads to misunderstanding, if any understanding at all. Skills require knowledge, and not vice versa. To teach otherwise is to put the cart before the horse.

The 2013 KS3 Science National Curriculum is better at enabling knowledge-based teaching than its 2007 counterpart, with substantial content covering the fundamental areas of Science (DfE, 2013). This provides the groundwork so a trainee teacher can plan to teach knowledge. During MTT I was taught how to write my own textbooks with knowledge, memory and assessment in mind, which enables the use of convergent teaching across our Science department and indeed the school. Our own Science booklets are effective and efficient vehicles of delivering convergent knowledge transmission, which guarantee that the scientific knowledge is always taught, tested, retaught, revisited, recapped, revised, and, ultimately, remembered. By contrast, individualised lesson plans tend to lead to divergent teaching and learning because they risk becoming discrete from one another, especially when inexperienced trainee teachers write them. There is a greater likelihood of using varied, mixed pedagogies throughout lessons and classes and departments when one uses many resources in contrast to using a single resource: one unified booklet. Of course, some knowledge can be regarded as essential, and some as challenging extension material, in which case a teacher may choose to teach certain additional knowledge to stretch certain classes.

As is often cited as a shortcoming of knowledge-based teaching, NTT has a tendency to emphasise the importance of planning for engagement and entertainment, with a heavy focus on practical experiments, collaborative group-work and project-based learning in Science. In actual fact, not only does this result in limited understanding of the actual activity, it risks rebranding Science teachers as 'edutainers,' a concept which, worryingly, is championed by the scientific community. The idea of 'edutainment' is patronising to and contemptuous of both teachers and pupils and there is no evidence to suggest it engages, or even entertains.

I was taught how to plan for subject mastery during MTT: keeping it simple with reading, explanation and practice, with the teacher as the expert and the focal point of the lesson. This was in place of planning for engagement and entertainment, as I did during NTT. As Doug Lemov asserts, 'true entertainment comes from the teacher's presence and the pupils' pride in their academic success.'

Autonomy vs. Convergence

An example of a training objective I met during NTT, which was a polar opposite to the objectives of MTT, was to 'understand the diverse needs of pupils and their barriers to learning and how to personalise teaching to address them.' This objective works on the premise that every pupil is unique in terms of learning. It then requires teachers not only to personalise their instruction, resources and assessment for the full variety of pupils in the class, but to offer personalised feedback for each individual pupil. This leads to pedagogical autonomy, a precarious position in which to place a trainee teacher and one that will inevitably lead to divergence. In addition, personalised teaching is unrealistic for a trainee teacher, mainly because of the vast amount of time it takes. It was something that I struggled with immensely. In fact, pupils are far more similar than they are different in terms of learning; they learn in the same ways. As far as cognitive science has been able to determine, there are not categorically different types of learners or learning styles, because learning is governed by long-term memory in the architecture of the human brain, regardless of our diverse personalities and infinite preferences.

Positive relationships with pupils are vital, and pupils' personalities are indeed unique, but MTT treats personalising the lessons themselves as inherently damaging. Why would a teacher abjure a highly effective teaching practice such as reading, writing or expert teacher explanation? It strikes us as counterproductive. At Michaela we believe developing relationships with pupils and endlessly personalising lessons to meet their individual needs do not necessarily go hand in hand. Furthermore, we believe that it doesn't damage pupils' individual experiences in lessons if we do not personalise learning.

Conversely, NTT focused me on generating lesson plans to include all manner of differentiation and, in turn, promoted more pedagogical autonomy. I was told that 'I should know what's best for each pupil' when of course I had no idea. I had to use huge amounts of largely unreliable pupil data to inform my pedagogy, which influenced resources and assessments and even techniques such as seating plans. This superfluity only detracted from what actually mattered: teaching! MTT focuses on improving the core teaching skills of instruction and feedback. Designing systematic resources and automating consistency in applying the behaviour system were priorities for me during MTT. I have limited autonomy over my pedagogy. Such a situation would have been ideal in my early weeks of teaching when I, like most new recruits, had absolutely no idea what I was doing. During driving lessons no one expects the driving instructor to ask them: 'What do you think the best way to drive is?' So why have I, and thousands upon thousands of other teachers, been asked to discover the best way to teach from the very outset?

The NTT objectives centred around differentiation are mirrored by the DfE's Teachers' Standards which state that 'a teacher must adapt teaching to respond to the strengths and needs of all pupils,' including an 'understanding of how a range of factors can inhibit pupils' ability to learn, and how best to overcome these' and an 'understanding of the needs of all pupils, including those with special educational needs; those of high ability; those with English as an additional language; those with disabilities; and be able to use and evaluate distinctive teaching approaches to engage and support them' (DFE, 2011). This standard reinforces the premise that every pupil is unique, and moreover promotes an underlying assumption that some pupils can, and should, do what others cannot, or should not. Excessive differentiation holds pupils back because it lowers the expectations put upon them by the teacher, whether consciously or subconsciously.

NTT taught me to limit the amount of reading dyslexic pupils did, because it was too difficult for them – instead, I had to provide images and visual clues. It also taught me to limit the amount of writing dyspraxic pupils did, because, again, it was too difficult for them – instead, I had to provide arts and crafts or ICT-based activities. By nature, differentiation requires a divergent approach to teaching. By contrast, MTT considers differentiation as inherently unhelpful, and instead adopts a convergent approach. Teaching methods other than reading and writing are not the best ways to get struggling pupils to improve their reading and writing. The more effective method lies in extended, deliberate, subject-specific practice, which is much more convergent than personalised differentiation.

Behaviour: Discovery vs. Consistency

The concepts of personalisation and differentiation overlap with the last main topic of this essay: behaviour. NTT professes that ADHD pupils must have different behavioural rules in the classroom because they are different to other pupils. As Katie Ashford explains in her chapter, at Michaela we believe that labelling pupils with special educational needs and disabilities of this type is often unhelpful because it reinforces excuses for poor performance and bad behaviour, thus limiting the pupils' chances of success in future. Moreover, it can be restrictive for pupils and lead to loss of self-esteem. Because of MTT, I treat all pupils equally and expect the same from each of them, thus raising expectations and improving their chances of success in the future.

During NTT there was no training objective focused on behaviour management. Instead my cohort of trainee teachers and I were told to follow our schools' own behaviour policies. Leadership at my placement school gave me guidance on how to manage behaviour and I tried using this for a few weeks, but had no success. I soon learned that every teacher in the school had developed their own individual behaviour policy. The reason that my placement school's official behaviour policy didn't work was because it simply was not being implemented. Teachers would just close their door and get on with their lessons, using whatever methods of behaviour management worked for them. This could not be a clearer indication of extreme divergence, and the reality is that it occurs all over the UK.

I was told by colleagues to 'keep trying different things' until something worked. I must have tried hundreds of different methods to maintain order. Some of the more notable methods included: sending pupils out of the room (which resulted in my Head of Department telling me 'Be careful not to be thought of as racist' because it just so happened all three of the pupils I sent out were Sikh), trying to develop friendships with the pupils in the hope that they would behave out of pity for me (which unsurprisingly made things worse), and spending an entire lesson waiting for them to be silent (by which point an hour of learning had been wasted). Bad behaviour was the main reason I resigned from my placement school. I went into teaching to teach children, not to shout and be shouted at.

At Michaela we believe that reprimands are a genuine incentive to behave and I must say that my own experience validates this. This doesn't have to translate into cruelty, or even necessarily having to shout. It simply means having clear and consistent boundaries and following through with sanctions, a concept which was completely foreign at my previous training school.

MTT requires the use of a very simple system of merits and demerits, with two demerits resulting in a detention for the pupil, and three demerits resulting in the pupil being removed from the lesson. The difference between my placement school and Michaela is not the system itself, but the implementation of the system. MTT taught me that as a school we must be convergent in our behaviour policy, and to do otherwise undermines Michaela and results in the bad behaviour witnessed in schools all over the UK. Consistent and strict discipline is also the linchpin for knowledge-based teaching and direct instruction. One cannot stand at the front and teach without strict discipline in the classroom.

One final issue is the importance of observations and feedback in both NTT and MTT. Whether I agreed with the training objectives set out in NTT or not, in order to achieve the end goal of QTS I had to 'jump through hoops' to fulfil the necessary criteria. In my case, a main 'hoop' was graded observations, a regime that strikes fear into the heart of every trainee teacher. Weeks, sometimes months of hard work are distilled down into less than an hour-long assessment with one's future as a teacher hanging in the balance. The stakes could not be higher, but paradoxically the impact on actually improving that teacher's practice could not be lower. Graded observations have more of a detrimental than an uplifting impact on improving teachers' practice. A set of comments stating 'what went well' and that the lesson would be 'even better if...', along with a grading of 1-4, once a month, does not constitute high-impact feedback or allow one to effectively improve one's teaching practice.

Conversely, as Jo Facer explains in her chapter on CPD, lesson observations at Michaela are never graded, and all of our classrooms have an open door culture, such that I am now completely acquainted with guests, our pupil guides, other teachers and members of the Senior Team wandering in and out as they please. My MTT took months of teaching one to two lessons every day, until I had automated Michaela's teaching practice. I was given candid feedback daily, not monthly. As a result, I developed more in one week than I did in a month under NTT. This is the epitome of low-stakes, high-impact observations.

The convergent pedagogy of MTT rests on one major fulcrum: the belief that there is an optimal way to teach and that this is what should be taught to trainee teachers. NTT not only promotes divergent varieties of 'discovery learning', skills-based activities and project-based learning, it leaves teachers to flounder because, in my experience, NTT offers little real clarity on how best to teach subject knowledge, only vague exhortations to discover your own style. A decision needs to be made on which method of teaching is best because otherwise new teachers will founder and we will continue to limit the success of pupils across the whole country.

Every year, thousands of perfectly capable teachers are forced out of the profession because they're let down by their training. I am testament to that. It is only through a random stroke of luck I found myself a training route that works. Whether one agrees with the teaching methods of MTT or not, at least it shows conviction and purpose: something that cannot be said of NTT.

Teaching Without QTS

Sarah Clear

Qualifications: a good thing, right? Whilst it isn't necessary to be qualified to teach, surely you would be better off spending a year learning how to teach properly before taking the plunge into an infamously challenging profession? Surely a school is better off hiring staff who have been trained, who have studied the literature and have proven themselves worthy of 'teaching status'?

I disagree. 30% of Michaela's teaching staff are unqualified. The average percentage of unqualified teachers in free schools is 15.4%, and 4.5% in the maintained sector. We, more than almost any other school in the state sector, trust the capable hands of unqualified teachers with the education of many of our pupils in many subjects, and we believe it has no detrimental effect whatsoever on the quality of teaching that those pupils receive.

I am an unqualified teacher, and proud. I'm not going to become qualified, at least within the next few years, and I do not think QTS is necessary. Since January 2016, I have been a Music teacher. Every day, Monday to Friday, I stand up in front of classes of children and I teach them. I am a form tutor. I run weekly debate club sessions. I am paid a good salary, by a school, to teach. This is despite the fact that I am completely unqualified. No university will vouch for me having satisfied the necessary requirements to be a teacher. I haven't completed the forms. No one has had to stump up £9,000 to buy me 'teacher status.' I have written no essays on pedagogy. And yet I have thoroughly enjoyed teaching for the last ten months, and I am good at what I do. In fact, I am convinced that the speed at which I have successfully adapted to teaching has been precisely because I have been spared the doctrine of progressive, constructivist education that is so prevalent in teacher training in England: a doctrine which results in low standards, ineffective teaching methods and cultural relativism.

Read Robert Peal's *Progressively Worse*, and you will find that progressive education is everything that 'The Michaela Way' is not. It is 'skills-based' discovery, child-centered 'learning how to learn.' It lowers your expectations for poor kids. I experienced this when I was at school. I experienced it when studying education modules as part of my undergraduate degree, and I experienced it when working for various educational charities. Whilst my teaching experience might be limited, I have seen plenty of evidence that confirms Peal's thesis: progressive education pervades the education system because progressive education pervades the teacher training system.

I was told by my mum, an Ofsted 'outstanding' Headteacher of ten years, that I should be trained before I teach. On her recommendation I visited outstanding schools, I investigated Teach First and I spoke to a variety of teachers and school leaders about routes into teaching. None of them suggested that I could teach without first becoming trained. All of them taught progressively. One charity I worked with places 16-25-year-olds into schools with a focus on personal development. They were trained by teachers and school leaders before they started and on every Friday throughout the year. Training was copious, and it was distinctly progressive. I spent a year for the charity in a difficult primary school. By the end of the year, we should have been capable and confident. Certainly enough time had been put into our training. But I felt like I had made no difference. For me, for the team and for the school, our training hadn't worked.

But with the right school training, an otherwise unqualified teacher can bring about impressive outcomes. All of my pupils have learnt grade one music theory. They can all read music, treble and bass clef. They can recognise major intervals by ear. They can look at a piece of Beethoven and identify the key, the style, the speed, the dynamics, the tonic triads, the intervals. They can complete simple dictation by ear. Pupils taught a progressive music education cannot do these things. Their education does not provide them with the knowledge nor the practice. That is, of course, unless their parents have funded private music lessons (perhaps explaining why, in music particularly, progressively trained teachers may have lower expectations for the poorer kids).

Now let me be clear: I am no teaching prodigy, as much as I would like that to be the case. At Michaela, I'm not alone – there are a number of us who are reliable teachers, but all unqualified. There are two reasons why we are able to teach effectively:

1. Progressive teacher training holds teachers back.
2. Good schools and good mentors enable teachers to flourish.

Combined, these are the reasons why, despite my lack of qualifications, indeed because of my lack of qualifications, I can teach just as well and bring out as good if not better outcomes as qualified teachers can.

QTS does not a good teacher make

The accounts of many struggling NQTs highlight a significant concern – that the training they received did not prepare them for the reality. They might have been receiving consistently positive feedback from lesson observations; they might have been rated outstanding at the end of their placements; and yet now they are failing as NQTs. Successfully completing training does not mean that you are able to do the job you have been trained for. The reason for this? ITT, in our current conception of it, does not work. Being trained to teach, whether through a PGCE or a school-based route, is not helping our teachers to teach well.

Too often, NQT years are not successful. The 2016 Ofsted report lamented the problems of teacher recruitment and retention, especially in state schools. To state what has been known in the teaching sector for a long while, 'many newly qualified teachers ... continue to leave to teach abroad, or in the independent sector, or decide that teaching is just not for them.' The workload, the pressure and, most often, the behaviour are cited as reasons that NQTs struggle, and consider leaving the profession before the first year is up.

Newspapers, blogs, and books are filled with the stories of survivors to help the newly initiated get through the first year in school. 'Eight ways to survive your first year in teaching' ... 'Life as a NQT: 10 survival tips from those who've lived to tell the tale' ... 'How to destroy NQTs' – does that sound like the life of trained professionals? One teacher records their experiences on a *TES* forum. The title of the thread is 'Failing NQT year' – a promising start. They describe the struggles they are having, the pressures of their observations, the crippling stress and anxiety. 'I have found this year to be one of, (if not THE) hardest years of my life,' they write. The advice given? 'Perhaps you should start applying for jobs in international schools.' Let me just reiterate that these are our qualified teachers. We have a chronic shortage of teachers in our country, and the ones that we have are leaving the country because they do not feel able to do the job that they have been trained for. Browsing the literature, you'd be forgiven for thinking that an NQT year was a test of human endurance, rather than the opportunity for graduates to put their training into practice and start making a difference in their chosen career.

Behaviour is the main complaint. There is plenty of evidence of the effect that poor behaviour in classrooms has on recently qualified teachers. A NASUWT report in 2008 found that 'more than a third of NQTs (41% in 2007 and 37% in 2008) reported that behaviour issues in their school had impacted upon their desire to remain in the teaching profession.' The same study found that 44% of NQTs who did not intend to stay in the career for longer than five years had experienced 'occasional physical violence.' The report concludes that 'poor pupil behaviour, specifically physical violence, is strongly associated with NQTs' decisions about whether to stay in teaching for the long term.'

'But this is the point!' I hear you cry. 'It takes time and persistence to change the story of a child's lifetime,' claims one teaching charity's website, justifying the trials and tribulations that new recruits will face as a necessary and noble part of the mission. Not everyone will be able to hack it, and that's ok. And yes, I've been drawn in by the 'if it wasn't difficult it wouldn't be worth it' arguments. I remember watching the BBC documentary 'Tough Young Teachers' back in January 2014, in awe of the commitment and strength of character that these new teachers had. If you wanted the easy life you'd work at a private school, but instead you're choosing to work with the most 'challenging' children; of course it's going to be hard. But if you can grit out the tough stuff you can make a real difference. That's how the rhetoric goes. By pushing yourself to the limits you will achieve things that you never thought possible. By taking on the biggest challenges in education you become a hero of underprivileged young people! It really is inspirational stuff. But it's not true.

Ironically, it is actually the case that the easier and more enjoyable the teacher's job is, the more successful the children are. If the school's policies are strong enough to keep the children behaving in the classrooms, the teacher will be able to teach. When the teacher doesn't have to worry about bargaining with and 'getting on the same level' as their pupils, they can concentrate on teaching. The idea that teaching should be a battle of wills between the tough-as-nails teacher and disenchanted teenagers – moreover the idea that a good teacher is one with the charisma and character to win that battle – is simply another damaging doctrine of today's teacher training. It lowers the standards and expectations of what teachers should have to put up with, so preventing school leaders from taking necessary steps to support their teachers ('So what if a teacher is receiving verbal abuse on a daily basis? It's not meant to be easy...'). It puts off people who could be perfectly good teachers from entering the career, and we have already seen how it results in swathes of teachers leaving the profession or leaving the *country*, having been worn down and disillusioned. It encourages failing teachers to take it personally, beating themselves up and overworking as they try to make a difference in a tough world. It encourages successful teachers to self-indulge, trying to become the stand-out hero teacher: who can put in the most hours? Who can build the most meaningful relationships? Who can fill their weekends writing the most personalised feedback in their marking? While all noble aims, teachers need to work as a team, and their time can and should be used more efficiently. Whilst the ITT rhetoric of the hero teacher might be virtuous, it is certainly not improving our education system.

Michael Fordham is one of a number of educational commentators who have critiqued poor teacher training, led by 'mentors ... who lack knowledge and who lack outstanding subject leadership ... who flail around for theory, and thus latch on to learning styles, or an attenuated version of growth mindset, or some other junk theory doing the rounds.' The Hillgate group, after extensive research into teacher training, concluded that it was 'at best an irrelevance and at worst a positive hindrance to good teaching.' John Hattie, in *Visible Learning* – a vast meta-analysis of the evidence-base – is entirely unconvinced that 'good' teacher training actually improves the quality of teaching, as judged by the effect on students' learning, concluding that 'there is not a lot of evidence that improving teacher education colleges has improved the overall quality of teaching.' How are we getting it so wrong that our teacher training, our teaching qualification, does not actually improve teaching? How can it be the case that training someone to teach can sometimes be a hindrance to good teaching? We are getting it wrong, and my experience has convinced me of it. As far as I can see, there are two key reasons why ITT and QTS hinders teachers:

ITT has formed an intellectual monopoly over trained teachers, constraining the workforce into the straitjacket of one orthodox doctrine.

In his thorough account of progressivism in the teaching profession, Robert Peal calls it the 'gospel of progressive education.' Teachers-in-training are given prescriptive reading lists, 'tending to combine the anti-authority, individualistic ethos of progressive education with revolutionary politics.' Macmillan studied the reading lists of 92 top teacher training institutions in Britain and found that they expose a 'staggering bias in current teacher training, a bias that amounts to nothing short of indoctrination on a very wide scale.' PGCE students required to complete essays and presentations know that, if you want a good mark, you'd best make it progressive. Teachers are not even exposed to the other options. Over the entire course of teacher training – the reading lists, the seminars, the conferences – a qualified teacher can have entirely avoided E.D. Hirsch's distinctly traditional 'Core Knowledge Sequence.'

One worrying consequence of this is that it streamlines the workforce of qualified teachers into pre-disposed advocates of one approach, alienating an entire group who could otherwise make extremely successful teachers. One *Guardian* exposé of the Roehampton University PGCE found that 'all the fourth-year students spoken to, without exception, were passionately in favour of child-centred learning. Part of the reason for this unanimity is that dissenters are likely to drop-out or transfer to other subjects, and thus never become teachers.' By shoe-horning our training teachers into a certain approach, we are pushing away people who could be very effective teachers.

One lived example of the potency of the progressivist doctrine is the late Chris Woodhead, the former Chief Inspector of Schools in England. A trained teacher from the mid-60s to 1974, he was a notable supporter of progressive education until 1974. But by 1994, when he was appointed head of Ofsted, he was a firm critic of the progressive methods which he had unquestioningly adhered to through his teaching career. Why the change of heart? Because, as he described, on passing out of initial teacher training the idea of an education which countered the child-centered method was 'abhorrent.' It was only when he left the profession that he could see beyond the doctrine. Teacher training preaches progressivism like a religion, meaning that qualified teachers become indoctrinated against traditional didactic instruction.

More concerning is the fact that progressive education is promoted so fervently in teacher training that qualified teachers will continue to practise it, even in the face of evidence which challenges it. A 2003 study by Russell Bishop demonstrates 'that teachers come into classrooms with very strong theories about students and often resist evidence that their students do not conform to these theories.' John Hattie, a passionate believer in the importance of basing teaching practice on evidence, points out the regularity with which teachers will use theories they have been taught in their training to dictate their teaching, 'even when the evidence of impact does not support their particular theories ... maintaining their theories becomes almost a religion.'

Teachers are taught the same way, unsupported by evidence. A Heath and Nielson publication in 1974 was already saying that 'the research on the relation between teacher behaviour and student achievement does not offer an empirical basis for the prescription of teacher-training objectives.' And yet still the single-minded doctrine of progressive education pervades our ITT routes. How can our education system improve when our teachers are indoctrinated into a single dogmatic orthodoxy?

The exclusively progressive approach espoused by ITT routes doesn't work.

Perhaps you're thinking that having a somewhat single-minded workforce isn't such a big problem. Maybe we all teach and think about teaching in the same way – that's just an efficient training system. But here's the problem. Aside from the concerns around the inflexibility of teacher training, the approaches which teachers are expected to master in order to gain QTS are ill-evidenced and don't work effectively in the classroom. I don't have the expertise to go into detail on the problems of progressive education (though Joe Kirby and Olivia Dyer point to the advantages of non-progressive teaching in this book, and as previously mentioned, I would highly recommend Peal's *Progressively Worse*). But I can highlight some of the problems with the progressive education which qualified teachers are being trained to teach.

Teachers are explicitly trained not to teach knowledge. So while I'm standing at the front of my classroom telling my pupils how to read music, what a tonic triad is, why it is important, and what it means when it says 4 over 4 at the start of the line, a trained Music teacher is much more likely to be allowing pupils to learn by creativity and discovery. I don't let my Key Stage 3 pupils compose – they don't yet have the knowledge to be able to do so meaningfully. A progressively trained teacher will be encouraging pupils to create their own compositions in almost every lesson, drastically reducing the time in which they can impart vital subject knowledge – particularly wasteful when most Key Stage 3 pupils only have one hour of Music each week. I can confidently begin every lesson with drills in note reading, dictation and harmony exercises. A trained teacher will need to begin each lesson with an interactive starter – card sorts would no doubt be a favourite. As my pupils gain five minutes of deliberate practice, the pupils of progressively-qualified teachers gain five minutes of music-related fun. Overall, I spend 120 minutes per week teaching knowledge to each class. For a progressively-trained teacher, it is probably closer to 30 minutes.

It is not only the pupils of qualified teachers who are missing out on subject knowledge in favour of pedagogical play-time. The training that teachers are receiving also lacks focus on subject content. It seems obvious to me that teachers need to know subject content. They don't just need to know it well enough to impart the information, but they need to know context, and they need to be able to sequence the subject. The evidence for it is clear, as demonstrated in Hattie's analysis:

> In the last 10 years or so, many observers have emphasised that teachers ought to have rich subject-matter knowledge, and there does seem to be some data that students of these teachers learn more, especially in middle and high school and especially in Maths.

Despite this, PGCEs have neglected subject content in favour of educational theory:

> The aim is to encourage the trainees to see the teaching of their subject in terms, almost exclusively, of recent educational theory ... That there are no subject studies, but something much worse, is one of the most disturbing features of the PGCE.

A teacher who has trained to gain QTS has been told that educational theory and pedagogical know-how is more important than subject knowledge. It is inevitable, then, that qualified teachers begin to neglect their own subject studies, knowledge and expertise, preferring to immerse themselves in educational theory. Qualified teachers are no longer experts in their subject, but simply 'experts' in progressive education. Unqualified teachers, free from the constraints of progressive training, can remain first and foremost specialists in their subject.

Not only does a focus on pedagogical theory distract teachers from their subject content, it distracts them from the real evidence of their pupils' learning – whether successful or not. Theory does not easily convert into practice in the classrooms of struggling NQTs, meaning a new teacher's attention focuses on their own teaching methods, and away from the evidence of whether these methods are actually working. Again, this is not just my own suspicion. Hattie's analysis found that in-depth theoretical and methodological teacher training has resulted in us being much more concerned with engaging activities rather than enduring learning: teachers aim to 'engage students in interesting activities, to excite them to participate in learning, and to ensure that, when the bell rings, they have completed the assigned tasks and at least enjoyed the activity. These are low standards – teachers need to take a cold hard look at the effects of their teaching and change their teaching accordingly... Too often teachers believe that theories dictate action, even when the evidence of impact does not support their particular theories (and then maintaining their theories becomes almost a religion).'

If you've included a starter, a plenary, and your activities were entertaining, but your pupils still aren't remembering what you're teaching them, what are you supposed to think? Are you to question the methods that were preached to you throughout your training? Surely not. And so many teachers conclude that rigorous high standards are wrong; they are too high. Adjust them to the individual child's needs. Lower your expectations.

Too many ITT routes are training teachers into a closed-minded system which is failing our schools. Too often our newly-trained teachers are willing to accept miserable lives in uncontrollable classrooms on top of ridiculous workloads because of ineffectual progressive training. Too many are hampered by graded lesson observations, performance-related pay and box-ticking rubrics, ignoring the evidence that suggests that these management methods are ineffective. Too often trained teachers have lower standards of what children can achieve after their training, because they value an ineffective methodology over developing genuine subject expertise.

That is not to say that this is always the case, whether school- or university-led. I will go on later to make the case that good in-school training is the best way to train teachers, but well-sequenced PGCE courses (courses which notably break away from the orthodoxy of progressive teacher training) also exist and are highly successful. One obvious but rare example is the Cambridge History PGCE, which has great prestige thanks to its rigorous knowledge-based training, ensuring that teachers have the vast knowledge base required to begin to impart this powerful knowledge to their pupils. Michael Fordham describes its 'unrelenting emphasis on the acquisition of knowledge' – 'ten novels, eleven history education articles and a raft of historical scholarship is the starting point for the pre-course reading.' When compared to the other prevalent ITT routes, whether schools-based or university-led, it is a 'withering critique... of the poor curriculum design, dodgy pedagogy or intellectually bankrupt assessment models.'

I am certainly not saying that having a teaching qualification can never work; Cambridge's History PGCE is proof that it can. But at the moment the prevailing doctrine holds teachers back. The good news is that it is beginning to be acknowledged that QTS, as it currently stands, is failing our teachers and our schools, because it promotes ineffective methods as gospel truth, lowering our standards. In the recent 2016 White Paper, outlining the changes that need to be made in education, there is an acceptance that the teaching profession has been 'forced to conform to an orthodoxy on teaching methods through national strategies,' or an 'Ofsted-preferred teaching style,' which has been based on 'un-evidenced material.' There is the admission that current QTS routes have been more focused on methods than outcomes, and that we should 'include more subject knowledge', and most importantly there is the demonstration of the need to raise standards:

> Currently, Qualified Teacher Status is awarded after ITT, often lasting less than a year. That means the bar is comparatively low – a new teacher needs only to demonstrate that they meet the Teachers' Standards at a level appropriate to the end of initial training, before they have acquired any significant experience of life in the classroom.

Where do we go from here? We can learn something from the experiments of free schools and academies which, by allowing the hiring of unqualified teachers to be trained up by the school, are offering up new and potentially more effective ways of training our teachers. Free schools can think differently, and they can hire and train previously untrained teachers to think differently too. Large academy chains can start to train up teachers in schools with subject specialists and good mentors, as many are already doing. We are testing the waters of different ways to train teachers, and it is beginning to reveal what really makes a teacher into a good teacher. If we accept that our teacher training currently isn't adequately preparing our teachers to educate the next generation, then what do we need to do to ensure that our children receive a quality education? If doing the current training and gaining the qualification does not make you a good teacher, what does?

Unqualified does not mean untrained; why good schools make good teachers

I might have saved myself the time, money and progressive indoctrination of QTS, but that still doesn't necessarily mean that I can teach. Apart from a good Arts degree and some experience with a charity in schools around London, there is nothing about me which would make me good at teaching. But I can teach, and I can teach well. I have been made into a good teacher by a good school. As have all the other Michaela teachers – qualified or unqualified. Ask the experienced teachers we teach with, and they will say that we (unqualified teachers) are better teachers after two terms than they were after two years. The advantage of being unqualified is that I have not been held back by teacher training. I have been able to learn from a school unencumbered by the burden of bad ideas, and so flourish as a teacher within a matter of months, rather than the two years or more which it would have taken to flounder and discover and then un-learn the progressive pedagogy of QTS in favour of the Michaela way.

I firmly believe that a school with strong leadership and unqualified teachers would be much better than a school full of teachers full of faith in progressive theory but without strong systems. It is well-thought-through school systems and strong leadership which enable teachers, qualified or not, to teach. From that strong foundation, new teachers can master their profession easily and effectively. There are three reasons for this:

1) Strong behaviour management routines create a level playing field

Let's be honest, some teachers are charismatic, others are not. We can read *Teach Like a Champion* ten times over, but some of us will just never be able to command awe and attention like 'that' teacher. As long as we train teachers to manage behaviour using progressive methods ('Get down on their level'; 'discover and develop your own personal systems'; 'ask why they're misbehaving'; 'let them take ownership'; 'reason with them'), the vast majority of our NQTs will be eaten alive in their first years. Even by the time they are experienced teachers, many will still feel they cannot make the impact they wanted because they cannot manage behaviour like the 'best' teachers can. And the most damaging part is that we are training teachers to believe it is their fault. Schools become crushing hierarchies, with only those at the top commanding respect from pupils and teachers alike, and with those at the bottom not only having to deal with the worst behaviour, but feeling guilty about it. Those with the least experience, those who should be most supported to focus on how they are teaching and what the pupils are learning, they are the ones who have the most chaotic classrooms. No wonder we have miserable NQTs.

This is happening all over our country. One 2014 Ofsted study found that 'only a quarter of secondary teachers agreed that the behaviour policy in their school was applied consistently by all staff.' Good, established and qualified teachers are 'aware of internal variations in their own school and want senior leaders, who should be monitoring and taking more effective action, to take more responsibility for putting a stop to this.' Across our schools, senior leaders are failing either to come up with effective policies or to properly train their staff to apply them consistently with pupils, resulting in worn-down and ineffective teachers. This is happening because schools are not taking full responsibility for training teachers effectively in their own routines, but instead are relying on an ineffectual, anti-discipline, progressive mindset. At Michaela, it is quite the opposite. We unqualified teachers are learning to teach in a school where all staff expect all children to work hard and behave themselves, and I can expect exactly the same in my classroom. The methods to achieve that are clear and simple. I have the authority, cognitive space and the confidence in the classroom to focus on my teaching practice.

Finally, if a school has a strong behaviour system and gives its teachers the tools to be able to apply it properly, it puts all teachers on a level playing field. Schools will inevitably have some less experienced teachers and, speaking as one of those teachers, I rely entirely on the school's behaviour routines and systems to allow me to actually teach anything. I know that I do not (yet) have the natural charisma to be able to control a classroom of teenagers, but I also know that I don't need to. I can expect the kids to behave as well in my classroom as they do in front of the Headmistress. There are no hero teachers. Pupils are learning in a school where all their teachers have been trained to work effectively together, and so know the expected standards and routines across all their lessons. If a child deliberately, persistently chooses not to reach that standard in a lesson, I will have the full support of Senior Team in getting that child out of that lesson and focusing on teaching the other 30 pupils. Pupils can't tell the novice NQTs from the veteran expert at Michaela, so they behave the same for everyone. New teachers to the school, regardless of qualifications or previous training, can learn the routines in a matter of weeks, earn the same respect from pupils as all other teachers, and get down to the much more important matter of what and how much the pupils are learning in their subject.

2) Simplifying and centralising procedures makes it much easier for teachers to store procedural knowledge in long-term memory, and make routines automatic

Teachers' brains work exactly the same way as pupils'. As the cognitive scientist Daniel Willingham explains, we learn by transferring knowledge from the short-term to the long-term memory; the more knowledge we have in the long-term memory, the more space we have in our working memory to process new information. For teachers, as Feldon concluded in a 2007 study, this means developing automaticity. We need as many routines stored in our long-term memory – automatic habits – as possible. The more routines, habits and, importantly, subject knowledge are habitualised and automatic, the more space we have in working memory to focus on what is happening in the here and now of the classroom – the fiddling at the back of the room, or the areas of misunderstanding. Subject knowledge, as we know, should be a priority for new teachers, and a focus of teachers' ongoing professional development, meaning the content of a lesson should be at the teacher's fingertips whenever they need it. Procedural knowledge must come from the school. Give a teacher strong, clear, and simple systems that the pupils know and respond to automatically, and the teacher's job immediately becomes simpler. They have the cognitive space to become much more effective in the classroom.

At Michaela, this means we learn a load of subject knowledge before we attempt to teach the topic, and we have consistent behaviour routines, with consistent narration from all teachers: 'That's a demerit, because we're distracting others from learning'; 'You want to be trusted? You need to change your habits'; 'That's a merit, for a lovely act of kindness.' Pupils know that they might be asked to read at any point, in any lesson, so they'd better be tracking the text line-by-line as we read together. It means consistent classroom routines, with strict time-limits to increase teaching time. '3-2-1 and SLANT' means you can have all pupils stop what they're doing and tracking you within four seconds. Passing out books takes eight seconds. Self-checking in green pen means that questions can be marked in a matter of minutes. If schools provide these routines, and teachers internalise them, we don't need to train teachers to invent their own individual routines, nor do we need to distract teachers from practical matters by training them in complicated and tricky-to-apply pedagogical theory. Teachers can quickly master the routines until they become automatic, and so gain the cognitive space to focus on trickier-to-master content explanations.

Certainly, at first this means that new teachers will only know prescribed classroom routines, limiting their ability to transfer their knowledge to other schools. But again we must remember that teachers' brains work exactly like pupils.' Our knowledge begins as hard-and-fast rules – inflexible knowledge – and as we master this knowledge we begin to understand the deeper structure behind it – flexible knowledge. What does this mean for teachers? As new teachers master inflexible classroom routines, that knowledge becomes flexible and transferable, meaning that when they move to a different school they are able to apply theoretical knowledge much more readily. In-school training may at first limit the teacher to only teach in one school, but as the teacher masters the knowledge they will become capable of applying their knowledge and so teach effectively across all schools.

3) A well-managed work-life balance allows for extended and deliberate practice over many years

A good school is able not only to simplify the teacher's life within the classroom, they can also significantly ease the teacher's work-life balance, and for a newbie teacher, this can be make-or-break. At Michaela, it is not an exaggeration to say I have been gently eased into teaching. At no point have I considered leaving. Unfortunately, the majority of qualified teachers have had quite the opposite experience. A recent ATL survey found that almost three-quarters of trainee and newly qualified teachers have considered leaving the profession, with 76% blaming heavy workloads. Almost four out of ten teachers quit within a year of qualifying. 98% of teachers say they are under increasing pressure and 82% describe their workload as 'unmanageable.' 73% say their workload is having a serious impact on their physical health and 75% on their mental health. I could go on.

But this is crucial not just for teacher retention, though that is a significant issue. It is crucial for the training and development of teachers. New teachers need more time to absorb their training, and even experienced teachers need to continue their professional development – one year of teacher training is simply the beginning of a teacher's education. Just like any other skill, activity or profession, practice is the only way to improve. Daniel Willingham deals with the issue in detail, emphasising the need for teachers not just to teach over and over again, but to make their practice deliberate – practice which enables the teacher to observe other lessons to get new ideas, to get feedback, to take note of what they find difficult, ask more questions and change their methods accordingly. It requires time and effort, and it should happen continuously, particularly for new teachers. It inevitably requires a manageable amount of work, time dedicated to improvement, and happens over the course of ten years! This isn't happening in our country. A newly-qualified teacher already spends unsustainable hours simply keeping afloat, let alone with time or energy spare for deliberate practice. Hattie has done significant research in the matter:

In much of the western world, teachers spend about 1100 hours a year in front of students. This is 36 per cent more time in front of classes when compared to 30 nations in the Organisation for Economic Co-operation and Development review. Darling Hammond argues that the countries that have made the greatest progress in achievement allow teachers with "15 to 25 hours a week.... to plan cooperatively and engage in analyses of student learning, lesson study, action research, and observation of one another's classrooms that help them continually improve their practice."

A good, well-planned school can give their teachers this time. When I started teaching I had two teaching hours a week. This increased to four, and then six. I was able to switch off outside school, meaning I could be 100% switched-on when I was in school. When I was ready I took on instrumental lessons and after-school clubs. Even now, after seven months, I am encouraged and I have the time to observe other teachers, read books and blogs, carefully plan resources and get feedback on them in advance. It is not the case that I spent a set amount of time qualifying and then took on the mammoth task of an over-burdened teacher. I have been – and still am able to – deliberately and effectively practise my teaching craft and develop my subject expertise. This is only made possible when teachers are given the extensive time at home to rest, and the extended time in school to focus on their own development.

It is clearly evidenced that good CPD within schools is far more powerful than a teaching qualification, from Hattie and Willingham through to the government's most recent White Paper – 'when teachers have extensive ITT in schools, they perform better.' When good schools train their teachers, QTS is at best unnecessary and at worst a hindrance. What new teachers need instead is for disruptive behaviour to be minimised by school systems, clear and consistent routines freeing up space in working memory for deliberate practice, and a school which reduces burdensome teacher workload to make time for effective CPD.

The next question is: how can this be achieved? Good leadership and useful CPD within schools is hard to come by, and it certainly isn't a quick fix to our education system. Perhaps the idea of trusting schools with the training of our teachers is unscalable – that sending unqualified teachers into many of our schools, hoping that they will successfully learn on the job, would end in disaster. In many schools, there wouldn't be those behaviour systems or those classroom routines. Unfortunately, in many schools there wouldn't be a strong leadership team supporting their teachers. Perhaps the PCGE, whilst not perfect, is a necessary precaution to ensure at least a certain level of proficiency in our teachers and to prevent disaster in our failing schools. But, as we can tell from the experiences of our trained teachers, PCGEs simply do not prevent this disaster. The lectures and theories of teacher training go out of the window, and weak leadership from within underachieving schools means that those teachers, whether armed with a qualification or not, will not become successful.

Currently, the experiment in unqualified teachers is just that: an experiment. Although private schools have always been free to employ whoever they want, in the state sector it has been a recent change, and a slow one. Michaela's employment of unqualified teachers is practically unmatched in any state schools. However, the number of unqualified teachers has been rising since about 2009. Free schools began employing unqualified teachers in 2010, and as of 2012, academies have also been able to hire unqualified teachers.

Certainly, as with all experiments, it may not succeed everywhere. Not all schools are like Michaela, and not all unqualified teachers are lucky enough to have had the experience I have had. But change is necessary, and what is clear is that as long as we still require our teachers to gain QTS as it currently stands – a prescriptive and progressive mould – we are holding teachers and, consequently, schools back. As Robert Peal describes, the freedoms given to academies and free schools, although limited, have taught us a valuable lesson: 'positive school transformation is best achieved outside the existing structures of state education ... breaking from the tired orthodoxies of state education is best achieved by breaking away from the institutions, such as local authorities, that have traditionally been the guardians of such ideas.' QTS is the scaffolding on which these structures and orthodoxies of state education rely. Whether intentional or not, the existence of QTS, for all of the reasons I have been writing about, has been preventing teachers from becoming effective, and has been discouraging schools from providing strong leadership, training and direction for their own teachers.

The experiment of scrapping QTS started in free schools and academies – schools like Michaela hiring teachers like me – and showed us that we need to raise our methods and our standards of teacher training by changing QTS across the country. And here's some promising news – in the government's proposal for future educational policy it was announced that they 'will replace Qualified Teacher Status (QTS) with a stronger, more challenging accreditation based on a teacher's effectiveness in the classroom, as judged by great schools. This new accreditation will raise the quality and status of the teaching profession, better recognising advanced subject knowledge and pedagogy that is rooted in up-to-date evidence.' Replacing QTS will not suddenly improve our schools, but it would be the first step on a journey of improving our school leadership, CPD and teacher experience.

So what's the future? Get good schools to train up good teachers. Get the teachers to immerse themselves in subject content; allow them the time to deliberately practise their subject teaching, guided by robust research evidence. Ensure that teachers can work successfully with schools and in schools, free from the prescriptive confines of QTS. We need to learn from the research evidence, and change our perception of what makes a good teacher. Teachers will still be trained, but there will be no longer be the prescriptive and progressive cookie-cutter of QTS. Great schools will train great teachers: focusing them on subject knowledge; using real evidence to develop successful teaching; maintaining high standards and ensuring that new teachers continue to deliberately practise, over time, in order to see real changes in their effectiveness in the classroom. I am lucky to be able to say that this has been my experience of teaching without QTS. For the sake of teachers and children around the country, I truly hope that the Michaela way is the future for teacher training.

Changing My Mind

Lia Martin

I went into teaching for many reasons. I was bored of the everyday office humdrum, exhausted by brand-led, advertorial cataloguing dressed up as 'magazine journalism' and, as unbearably clichéd as it sounds, I wanted to dedicate my work to something consequential: something that would have a tangible impact on people's lives.

I joined Michaela Community School in September 2015 and was struck by what I encountered. A world away from my own grammar school experience, the consistent discipline, silent corridors, polite pupils and a staff group with an unwavering loyalty and commitment to their work were things I had never witnessed. From day one, I had no doubt in my mind that the school was doing something of magnitude. With a typical inner-London intake comprised primarily of pupils from socially disadvantaged backgrounds, it was remarkable that they were so engaged with their learning and eager to show off their vast reams of acquired cultural literacy. Michaela stood polarised from the overarching narrative seen in the media: *poor kids usually fail*. I knew instantly that it was a revelation in the educational landscape.

Having recognised this immediately made my ensuing doubts harder to come to terms with. I wanted the same outcomes as the rest of the team: happy, successful pupils with the opportunity to forge their own paths in life and compete for the best. However, I was uncomfortable with some of our methods, and I knew why. As a self-confessed liberal, some of the theories underpinning our practices made me wince. Zero-tolerance behaviour policies, an entrenched 'no excuses' ethos, public reprimands and a sense of elitism: these ideas were difficult for me to grasp. Everything about my upbringing, schooling, university and general life experience had reinforced ideals of fairness and individual freedom – ideals I continue to cherish. It was not until I started researching the subject, talking it through with respected colleagues and, crucially, visiting other schools, that I understood that these ethics in education cannot be achieved without the tough stuff: the authoritative, disciplinary environment that liberal progressives so often wrongly condemn. As Hirsch points out, 'political liberals really ought to oppose progressive educational ideas because they have led to practical failure and social inequality.'

In Jonathan Haidt's *The Righteous Mind*, he explains that once we 'accept a particular narrative' we 'become blind to alternative moral worlds.' I had to work hard to reawaken an open mind and alter my perspective to understand why Michaela works and why we do what we do. Here is how it happened.

'Top of the pyramid'

At Michaela, we use the phrase 'top of the pyramid' recurrently, encouraging our pupils to strive for the best. We tell them that they are not the same as other pupils from other schools; that they can be different. This was something I found difficult. 'Isn't it elitist to tell them this?' I asked the Headmistress early on in her office, my head shaking, my brow furrowed disapprovingly. Viewing the world through a progressive lens, I considered this an opposition to the fundamental principles of equality. After many conversations, however, I started to realise that promoting self-belief is paramount to children's success, especially for children with a challenging background. I would listen to assemblies given by the Headmistress where she would repeatedly say that success is not about wealth or social class, but can be achieved through the children's own behaviour. I would watch them size themselves up next to the children from other schools outside. They would watch others behave badly and want to be better than them. The children internalised this message: your behaviour determines your outcomes.

We want them to take pride in their school and understand how valuable an opportunity they have been given. We want them to feel gratitude for the high calibre of teaching and support, which some pupils in Britain are not fortunate enough to receive in the state system. We tell them that privately educated pupils take up a disproportionately large number of top university places in this country and, as a result, acquire top jobs, and resulting fulfilment and affluence.

It is those hailing from leading public schools that possess unequivocal self-assurance. Etonians do not need to be told they are the best; they know they are. They have got the historical gravitas and the legacy of a hefty heap of success stories behind them, proving to the world again and again that they are capable of high achievement. It is this self-confidence that we need to encourage in our children, alongside the value of hard work.

Self-confidence is, of course, different to hubris. What we reinforce even more is the notion that our pupils have to work incredibly hard to be 'top of the pyramid' people. They do not automatically adopt that right away. In our year 7 bootcamp week at the beginning of the year, we teach them that perseverance is the key to success, and that the competition out there is fierce. If we do not tell them that they can do it, then who else will?

Tough love

I struggled with a 'no excuses' approach. It is instinctive to defend, for instance, non-completion of homework because of trouble at home. When little Ahmed, sheepish and glassy-eyed, explains that he did not bring his book because he was visiting his mum in hospital, it is hard to sanction him. I grappled with this, upholding our sky-high standards but always feeling the impending guilt. I began to understand, though, that letting Ahmed off in the short term would only impact negatively on his long-term success.

In his book *Progressively Worse: The Burden of Bad Ideas in British Schools*, Robert Peal notes that when 'teachers and schools take on the belief that certain social groups can only be expected to achieve so much, such crude assumptions inevitably fulfil themselves in reality.' Not having set foot into another secondary school since leaving my own, I did not truly understand that our British education system is permeated with these beliefs. Even in good schools that have higher expectations of pupils – where lower standards are not always starkly obvious – excuse-making is rife. But until spending time in an ordinary inner-London secondary, shadowing pupils as they navigated their boisterous school terrain, I had not seen what Peal and my Michaela colleagues had so often described. Time and time again I observed teachers making excuses for their pupils and overheard fatalistic conversations about lower sets 'only aiming for a pass.'

In one History lesson, the teacher asked all pupils to complete a written task. Many acquiesced, intermittently writing sentences punctured with laughter and chatter. Some diligently refused. One boy put his head down on the table and doodled over his book. 'Sit up,' I asked of him. 'Let's have a look at the first question.' I assumed his lack of compliance was down to lack of understanding. No sooner had he sat up and picked up his pen, the teacher interjected: 'Leave him. He never does his work.' Then, in a troubled whisper, 'he has a lot of issues. I always leave him to it, poor thing.'

This ostensibly insignificant moment characterised so much of what I have read and heard about our British education system: differing expectations for pupils labelled with 'issues,' an admission of defeat, of letting pupils off; a culture of perceived kindness that, too often, kills pupils' potential before they have even had a chance to try. I watched as he returned his head to the table nonchalantly and resumed his hour of utter, uninterrupted boredom. In that lesson, this year 9 pupil missed out on integral knowledge that would have helped him not only in future exams but, perhaps more importantly, in the cultural framework of his future life. This is an outrage. It is a dereliction of our duty as professionals.

'What if they have troubles at home?' my mind used to wonder. Now I see that these are the pupils who need our high standards the most. Doing what is most caring may not always feel 'caring' in the moment but, at Michaela, we will not let children fall by the wayside by having lower expectations of them.

Harmony

Visitors to our school are always taken aback by the painstaking, precise harmonisation. We have many rules and routines that the children follow. The pupils transition between lessons in silence and enter classrooms in single-file in less than 30 seconds. Teachers use countdowns to hand out books efficiently and, when any teacher raises their hand, every pupil will immediately do the same and proceed to 'track' them. I initially queried whether it was right to insist on such obedience. I erred on the side of progressivism, finding it hard to shake the idea that stifling freedom was bad and autonomy was good.

But stringent rules are essential to the day-to-day functioning of a school. Many schools in Britain, particularly with a 'tough' intake, will insist on adherence to such procedures. It prevents pandemonium and maximises learning time: something these pupils desperately need. Spending time in other schools showed me what corridors can look like without strict rules – a chaotic no man's land rife with disrespectful behaviour. Reading Robert Peal cemented my understanding: he recognises that pupil compliance and their ability to follow school rules demonstrates that 'such structures are vital in building the sort of orderly school community within which freedom and self-expression can ultimately emerge.' When there are rules and boundaries, it is easier to build relationships and have fun with the pupils because they know where the line is drawn. They learn far more in lessons because there is no time wasted. When there are boundaries, pupils feel safe and happy. I see this in action every day at Michaela.

The hardest realisation

Perhaps the hardest transition was one of self-acceptance. At Michaela, we strive for our pupils to value personal responsibility and treasure the belief that they are masters of their own fate. From day one of year 7, they learn William Ernest Henley's poem 'Invictus' and Rudyard Kipling's 'If' by heart, inspiring them to never make excuses for their own bad choices and to persevere through life's many challenges. They learn to accept responsibility and gain insight from their mistakes.

It took a while for me to come to terms with the fact that my discomfort around this stemmed from my own lack of personal responsibility. In my teenage years

I was an excuse-maker; I was someone who would take criticism badly and deflect blame, insisting my lack of motivation was someone else's fault. I was someone who got through the system with homework rarely completed yet secured a place at a Russell Group university. I never strove for the best because doing 'well' was good enough.

But what I hadn't realised was that I could get away with this because I was privileged enough to come from a middle-class family who engaged me in political debates around the dinner table and exposed me to classic novels, galleries and museums before I had even entered my secondary school's gates. Many of our pupils are not so fortunate, needing to exercise great levels of resilience and self-control to have a chance of catching up and to secure the same kinds of opportunities. That is the reality. They have a much higher mountain to ascend. Why shouldn't they have the same opportunities that I had? Why is it acceptable to let poor children fail? It is not, and that realisation made me determined that we should have the highest expectations for our pupils.

Nothing makes me prouder than having eloquent conversations with proud, beaming pupils who are kind to each other and have genuine ambition. This is possible because our pupils thrive in their school environment, which is warm and strict in equal measure. When visiting other schools, I was shocked by pupils' rudeness and the palpable disregard for their teachers; our explicit emphasis on kindness, our constant narration of the 'why' behind all of our rules and, perhaps most crucially, our firm, 'no excuses' methods make this behaviour inconceivable. Progressive teachers: be open-minded to 'alternative moral worlds.' You can achieve your goals and allow poor pupils to flourish. Doing the right thing is not always comfortable, but for our children to succeed, we are determined to do it all the same.

CPD at Michaela: Question Everything

Jo Facer

Every day at Michaela, teachers watch their colleagues teach – five minutes, ten minutes, 30 minutes perhaps. Teachers receive feedback on their practice from every member of staff – teaching fellows, Heads of Department, SLT, and admin staff will chip in what they notice. Every teacher will watch and be watched hundreds of times in a year. No grades, no top-down feedback, just teachers, trying to get better at teaching, by looking, learning and receiving feedback.

Every week at Michaela, departments sit together and look at the upcoming week's lessons. They talk through the context and how it will be delivered together. They anticipate misunderstandings, consider links to be made to prior learning, and spot opportunities for additional examples, together.

Every week at Michaela, all our teachers and teaching fellows sit for an hour and talk about issues, values, and ideas. We grapple with our fears, our doubts, our outlooks, and come together as a team through these discussions.

That is CPD at Michaela.

The challenge of CPD

Developing teachers, or fostering their 'continuing professional development' (CPD), is a notoriously tough balance for schools. In a hall of 80 to over 100 professionals, one session can rarely provide what each teacher needs. Teachers aren't streamed or set like pupils are; within any school there is a range of 'need,' from NQTs struggling to control behaviour to maverick teachers struggling to 'step in line' with one new policy or another, to the seasoned sages who have listened to group work come and go and wonder whether they should be similarly heedless of the new jargon being presented to them on hastily knocked-together (or splendidly artistic) PowerPoint slides.

Couple that with *when* CPD is being delivered: usually after school, and in an increasing number of schools, more than once a week. Or during an inset day, which teachers have secretly marked out to do the million and one tasks they could never accomplish in the haze of a normal school day. Or, more painful still, the current trend of 'breakfast CPD' sessions, with teachers cramming into a hall or staffroom for a ten-minute whirl around the latest gimmick. Nobody, but nobody, wants to be there – not even the person presenting their wares. Everybody would rather be finishing their photocopying, which is saying something.

The reality is that no single CPD session will directly or immediately improve anyone's practice. Doug Lemov's movements towards 'practice'-based CPD, whereby tweaks to teaching are not lectured on, but enacted by listening teachers, is an excellent development, but it is not enough. There is still the boggling range of knowledge and capability in any room of teachers.

Ask any teacher what made them the teacher they are today, and I guarantee two trends will come up. One: mentors. Many teachers learned in their early years from extraordinary teachers who taught them the fundamentals of classroom management and the education of children. Alternatively, teachers will reach back into their past, finding a touchstone teacher of their own history who inspired them during their own school days who they seek to emulate. Two: observing excellent colleagues. I have never (yet) heard the teacher say that 'a CPD session on [insert latest fad: perhaps, dialogue marking?] revolutionised my teaching and made me the awesome professional I am today.'

At Michaela, we reject standard, one-size-fits-all, hall-based CPD sessions for a different approach.

Subject CPD

To begin with, we conduct the bulk of our development of teachers within departments. At Michaela, the subject is at the heart of everything we do, and we know a brilliant Maths teacher will look slightly different to a brilliant History teacher. That difference will be knowledge, and that is the cornerstone of our practice.

We have absolutely no graded observations, ever. The literature on graded observations is readily available, but just to summarise: making an observation formal and high-stakes fundamentally changes what you see. Anyone can pull out tricks they know the inspector wants to see and teachers can 'turn it on' and do something different. Most teachers know this because they *have done this* in the past (many is the proud current Michaela teacher who has been graded 'requires improvement' in past schools for eschewing such tricks). Tom Sherrington, Head of an Islington comprehensive, says of ungraded observations:

> The lessons are more normal. You see regular lessons. People tell me so; they fret less about putting on a show and I'm more confident that what I see is what the students get on a normal day. There may be some tidying up but it's not a performance. The process encourages a stronger focus on learning than

teaching. Grading could only be about the lesson snap-shot and that led to a focus on teacher-performance during an observation. Learning is long term; without grading, the discussions are about the whole process – what goes before, what follows and how a lesson fits into a big picture. Grading could never meaningfully capture that.

Coupled with no grades, we also have absolutely no formal observations, ever. We just wander in and out of each other's classrooms, pinging a quick email with thoughts for improvement afterwards. We've taken this approach from Paul Bambrick-Santoyo's *Leverage Leadership* coaching model, which relies on frequent, low-stakes observations with immediate, actionable feedback.

In the early days, such observations are incredibly frequent: in my first two weeks as a Michaela teacher, I was observed an average of twice a day. The email would ping into my inbox as I was still teaching, and it would read something like this:

> Lovely, warm affirming presence, combined with sky-high standards for their focus, concentration and attention, minimising fidgeting with effective pauses. The automaticity of your subject knowledge has really boosted how commanding your presence is.
>
> A couple of tiny tweaks:
>
> **Use 1-2-3 choral response** to give more of them a chance to contribute when 50% or more have their hands up for a one-word answer. On 'imperatives,' for instance.
>
> **Number** those with hands up so that they're not waiting there with hands up but know you'll see them within a minute or so. "Karim, 1... Sarah... 2.... Khayyam, 3... I'll be with you in just a bit."

Occasionally, it was as simple as this, which I received from our teaching fellow in English:

> I noticed Elena doing a lot of backwards glances at Laureth (back, your left-hand corner). I noticed this and smirking particularly when you mentioned Medusa. Just flagging as you may want to move them so they can't see each other. They're a tricky pair!

And occasionally, it was interventionist: someone would come into my room as I was teaching and say: 'Sorry, Miss – can you just log a demerit for Ryan? He just looked around as you were speaking.' This is invaluable, as the new Michaela teacher doesn't have the radar needed at our school. A slight head-turn would definitely not be picked up on and sanctioned at any of my previous schools, and this kind of polite flagging was absolutely crucial in allowing me to adjust to the higher standards of behaviour. Importantly, the final two examples were from a teaching fellow: someone who is employed to assist the teacher and learn how to teach. Observations at Michaela are not hierarchical: for the new teacher, however seasoned, an existing Michaela member of staff will always know better the methods, routines, and expectations.

So a lack of ego is crucial to thriving. I could have received any of the above, all examples of feedback from people who have been teaching for less time than I have, and been resentful: 'How dare they? I have the experience; I have been graded "Outstanding," I have got great results for my classes.' But this is not the way to learn. To succeed as a Michaela teacher, you leave your ego at the door, and take on feedback with humility. I'm not saying it is easy – for me, beginning at Michaela and taking feedback from two of my closest friends, was at first embarrassing. But after about a day I got over that. If you focus on learning, improving and aligning to the organisation, you start to see that feedback in a different way. In fact, I now actively seek the feedback: often, someone who comes into my room to grab a work pack or exercise book will find themselves collared later: 'What did you see? What can I improve?'

The other paradigm for learning is to observe others. Michaela has teachers like no other. In our free periods, we are all observing each other for learning – even seasoned Michaela founders. Going into Jonny Porter's classroom, Olivia Dyer's classroom, Joe Kirby's classroom, Katie Ashford's classroom, Barry Smith's classroom, is something visitors frequently say has redefined what they thought possible for education. Imagine being able to enter those teachers' classrooms any time you wanted! There is no CPD more inspiring than a five-minute jaunt down the hall to watch children's lives being changed.

Our CPD in terms of teacher actions, therefore, is delivered one to one: through emails or conversations where necessary. Department meetings are given over to subject content. We bring our booklets for each year group and go through the following week's lessons. In English, we could have annotated the poems, and we turn up to share the key aspects we want all pupils to be learning. This helps to promote consistency. For example, looking at Shelley's 'England in 1819,' the opening line reads: 'an old, mad, blind, despised and dying king.' While I might say: 'let's note the listing of the first line,' Katie Ashford would say: 'can we teach them "congeries", the rhetorical term, instead of listing?' And we all note it down. Someone might know the context, and would say: 'let's flag up the context before we annotate: this poem is a reaction to the Peterloo massacre.' And others annotate their poems similarly.

This means teachers go into their lessons knowing exactly what to teach: we have clarity on the key aspects of form, language and context, and are all reaching a consistency I only dreamed of in the other schools I've taught in. One Maths teacher on her wander around the school remarked to me: 'I came out of Katie's classroom as she finished a sentence, and walked into yours across the hall where you were finishing the exact same sentence!' Katie and I hadn't 'co-planned' that lesson, but we had discussed the poem together, and we had seen each other teach so many times that our methods and explanations were converging. Frequent observations and knowledge-based department meetings are the key to true consistency.

But what about performance management – how do SLT judge teachers? This is a question visitor after visitor has asked me about Michaela. And I explain that we don't do performance management: it is the wrong paradigm. How many hours do teachers spend every year in performance management meetings? Setting targets, reviewing targets? All of this hinging on a single observed lesson performance? Perhaps creating the dreaded 'action plan' to go along with their monkey dance? (An aside: at a previous school I was already won over to the bureaucracy-light side, and spent an entire weekend shrinking my hated action plan to what Joe Kirby calls 'a one-pager' – because there's never a need for more information than that. I was told to go home and radically 'improve' it – aiming for at least five pages. Otherwise it looked like 'I didn't care.') Action plans are flawed, because schools change more swiftly than a one-year cycle. In fact, my aim for this week will probably be different to my aim for next week. And ultimately, we all want all of our children to excel in their exams. So what is the need for all teachers to be filling in pieces of paper? The costs of performance management – the stress, bureaucracy and incentive to lie – all massively outweigh the benefit of leaving a paper trail for Ofsted.

Long term impact

At Michaela, we spend our inset days resourcing our curriculum. We come into school and we work on making our curriculum better. This requires some forethought from department heads, who might ask teachers to tweak questions, or add recap questions, or create practice drills. We might be improving past units; we might be writing new units – as we grow every year, there is always new content to resource. We are abridging novels and biographies and historical surveys; we are scripting the perfect questions to ensure all pupils understand the content. We are writing model paragraphs to show pupils the high standard we expect them to reach when they write their own. This takes time, and we use our inset days to complete it.

Tiger teachers

But beyond the craft of classroom instruction and the intellectual rigour of improving our subject knowledge lies a deeper aim to Michaela's CPD: to hone the 'Michaela Mindset.'

This book celebrates all that we do in our school; we are the Tiger Teachers of the title. We take the term from Amy Chua's memoir: *Battle Hymn of the Tiger Mother*, which is a key piece of reading for staff and parents of Michaela's community. A tiger parent is roughly defined as someone who has radically high standards for their children, and is relentless in getting them to meet them. The tiger parent does not rely upon compassion alone, however, but also compulsion, accepting that children are often complacent and lacking in knowledge, and in need of external incentives and sanctions to rise to our high expectations. Rare is the child who defies all expectations through woolly 'You can do it!' comments alone.

Being a Tiger Teacher is tough — no question. The weakest children, the naughtiest children, they are still children — adorable, loving children, full of hopes, dreams and boundless potential. It is hard to discipline these loving, lovely beings. But it is crucial. When a child who has defied every expectation to come to school despite facing significant personal challenges, has turned up in full uniform and sat in five out of six lessons doing exactly the right thing, working hard and being kind, decides to whisper to their partner, it feels just plain mean to give a demerit to such a child.

What does a Tiger Teacher do? They give a demerit. Because we know that what seems 'mean' in the short term is *kind in the long run*. Compare this approach to that where a child in the same situation at a different school was removed from a detention by the Head of Year, who explained: 'he's had a terrible day — no child should have to go through that.' That same child turned up to that teacher's every following lesson hurling a string of expletives at the door, and being hustled to the office for some TLC and time out. That child was denied their education because of their circumstances. At Michaela, this would never happen. We are compassionate, loving and kind; we are also firm, strict, and ruthless with our standards. A child who has grown up in care, a child who has grown up in poverty, a child who has come from a war-torn nation with only the clothes on their back, they are the ones who most need our rules. If we keep our expectations sky-high, they will rise to them.

And let us find some perspective here: what is the worst that happens to that child? Are they thrown in the chokey? Beaten by a belt-wielding housemaster? No: they sit for 30 minutes in detention, quizzing on their learning. Detentions are not that bad. Even our most emotionally fragile pupils can surely bear to sit in silence and revise for half an hour.

Tiger Teachers expect more of pupils, and their pupils prove time and time again that they are capable of rising to the challenge. Children are remarkably resilient, and remarkably opportunistic. Give them an inch, and they will run with it. Give them boundaries, and they will respond. Give them sky-high standards, and they will rise to them.

Being a Tiger Teacher comes naturally to only a few professionals, in our collective experience. We don't only hire Tiger Teachers! We hire excellent professionals who are dedicated and smart – but these same professionals are often, as I was, compassionate and progressively-minded. We want all our teachers to become Tiger Teachers, to see through a new paradigm: the Michaela Mindset.

Question Everything

Everything at Michaela, it seems, is thought of in a different way to other schools. Many of the chapters in this book illustrate this: we don't plan for engagement, we plan for learning – and the children come to be engaged and love and have fun in lessons which are purely content-focused. We don't differentiate for the needs of different children – we teach the whole class, and find that children learn in the same way, and they all do learn. We don't think it is our responsibility that children progress, but the pupil's.

A cornerstone book for the new Michaela teacher is Jonathan Haidt's *The Righteous Mind*. In it, Haidt explores the idea of morality as being like a tongue with taste receptors. While liberal, compassionate teachers tend to identify with the receptors of care, fairness and liberty, we at Michaela need teachers to also understand the receptors of authority, loyalty and sanctity. Schools are not about snowflake-like individuals, but the community – to use Haidt's metaphor, they are 'bee hives,' where we all need to follow rules for everyone to prosper. And, again as Haidt says, 'you don't help bees by harming the hive.' Authority, discipline, tradition and loyalty allow us to build a strong community and a strong ethos, so that all the pupils can prosper.

Induction

Before joining Michaela, we not only set our new teachers up with all the knowledge organisers to learn by heart, we also provide an extensive reading list. This includes articles, books and blog posts, including many by current Michaela staff, to help them understand what it means to be a 'Tiger Teacher.'

Jess Lund's blog, 'Confessions of a soft touch,' is a great example of this:

> I was approached by several pupils who had just been given detention by another staff member for rudeness and inappropriate behaviour. Why did they approach me? Was it because I was their form tutor, or the head of the department, or some other person of pastoral or disciplinary significance? No. I, Jessica Lund, am a Soft Touch. I gave them the opportunity to air their grievances. It wasn't fair, they said. They weren't guilty of what they had been punished for, they maintained. This teacher had it in for them, they moaned. I probed a little and ascertained that, actually, they had been guilty of about 60% of what they had been punished for, but that the actual detention they felt was the unwarranted bit. I said I would speak to the teacher on their behalf. "Leave it with me." I can hear the voice of my new Headmistress now – WHAT?! That is outrageous. That is completely and utterly unacceptable. And she's right. What I did was completely and utterly unacceptable. I, Jessica Lund, am a Soft Touch. There are innumerable similar instances of such behaviour. The moments I would excuse non-completion of homework because of illness, technical problems with computers, trouble at home, trouble at school, bad hair days. The instances in which I would accept that a child would only learn 2-3 words in the course of a lesson because 'oh, they have issues.' The times when I would listen to pupils saying that I, or another teacher, had unfairly punished them, and would (in some cases) reverse decisions. The moments when I overlooked equipment sanctions for the chronically disorganised child, or gave a pupil an extra chance to tuck in their shirt en route to a lesson. I was proud to be a teacher that pupils would come to in order to seek justice or discuss their problems. I, Jessica Lund, am the embodiment of the Culture of Low Expectations.

What Jess so brilliantly describes in this post is the movement from being a 'soft touch' to embodying the high standards required at Michaela. It is tough – no question about it. But it is essential for us to challenge everything we have previously thought in order to become a Tiger Teacher. We are tough at Michaela with the children because we expect more of them: like Amy Chua, it comes not from hating children (as our detractors would have you believe), but *loving them*, and from *expecting more from them*. When our children misbehave, we tell them off: the responsibility for their behaviour lies not with the teacher for teaching boring lessons, not with society for keeping that child poor, but with the child. Only children who can accept personal responsibility really have the chance to exceed expectations, because those children will *stop blaming others and start working harder*.

Our approach: yes, life is tough, so you need to work harder. We know you can work harder, so we will make you. We know it is easier for us to let you off, and we know it is easier for you to be let off, but we don't choose the easy way. We choose the tough way, because being tough now means you have more chance of achieving your dreams in the long term.

And the children who were given demerits, detentions, whose circumstances were ignored? They are excelling. They love the school. They are paragons of what it means to be Michaela. In the short term, habit change is tough, but in the long term, it is life-changing.

Weekly Seminars

Teaching at Michaela is not just about learning our systems, rules, or curriculum. To become a Michaela teacher is deceptively difficult, and that is partly because our values as an organisation often diverge from the values prevalent in the current educational landscape. While teachers like the results of our strict behaviour system, liking a system in theory is not the same as enacting it. For new staff it can feel 'cruel' or 'mean' to give detentions and demerits for incidents that would barely register in their previous school. (One new teacher commented to me on his visit to the school before beginning: 'I watched lessons, and heard teachers giving demerits for things I couldn't even see. I sat there, trying to work out what the kids were doing. I'm scared!')

Even for established staff, 'being Michaela' requires effort. In a year 8 class I was teaching last year, one particular boy was especially keen: always putting up his hand, sending me emails asking for extra work, embodying the politeness we expect throughout the day and in every interaction, and diligently focusing 100% of the time. But, being tall, he tended to slouch in his seat. Slouching is something that warrants a reminder, and then a demerit. We want our children to sit tall and proud: it makes it much easier to focus when we do so. So, when this lovely, kind, keen boy starts to slouch, I wonder: should I do it? Should I give him a demerit when he is doing everything else correctly?

The Michaela solution to the problem is to ask: 'Do I care about this child's future enough to give them a demerit?' If a child is 99% compliant, why not ask for the final per cent? Why not allow that child to meet your highest expectation, and remind them when they don't?

At our school, we want there to be no gap between founding teachers and new, inexperienced teachers. We want office staff to be respected as much as the Headmistress. A crucial component in creating this culture is to row together. At Michaela, we don't value those with good intentions who choose to bypass the excellent systems that we know work. When some teachers use systems and others get by on charisma alone, a chasm opens. Soon, children will behave for some teachers, and resent others for detentions, which suddenly seem punitive.

To flourish at Michaela, almost everyone has to change their mind. This doesn't mean that we all think in exactly the same way. But no matter who you are, no matter where you have worked, it is almost certain that your standards won't be high enough and your instincts will be wrong. A successful Michaela recruit is open to learning, and keen to understand what makes us so successful. As Katharine Birbalsingh tells new staff on their first inset day: 'You might not get it at first. It might feel unusual, or even uncomfortable. Trust us. You have to trust us.'

To assist teachers to adopt the Michaela Mindset once they arrive at our school, we hold weekly seminars with all staff. Teachers are given the reading a week in advance, and arrive at the seminar to listen and discuss. We talk about culture, authority, sanctity, loyalty; we talk about how hard it is, but reiterate why we do what we do.

The seminar reading is a mixture of articles and books. As I've mentioned above, one cornerstone text is Jonathan Haidt's *The Righteous Mind*. Haidt helps us to see that our values are a prism through which we view the world. By recognising that there are alternative narratives, we can ensure we are not 'blinded,' as Haidt says, to our own narrow views, but aware of the multitude of narratives available, allowing us to choose the values which serve our children and community best. We read texts like Roger Scruton's *Culture Counts*, where he explores the formation of the curriculum in modern times and all the implications of learning in contemporary culture.

Throughout the year, we discuss our transition towards the Michaela Mindset. Teachers, old and new, are encouraged to share the beliefs they have previously held, based on our experiences and initial training. For example, many of us, before joining Michaela, believed when planning lessons that we needed to keep pupils 'engaged;' we wanted to use a variety of teaching methods to please those observing us, and thought we might 'lose' the children if we weren't edu-taining them. Instead, at Michaela, we reject this complexity, and focus on simplicity: reading, explanations and pupil practice. We still believe in joy and engagement, but want this to come from the pupils' pride in their academic success; their genuine enjoyment of academia. Teachers revisit these comparisons in our staff conversations throughout the year, and it can help to track the development of their mindset to see old beliefs they have cast off and new ones they have begun to hold.

Teachers find themselves opening their minds to a new way of thinking. It helps us compassionate liberals to be able to give the demerit of kindness and the detention of kindness.

The aim of our CPD programme of reading and discussing is to build our ethos, and build our staff culture. When we row together, we go further. When we understand *why* we do things the way we do them, we begin to see what we do in a new way. Our Michaela Mindset means it is easier to deploy the tough love methods that lead to such astonishing results for pupils. We are all responsible for nurturing the Michaela beehive, where all pupils have a chance at reaching the stars.

Je ne regrette rien

Fadila Bettahar

Moving from France to London wasn't a decision I took lightly. I first applied to work as a French teacher at Michaela Community School, but I was unsuccessful. Katharine Birbalsingh was, however, willing to take a chance and offer me a position as a Teaching Fellow. I understood her caution. I was an unknown quantity. This strange French woman who was willing to up sticks and leave her entire life behind to come work in a tiny little school, with a small body of staff, in one of the world's most expensive cities. Could she count on me? Would I stay?

Had it been any other school, there is no way I would have left France and everything that I knew behind. But I knew instantly that Michaela was something special.

Why did I decide to leave France to come to a school that had only opened a few months earlier, a school with no real track record, a school breaking every rule imaginable? The answer is easy. It was '*un coup de foudre*'; for English readers, that's 'love at first sight.'

When I first came to visit the school in January 2015, only four months after Michaela had first opened its doors, I saw the enormous potential of the school. I was blown away by the discipline, the silence in the corridors, the politeness and enthusiasm of the pupils, the sense of industry everywhere I went.

But what really convinced me that this school was special, in every possible way, were the French lessons. I was amazed by the pupils' accents, by the range of structures, proverbs, idioms and expressions that they trotted out so confidently.

I have to admit that, at first, I was more than a little thrown by the style of language teaching that I encountered at Michaela. It wasn't like anything I had ever seen before. I was no newbie to language teaching when I came to visit Michaela. My degree is in Teaching French as a Foreign Language, and I'd been doing just that since 2007. I was well-versed in MFL 'good practice.' I was used to the standard fare of choral repetition, games, pictures, ropey pronunciation and snail's pace progress.

At Michaela, I encountered something completely different. Every word was dissected, every vowel combination noted, every prefix and suffix analysed. Silent letters, instead of being a perennial stumbling block, were a springboard for perfect pronunciation. Pupils beamed with pride. They loved reading aloud; they revelled in the frisson of rolling their Rs and demonstrating their familiarity with liaisons.[1]

Pupils really understood how the language worked. They understood every single word. They giggled at the literal translations and they remembered them too. They understood how to break a sentence down and then build it up again. They wondered at the jigsaw complexity of the language, yet they basked in the transparency of everything they heard and read. They readily told me that learning French – '*c'est un jeu d'enfant!*'

What really knocked me off my feet was when pupils, barely into year 7, would confidently announce in perfect French: '*Aaaah mais c'est évident, il y a un accent grave sur la lettre E.*' Pupils in year 7 were able to differentiate an '*accent aigu*' from an '*accent grave*' with startling precision.

No pictures, no games, no guessing, no PowerPoint. Was I really in a French lesson? And yet, pupils would listen attentively to Monsieur Forgeron's (Barry Smith's) explanations of the language, they would read with their best accent, they would really make enormous efforts with pronunciation and intonation. Pupils demonstrated rapt attention: they were delighted to show off their knowledge of the language, its nuances, its sophistication and its cheeky bits too. They were playing with the language, deconstructing and reconstructing, toying with it, really grasping the building blocks. They were thinking like linguists!

But as Barry explained, 'Teaching is easy here. In lots of schools you see kids Period 1 on a Monday and then you don't see them again until Period 5 on a Thursday, and God knows the chaos that has ensued in the intervening period. But here, the kids leave me and I know they are going to have lesson after lesson of brilliant teaching in an atmosphere where success and aspiration permeate everything. It's the quality of teaching in every lesson that makes my job so easy.'

When I first visited Michaela, I couldn't help but think of my own education in France. Michaela was, on the one hand, shockingly innovative. In lesson after lesson, I saw the orthodoxy of accepted wisdom swept aside. I saw teachers who taught from the front with poise and confidence. I saw teachers who taught with the self-assurance of subject experts: teachers who didn't pander to the vagaries of fashion. They were free! The yoke of 'good practice,' of 'being seen to do the right thing,' had been lifted. There was a lightness in their style,

---

1   'Liaisons' refers to words in French where one word is elided with the next in their pronunciation.

a genuine joy in just teaching, just being the adult who reveals to children the wonders of their subject. I saw teachers bringing their subjects to life. The teachers were loving it. The pupils were loving it. The atmosphere was electric.

But, for all of Michaela's apparent innovation and break with contemporary traditions, watching lessons at Michaela took me back to my own school days, to my lessons with Monsieur Farque – the best teacher I'd ever known.

Monsieur Farque embodied strictness, expertise, humour. He was the adult; he was the sage on the stage. We knew where we were with him and we loved being there with him. We had a healthy respect for him and a certain admiration. We were, most definitely, kept on our toes. That's why we loved his lessons so much.

M. Farque was our form tutor and also taught us French and Greek. From our first meeting, he let us know that his standards were sky-high and that they would always be constant – there was no compromise with Monsieur Farque.

How did we know he took no prisoners – that he meant what he said and he said what he meant? In our first lesson he made us copy a list of books, four pages of book titles in total, and explained that we would have to read these books. We would have to do fortnightly book reports. We were set holiday homework, two books to read in two weeks. We copied in silence; we never even contemplated the possibility of slacking. From that first moment, we knew we were safe. That was 20 years ago, when I was in year 10. Monsieur Farque's intractability set the course for the rest of my education. I knew where I was going. He showed me the way.

At Michaela we might call Monsieur Farque's approach 'no excuses' or 'tough love.' We knew he was there for us. We knew that it was a two-way street too. He expected a lot from us, and he gave a lot too.

Again, I look back at my best primary school teacher, Madame Baujeux. Her attention to detail was extraordinary. She was also extraordinarily demanding of us too. We'd stand; we'd read aloud. We'd project to the entire class. She would correct every error, she would teach us to perform, to really deliver a speech, to really read for an audience; every pause, every breath, every liaison. She never held back. We knew that every word of advice was gold dust. We drank in her words. To this day I remember her advice. I catch myself sometimes being Madame Baujeux myself. Or at least trying!

The education system in France today is not what it was. I am 34 years old. I am a product of the French education system as it was: elitist, traditional, didactic and grammar-obsessed. You may accuse me of being overly nostalgic, but there are some simple facts that are undeniable. Over the years, as E.D. Hirsch attests to in *Why Knowledge Matters*, there has certainly been a move in France to make teaching harder for teachers and more playful and fun for pupils.

When I was at school, the system was proudly elitist. You worked hard, you got to the top. More recent reforms have purported to work towards equality of opportunity. I can understand the desire to help the socially deprived – I come from a solidly working-class background myself. But my parents believed in a strict education, in effort. They pushed me and my sister and brothers. They didn't allow excuses. They stood by the school. Neither of my parents had been to university but both of them read voraciously and we knew the value of knowledge. My mother would always say, and still says to this day: '*Ce que tu apprends, ce que tu as dans la tête, personne ne peut te le prendre.*' A rough translation might be 'Knowledge is Power'!

The reforms I see in France today don't help the deprived; they don't raise the aspirations of the poor. If anything they stymie ambition, and they shelter pupils from the inherent complexities of the French language. Instead of teaching pupils to really grapple with the language, the latest fashions dictate an over-simplification of everything. Everything must come easily; nobody must have to try too hard.

But what does that teach children? It teaches them a lie. It teaches them that success is easily won. True success is never easily won. True success is the journey. True success is struggling, persevering, falling down again and again and still getting up.

The best parts of my education gave me that. Michaela gives pupils that. The current reforms that are so in vogue in France don't prepare children for the vicissitudes of life: the ups and downs, the hard knocks.

Michaela echoes so much of the best elements of the French education system as it was: the strictness, the attention to detail, the focus on personal pride and perseverance.

I am so thankful to my parents and to those strict teachers who cared enough to be demanding of me. They taught me discipline, self-respect and a love of knowledge. Today, working at Michaela, I have the opportunity to follow in the footsteps of those great teachers I was lucky enough to encounter on my journey.

Top of the Pyramid

Barry Smith

7:15am. That's when the Michaela magic begins. Every morning at 7:15am we are out there. We believe in personal responsibility at Michaela, and it starts early in the day. Kids and parents are told that every Michaela pupil must be in bed and asleep by 9pm. They're told that they should be up at 6am. They're told that they need a fresh, clean white shirt every day, clean pants, clean socks, they've got to wash their 'bits and pits' and brush their teeth. A healthy, filling breakfast too, before they leave the house. No calling in to Subway – that's where the rough kids hang out. We remind our pupils: 'You're not like them. You're Michaela. And remember, every Sunday night at 7pm I should be able to open my window and hear 360 Michaela pupils polishing 720 shoes. That's your job! It's not your mam's.'

We're out there at 7:15am because we want our kids to be safe. We tell them to aim for a 7:30am arrival at school – that way they will never be late. Officially late is 7:56am. But if you aim for 7:30am and the bus is a bit late you'll be alright. And if you arrive at 7:30am you can go to the toilet, you can go to the stationery shop, you can talk to your mates. Don't go thinking, 'That bus will get me in for 7:45am, I should be fine.' That's not Michaela. You plan ahead.

So 7:15am we're out there. We're mingling. We're chatting. We're checking on uniform. We're having a bit of banter. By about 7:30am I stand up on one of the street benches recently vacated by a rough sleeper. I gather the 200 or so kids who've already arrived around me and I start my daily 'Sermon from the Bench.' The sermon often goes something like this:

'Ladies and gentlemen, gather around please. All eyes on me. Headphones out, phones off. Remember, if we hear it or see it, we take it. And we can keep it for up to 17 weeks. Don't bother sending your mother in to complain. You know the rules. So does she. The rules won't change.

'Firstly, excellent time-keeping, ladies and gentlemen, I cannot fault you. Well done. That's what makes us Michaela. We take responsibility. We might not want to go to bed early, we might not want to get our clothes ready the night before, we might not want to check that we have all of our equipment, we might not want to get up at 6am when it's cold and wet and dark – but we do it. We do it because we are Michaela. We do it because we are Top of the Pyramid.

'Do you know what Top of the Pyramid means? It means that when there are tough choices to be made we do the right thing. There are millions of people at the bottom of the pyramid. Millions. When things are tough they take the easy choice. When things need perseverance and effort, they take the easy way out. When success isn't instant, they just give up. That's not us. That's not Michaela. We're Top of the Pyramid.

'Top of the Pyramid people – there aren't many of us. We're special. We make the right choices. Even if it's difficult. Especially when it's difficult. We don't hang around "Sam's Chicken." We don't drop litter. We don't swear. We don't swarm at the bus stop. We don't pull our shirt out and take our tie off. We don't have two haircuts on one head and we don't wear trainers with our uniform. We are Michaela.

'We're not normal. Make no bones about it. We are NOT normal. You know what normal kids do? They shout in the street. They push and shove at the bus stop. They never say thank you to shopkeepers. They never give up their seat for older people on the bus. They don't know how to shake hands properly. They don't make eye contact or smile when they speak. I don't want you to be just normal.

'See all those empty bottles and cans of lager on the ground? We would never do that. We don't drop litter. In fact, when we see litter we pick it up. We didn't drop it but we still pick it up. I don't want people arriving outside school and seeing all this rubbish and thinking, "Rubbish people live here." Wembley is our home. We've got to look after it.

'When we walk across the bridge over the tracks we walk in single file. We respect other members of the public. Kids from other schools don't do that. We see a lady with a buggy – we help her. We see a lady with shopping bags – we help her.

'Tonight, just stop and look and listen to the kids from other schools. How do they dress? How do they talk? We don't talk street. We don't use slang. "You get me, blood?" When we wait at the bus stop we wait by the wall or the railings. We keep into the side. We let people pass.

'When it's hot we still keep our shirt tucked in, we still wear our tie with pride. I want people to see you at the end of the day and ask, who are those posh kids? I wish I had the money to send my kids to a posh school like that!

'There are nice kids at other schools. Some of you went to other schools. You know what it's like in other schools. You know that, when you're Michaela, you do the right thing, because it's the right thing. Because we are Top of the Pyramid. Because we are Michaela.

'Remember too, ladies and gentlemen, that all of the local shopkeepers have my number. Every week I go to McDonald's and I check the CCTV to see if anyone has been rude. I've told the McDonald's manager and the shopkeepers that if you're cheeky they take a photo and send it to me.

'Some schools have a police car outside every night. You know that. That's not us. Remember who you are. You are Michaela.'

So that's our morning routine. I gee them up for the day. I remind them who they are. They are Michaela. And all of this before we even enter the school gates. We'll often get a little gathering of passers-by. They stop, they look on, amused or bemused. I'm never quite sure which.

The other day, at the very start of term, with lots of year 7 parents waiting outside the school, I was doing my sermon. This time the sermon was largely, though not exclusively, aimed at the assembled parents. I wanted them to get a sense of who we are. It was the first day when all three year groups were together. This was the first day back for year 8 and 9 after almost two months away. The year 7s had already had seven days of bootcamp. With about 300 kids outside on the pavement I raised my hand. I didn't say a word. Everyone went silent. I then instructed the kids that, on the count of three, they were going to circulate, they were going to go up to people they didn't know, make eye contact, shake hands and introduce themselves. I counted 1-2-3. They did exactly as instructed. I raised my hand again. 300 kids all immediately fell silent. I then addressed the parents and kids.

'There's not another school in the world where you'd get that. Nowhere. The new year 7s are very lucky indeed to be joining a school where the year 8 and 9 are such excellent role models. Harrow, just up the road, charge £37,000 a year. You wouldn't get that there. Ladies and gents, because remember, you are ladies and gentlemen, you're not hoodlums, you're not ruffians, you are ladies and gentlemen of Michaela, on the count of two, 1,2.' And 300 kids clapped twice in unison appreciating one another in the Michaela manner.

I then turned to them again and simply said one word – 'Out.' 300 kids recited the whole of William Ernest Henley's 'Invictus'. Clear, loud, proud, in unison, all eyes front. It was very, very hard not to choke up. Even as I write this, it is really very hard not to choke up. In 20 years of teaching, in ten years of teacher training, having visited hundreds of schools and having worked with thousands of teachers, I've never even come close to experiencing anything like Michaela.

The other day I was taking the tube home and a smartly dressed woman in her 30s was staring at me. She kept staring at me. As we both got off at King's

Cross she approached me and said, 'I just want to tell you that I pass your school every morning and I wanted to say that I have never seen anything like it. I really appreciate what you all do. I really wish you luck. You're all doing an amazing job.'

She then said, 'It can't be easy.' To which I replied, without really thinking because it seemed such a natural response, 'Well, actually, it is easy. We love it. We love those kids. We believe in them.'

I don't think that was the response she was expecting. It came from nowhere. It was the most spontaneous and honest response I could have given.

A few months ago a man on a bike approached me as I was crossing the road outside Wembley Park Station: 'I just wanted to say that I go past every morning. I'm a community policeman. I've never seen anything like your kids. The way you all handle them. Their behaviour. It's incredible. I've worked with so many schools. I've never seen anything like it.'

Last summer, it was a warm evening, about 5:15pm, and we were still chivvying the kids along, making sure they went straight home after detention, when a stranger approached. 'I just want to say what a lovely relationship you all have with the children from your school. I've never seen kids and teachers talk like that before. Get on so well. Be so polite.'

Again, last summer, we were taking 120 kids to Powerleague, a brisk ten-minute walk away. There in two perfect lines were Michaela year 8s: 60 boys, 60 girls. They marched past a group of teenagers drinking lager in the street. The teenagers congratulated us: 'I wish my teachers had been like that, man.' Our kids didn't turn their heads. They proudly kept their eyes to the front. The teenagers looked on in genuine wonder.

The caretaker at the Powerleague pitches where we do sport sidled up to me: 'How can I get my daughter into your school? Your kids aren't like the kids from the other schools. Those other kids are bloody awful. My daughter's going off the rails. She needs a school like yours.'

Just last Saturday, I was talking to the receptionist at the dentist, 'Wembley? I live in Wembley! Which school you say you work at? Oh, I've seen your kids at the bus stop. That's a good school, that is.'

There are countless tales like this. I always gather the kids around and tell them what people have said. I always remind them we are Michaela. We're different. We're definitely not normal. We work hard and we are kind. Being kind is key to everything we do.

'Imagine where you're going to be in ten years' time! You will have graduated from a great university. You might be taking a year out. You might be living in Europe. You might be travelling around Australia. You might be starting your dream job.'

'I have this fantasy! You're all about 30. I'm there with my wheelchair, tartan blanket and Werther's Originals. We have a school reunion and you all come back and you're all telling us about the great jobs and great lives you've got. There'll be doctors and lawyers and politicians and, I hope, some of you will be back here, teaching at Michaela. I'd love that! You lot would be brilliant Michaela teachers!

'Where do you think the kids that hang around McDonald's will be? The kids with the shirts hanging out. The kids that push and shove and spit and swear?

'When you got your place at Michaela you won the Golden Ticket. You won the lottery. In fact, what you got was better than any lottery win. Being Michaela is being grateful. Being Michaela is investing in your future. Successful people don't necessarily want to work hard, to keep going, to slog, either. But they do it. When there's a tough choice and an easy choice they take the tough choice. It's who we are. It's what we do.

'And remember, there'll always be people who want you to take the easy route, to be normal, to be ordinary, to be like them, to be Bottom of the Pyramid. Remember who you are. You're Michaela. We're a family. We stick together. It's us against the world.'

So, think of us 7.15am when it's wet and windy, cold and foggy, sunny and bright. Whatever the weather, we'll be there. Fresh clean shirt every morning, shiny shoes and climbing up to the Top of the Pyramid.

Parenting the Michaela Way

Chashe Musarurwa

There is no qualification required to be a parent. No certificate, not even a test. They kick you out of the hospital after 48 hours with a little *person* and you pretty much hope for the best. I did my best to read up on what was coming at every developmental stage, and what I should be doing as a good mother, but none of that really prepares you for the reality of hard work and endless nights. Those early years are like nothing written in books! In retrospect, however, I now find those early years were actually *easier* since most of the job was very straightforward: feed, change, clean, nurture and, in general, keep them alive. After you're done with all of that though, you're left with shaping a person, and that is one of the biggest puzzles of human life, on which millions of contradictory books have been penned.

Shaping people, as it turns out, can lead to even more sleepless nights than the previous 'keep them alive' phase, and is harder, more ambiguous work. I say ambiguous because all of the *help* out there gives many mixed messages. Needless to say, I've been worried about getting it all wrong. I am the mother of a five-year-old heap of joy, and this is my story of how it's all been coming together.

I was born and raised in Zimbabwe, where the way children are brought up is vastly different from how things are done in the West, due to various cultural differences and values. In Zimbabwe, for instance, the theme of respect and discipline runs through all fabrics of society, from language to table etiquette. There is a respectful and non-respectful way to say everything. There is an order to who begins eating a meal in a group setting. Parents are very strict; teachers are even stricter. As an adult I would still never dream of raising my voice to someone my elder or, God forbid, interrupt while they are talking.

My husband, Alex, was born in Australia and raised in England, where values diverge from those I grew up with in Zimbabwe. Naturally, he was worried I'd be running some kind of militant dictatorship when the baby came. Where I thought he was bonkers to believe in time-outs, he thought I was bonkers to even consider corporal punishment. I think we both stared at each other in disbelief the first time this disagreement came up. Both of our versions of discipline seemed normal and obvious until they were said aloud. It's hard work to be a team and we engaged in continuous convincing of one another.

A big change in our parenting experience has been me beginning a career in teaching at Michaela. After just one visit to the school when interviewing, I realised it wasn't just that Michaela's values resonated with me, but that they are so well articulated and practised. Seeing these values affect kids so positively in a reality removed from my own has really shifted my own parenting goals, and has helped me to finally express my values to others.

There are six main principles of life at Michaela that I've been applying – and they've made life at home better than it's ever been:

- Gratitude
- High Standards
- High Support
- Discipline
- Work-Life Balance
- Rowing Together

Gratitude

Instilling gratitude in pupils is at the heart of Michaela life. Contrary to popular belief, it is not naturally a part of who humans are. People have to learn to be grateful and appreciative. At lunch, pupils are given an opportunity to give an 'appreciation' to someone for an act of kindness that they noticed in the day. This sort of thing is exactly the sort of thing I immediately jumped on to take home.

I hear young kids whining all the time about things that really do not matter in the bigger picture. We've all heard them, tots screaming in Sainsburys because they didn't get the exact type of chocolate they wanted. My daughter, Lindie, knows my biggest pet peeve is whining. When it first started, I would tell her to cut it out because she was being unpleasant – to the horror of onlookers! Emphasising gratitude, however, has really changed the game when it comes to curbing unpleasant, unnecessary and ungrateful behaviour like whining. Take for example:

'Mummyyyyy, I'm still hungry.'
'Okay I can cut you up some cucumbers and carrots.'
'Noo, I'm hungry for something yummierrrr mummyyyyy!!!'

This sort of thing can drag on, as you can imagine. The last time this whine episode happened, however, I adjusted my approach.

'Do you remember that man who was sitting outside the bank on his blanket on the way home from school? He's been hungry *all* day with nothing in his belly. You have already eaten three times today, you should be very happy to have the extra serving of cucumbers and carrots. Some children didn't even eat today!'

The result? She ate the darn cucumbers and carrots and thought about the fact that others don't even have this option. Over time she has become more grateful for what she eats. The more I bring up that she's lucky, the more she sees it as something to appreciate. It's not an automatic part of development; kids really do need to learn this. In fact, many adults could do with a reminder. When I say these sorts of things in public, I sometimes get dirty looks from people, as if I'm traumatising her somehow. Sometimes I whisper it to her to spare myself the judgement! I wonder how some of these people go about life not believing that ungrateful behaviour is something awful to be squashed.

Nevertheless, I'm not stopping: everyone should grow up actively knowing what they should be grateful for, because when we are not grateful we take things for granted and grow to be rather self-centred.

On Sky-High Standards

At Michaela, we talk a lot about having 'sky-high' standards for all pupils, all of the time, no exceptions. There should not be a cause for low standards just because a kid struggles with Maths. In fact, keeping high standards for those who struggle helps them to achieve more. You're saying you believe in them, that they can achieve, and that there isn't a ceiling on what they can learn.

Naturally, this is a winner to bring into the home as there are a lot of low standards to go around when it comes to parenting. A popular misconception is that, whatever happens with our children, we have 'done our best' and it is 'not our fault;' whether it's childhood obesity or that your child has become a bully. We are often tired and stressed from work, and it is easier to do the minimum. It is easier to believe that children will ultimately be who they are, but this is simply not true. Our standards influence not only our children, but the people around us, and we are responsible for who they become.

For instance, before my daughter Lindie began school we used to read one book every few days. I presumed that this was enough to produce a great reader. This was at the stage where books only had a line of text per page. The school's reading curriculum was two short books for the entire week and I thought this was good. However, the more time I spend thinking of raising standards the more I realised that two books a week was hardly a challenge at all.

I began to fill this gap by signing up at the local library so we would have a more interesting variety of stories to read at home. I would go towards the 'easier' books that I thought she could 'manage.' Throughout the summer I thought this amount of reading was good.

In the mornings we play a game where she is the mummy and I am the kid and she reads to me while I'm in the shower. On one summer morning I stepped into the shower before choosing an appropriate book, and so she was left to go choose a book herself. She came back with *The Cat in the Hat*, which I immediately thought was a lost cause given the amount of text. As I showered, my jaw dropped to hear her on the outside getting through the first page, and then the next, and then she was on page 22! My standards for what her reading could be were far too low, yet again! Imagine where she would be now if I hadn't set the ceiling on her capabilities.

Good is not good enough. Whenever we give in and settle for less, we do our children a disservice. Lindie is endlessly showing me that my expectations are too low and that she is far more capable than I allow for. The higher I push those limits, the further she goes.

I've cut out the excuses, and we now read every day. Even when I'm sick, even when she's tired. Real support is doing the hard things *especially* when it's difficult.

Sky-high standards at home should apply to everything as they allow children to be the very best versions of themselves that they can be. This is not left to the gods or unseen forces; as parents, it is left to us.

On Being a Supportive Parent

The more time I spend working in a school, the more I realise just how easy it is to be an unsupportive parent without meaning to, and without even realising it. The more I think about it, the more I am aware that at times I fall into that bracket of parents that make it difficult for the school to do its job. Initially my instinct was to defend parents that don't support the school, arguing that perhaps they were too tired from work and too busy. But then I realised that it is our duty as parents to do what is right by our child, to help the school when the standards are held high, so that the child can fulfil their potential.

It's also not enough to only do the minimum of what the school sends home. After reading Amy Chua's book *Battle Hymn of the Tiger Mother*, I learned there are so many more extracurricular possibilities than I had previously been aware of which help children to advance. In the past I made excuses like 'She's too young,' and that she should just 'get to play.' But play alone doesn't get anyone anywhere in life, if we're being honest. I want my daughter to have as many open doors as possible for her in the future. So she does extra Maths practice, extra reading from books I pick out, and she will begin an instrument this year if it kills me! And guess what – it's not traumatising and harsh. Lindie has so much fun, is feeling more and more competent, and above all we have a new opportunity to bond. Doing these things together really doesn't take that much more time or effort out of my day.

Support means more than creating a happy environment. It means pushing someone to be the best version of themselves they can be. I know in my heart she will be thankful for it later.

On Discipline

A hard conversation I'm often having with friends and family is convincing them that discipline and respect for authority are not things that take away from a person, but rather add to them. When many people in the West hear the word 'discipline,' they think of adults trying to prove they're in control. They think of damaged children who are emotionally stunted and afraid. They think of mindless robots. They think of abuse. In fact, real discipline is nothing like that.

In the midst of fighting against abuse and promoting children's rights, society has become so lost in 'saving' them that we have forgotten that we also need to *guide* them. Guiding children is not all about praise and positivity; they are young and need our guidance to become better people. It comes from a place of love, not control and not power.

One of the worst things anyone can do with discipline, however, is be inconsistent: 'Yes' today, 'No' tomorrow, and worst of all 'No' with no follow-through. Working at Michaela, it became apparent to me that discipline at home was not nearly as good as it could be, mostly because my standards were not high enough. Children learn fast, and mine had learned to recognise that she could get away with more if her mummy was tired. The words 'We are what we repeatedly do' are written in giant letters right as you enter the Michaela building. If I am inconsistent about my own boundaries, then the things I say cannot truly be counted on. The things I say are thus subject to my mood, and good relationships cannot be founded on emotional inconsistency. Being in an environment where excuses are not acceptable, even for myself, has been improving that aspect of my parenting.

The result of it is that I have become much more consistent in the most important relationship I'm likely to have in this lifetime. I need to be the solid ground that my daughter can count on, in all moments, whether it is for discipline, for fun or for promises.

My daughter says to me, 'Please can I have some more ketchup?' Yet I sometimes hear her say to others, '*Get* me ketchup.' No big deal, you might say. Kids should be kids, you might say. But now, I see absolutely no reason we can't let kids be kids who are *also* respectful and kind. Discipline is the difference between the child who demands and the child who asks. As adults, the onus is on us to set that boundary.

The most important part about discipline I've picked up from Michaela is the importance of acknowledging my own mistakes. Katharine Birbalsingh talks about how important it is to 'mend the relationship' after disciplining someone so that the relationship does not begin to break down. This means both fixing it when you're in the wrong, and talking through it when you're in the right. Thorough narration of what went wrong to warrant the discipline is key because, again, it comes from a place of love, not power. We discipline those who we care for enough to help them improve.

On Work (or parent!)-Life Balance

Cabin crew on an aircraft always state that in the event of an emergency or loss of air pressure, 'First secure your own oxygen mask, and then that of your child or any other passengers in need of assistance.' My very first flight with my daughter was the first time I ever paid close attention as they played us the safety video and my instinctive reaction was to think 'That's madness, my baby has to breathe before I do!' In this irrational thinking, I totally bypassed the fact that I need to breathe before I can help anyone else to do it. That if I allow myself to stop breathing for other people, I become useless to them and put them at greater risk.

Like teachers, many parents have been told that they must do whatever it takes to help their children and keep them safe. However, there is a point at which 'whatever it takes' is counterproductive: a point at which that sort of thinking damages both the parent and the child. Parents are people: we burn out in over-extending ourselves. Equally, and when children are accustomed to having people bend over backwards for them, they tend to take advantage and can end up somewhat handicapped.

With the overwhelming pressure to be a 'good mum,' this can be difficult. When I began my first full-time position as a teacher I quickly became exhausted – physically, mentally and emotionally. I worried that I was failing my Lindie. I was told by various people that I was 'putting work first' and I wondered if I'd made a mistake. Six months in, I felt like I was drowning and losing myself entirely to work, parenting, marriage, cleaning, everything else but me. I went over to Katharine's office. As a fellow working parent who balances these aspects so well and still remains healthy, happy and vibrant, I had to find out her secret. She doesn't just stay afloat; she is a champion swimmer. I was tired of treading water. Before we talked I had many ideas in my head of what she might say, but her advice was nothing I'd imagined. As it happens, the problem was *me*.

In school we talk about work-life balance, and I had been lacking in what I like to call parent-life balance. I was putting a lot of my energy into things that do not matter because I genuinely believed they were important, but they were taking away instead of adding to life. In all of this I was not leaving any room for me the individual. It turns out the way that I was neglecting my child was actually by neglecting myself. In the same way that teachers who try to give *all* of themselves to their pupils start to lose it and become average at best because they don't take a break to live.

It doesn't matter how quickly laundry is folded away or how often the kitchen floor is mopped. I used to believe such things made a home a 'better' place to be in, but the truth of the matter is that it simply doesn't. Happiness is not improved by shiny floors and clean closets. Cutting out the long list of things we have to do to supposedly be good parents has left huge amounts of time that I now spend actually catching up and bonding with my daughter after work.

The bed-time story is no longer a stressful and rushed event because 'she must be asleep by 8pm or I've failed.' Reading is relaxed and enjoyable, we can pause and discuss interesting plot lines in the book, and even take a moment to do some handwriting after. Never again shall I be bound to what the world tells me is a good bed-time.

The list is long: chore after chore every day that do not add to anyone's happiness. But many of us do these things because we've been told they are best. We bend over backwards without any balance. I still have a long way to go cutting out the clutter that clouds up my life, leaving more room to be a more supportive parent and to also retain my sanity. As with everything, moderation is key – I am not suggesting that parents put their kids to bed at 11pm so that life can be more relaxed, just that it is worth re-evaluating arbitrary things we use to measure how well we are raising our kids. It's worth re-evaluating whether doing 'whatever it takes' in the home is really going to lead to a happier family dynamic. It's worth re-evaluating what really matters and what does not.

Rowing Together

At Michaela, we all do what Katharine refers to as 'rowing together.' This is firmly based on the idea that in order for any behaviour system to successfully work with children, all of the adults involved need to do their part at all times, and, most importantly, they must be consistent in this.

It is often said that it takes a village to raise a child. Any parent would agree that 'going it alone' is not a way to live. The adults in your child's life provide relief, assistance, perspective and role models to look up to. It goes without saying that we must be careful in choosing who we allow into their child's life. But it is most important that you and the village are in sync. The village needs to row together or there can only be chaos.

When adults don't row together, one of the first things that happens with the child is resentment. There grows a sense in the child that one adult is better or nicer than the other, because the 'nice' one has a different set of rules. Naturally children prefer behaviour systems that give them the most liberties and so the adult that lets them get away with more automatically becomes the 'good cop.' It will start to seem unfair and confusing for the child when the 'bad cop' disciplines for something the 'good cop' would not. Take for example this typical school problem: Teacher A is very strict and holds pupils to account; Teacher B believes kids should be kids and allows them to get away with a lot. Pupils will behave and be happy in A's rooms, they understand A's boundaries. But as soon as B is introduced, suddenly there is a feeling that A has become unfair and unreasonable somehow. Naturally the sentiment shifts towards adoration of B and negative feelings towards A. The only thing that has changed here really is that the standards have become inconsistent leaving pupils confused and frustrated.

Ultimately, rowing alone can lead to dents in the relationships between the adults who hold different standards. The adults in question need to agree on the rules in advance, and, once settled, everyone involved needs to sing the same tune. I have found that working at being on the same page with the people in my child's life really helps us all to do better for her. We have to communicate, constantly, and with candour and clarity. In my village, we disagree a lot. When you mix the cultures of Zimbabwe, America, Australia and England, that is bound to happen. But eventually, we do balance each other out somewhat.

Recently my husband took Lindie to Disneyland. They went on their own – perhaps foreseeing that my presence would turn it into a nightmarish commentary about safety and the environment and 'Why is nothing educational going on!' They went to one of those Princess lunches Disneyland is famous for, and Lindie got to meet Cinderella, Snow White and the others. Princesses are her thing at the moment, and she was deliriously happy. This was hard for me, because I want so much for her thing to not be princesses. When princesses are happening, I worry that I'm losing her to that world where women only need to be beautiful and 'marry well,' they don't need to learn and work hard.

As I began to have a slight meltdown about the lunch, I recalled the morning they were leaving: I had overheard her telling my father-in-law 'I love doing Maths with Mummy on the weekends because we have more time and I can keep up with school work and get medals and...' The memory made me proud that she no longer sees Maths drills and practice as something we *have* to do, but rather something important and fun, something that helps her improve herself. I said a silent '*Yesss!*' to myself. But there is balance: my husband, Alex, lets her love what she loves, which is paramount to her own character development, while I stay up and worry about her GSCEs! She gets the best of both worlds.

Environment and influence changes a lot about how well we do our jobs as parents. We'll hopefully all arrive there differently, but I am relieved and happy to be surrounded by Michaela people every day, because every day I am challenged to be a better version of myself.

When Parents Push Back

Katharine Birbalsingh

Last September, Korey joined our school. He is black, has special needs, and lives on an estate. His mother and grandmother were desperate. His father was absent. His primary school said that he was the worst-behaved child they had ever seen. Our SENCO visited his primary school to watch Korey in a classroom and confirmed that the description of 'worst child ever seen' was not over the top. We then happily invited Korey into Michaela.

Thanks to Michaela's reputation for strong discipline, families with challenging children will often choose our school because they hope it will transform them. While detractors of our no-excuses approach to discipline insist that it excludes children, in fact precisely the opposite is true. Parents who are at their wits' end come in search of a solution to their child's unruly behaviour. And we are happy to help.

100% Support

I told Korey's mother, as I tell all parents, that we need two things from her:

1. 100% competence
2. 100% support

I also say, 'You would not tell a doctor how to cut you open, move your organs around and then sew you back up.' This is when parents normally laugh, which is my cue to say, 'Ah... you laugh now, but I promise you, the day will come when you won't like something at the school and you will tell me how 99 of the rules are fine but that you want to me change this one rule. And I will tell you no. It is not your place to tell me how to run the school.'

I then explained to Korey's mother how the school works, why we have silent classrooms with hard-working children, learning more than anyone could ever have imagined possible, even more than their counterparts at private schools. I point to our silent and orderly corridors, our toilets and lunch halls that are free from bullying, our playground where children are able to be children. It works because we do not pander to every parental whim, trying to please everyone, trying to be diplomatic, always making exceptions in order to 'accommodate.'

Schools need a clear vision that is not constantly compromised by different parents wanting different things. As a leader one needs to know in one's soul that one cannot please all of the people all of the time: know thyself and hold the line. Our school works well because parents understand our expectations, and they know that they also have a job to do. I believe some of the new-model charter schools in the US where teachers run around doing everything for families is a flawed (though extremely successful) model that is not sustainable or scalable. It can only succeed in the short term, with incredibly dynamic young staff who give over their lives to the school. But eventually those staff leave, burnt out after a few years, or they simply want to have a family of their own, and then what do you do?

I give parents the option to turn us down. I understand we are not necessarily the right choice of school for every family. Usually, the more middle-class the family, the more likely they are to reject what is on offer at Michaela.

But Korey's mother was not middle-class. She was a black single mum with two jobs, about to have a breakdown because her boy was so out of control. She cried. Korey's grandmother cried too. 'Help us, we don't know where else to go,' was what they told me.

'I'm not going to lie to you,' I said, wincing. 'This is going to be hard. The question is whether you have the stomach for it, whether you are going to see it through.' They nodded. 'I need your support, 100%. By that I don't mean 99%, I mean 100%.'

Parents everywhere often say they support their child's school because otherwise they would pull their child out. But they misunderstand what '100% support' means. It means backing the school's decisions even when they don't seem to make sense. It means never criticising the school in front of one's child. It means keeping an open mind.

Why? Because if a parent's mind is set against the school, then their child is bound to fail there. Seek clarification by all means, but always remember that it is not a parent's place to tell a doctor how to do their surgery, and neither is it their place to tell the Head how to run the school.

Of course that does not mean that we do not listen to parents. We have changed many things in the school thanks to feedback from our parents. We have made our online behaviour system easier to check and we have established an ICT support club for homework to help parents who do not have the internet at home. We have put more photos on the website to help support parents with uniform and we open the gates earlier in the mornings so that parents do not have to worry about their children having to wait outside in an inner-city environment where drunks lie asleep outside our school. We listen to parents and go above and beyond to accommodate their concerns. But what we haven't done is change our values, the soul that makes the school tick.

I explained to Korey's mother what I say to all parents whose child is struggling to meet Michaela's standards. 'If you back us 100%, I guarantee you success. But if you question our decisions or judgements, even slightly, I guarantee you failure.

'Are you able to give me 100%?'

The ladies nodded eagerly.

Now, of course, all parents agree to give 100% support at the start. I suspect we are like other schools in this way. Where we might differ from some other schools is how we deal with families when they do not follow through on this promise.

Clarity at the start for pupils and parents is crucial. Parents need to understand before they choose our school exactly what they are taking on board.

So later, if the parent reneges on our home-school contract, one can always refer back to what was said and then agreed in writing when the child first joined the school. Our home-school contract is very detailed and demanding. We make it clear that we will hold not only the child to account, but the parents too. Too often, schools have parents sign home-school contracts that are vague and then never refer to them again. Not only do we refer to them time and time again during a child's time with us, but before the parent signs, we emphasise just how important that signature is.

100% Competence

The second part of the bargain can be harder. Not all parents are able to give 100% competence. And with this, we are a little more forgiving. We ask parents to be 100% competent and all of them try to get there. Not all of them manage it.

Parents are generally happy when you tell them that X-Y-Z will happen to their child if he doesn't toe the line. But we make it clear that Mum (or Dad) will be hauled into the school if the homework isn't done, and that parents will be held responsible for checking to see if the homework was done. If necessary I tell parents right from the start that they are not being a very good mother or father and that things have to change. 'Think of us as a personal trainer,' I say. 'You will get better at parenting if you stick with us. We do not shy away from the truth. If you don't want to be a better parent, then we aren't the school for you.'

It isn't easy to say this of course. Some parents, despite having been warned, can get very angry when they are told they are not doing their job as a parent very well. They can demand that I not say such things. They can tell me that, in my role as Headmistress, it is inappropriate for me to say this. My response is always the same. I explain that as a Head it is my duty to highlight their failings as parents. To do otherwise would be to let their child down. It is my responsibility as the leader of a school to be clear with parents what good parenting looks like and to point out where their efforts are lacking.

If we as school leaders do not point this out to parents, then who will? A mother who is more interested in recovering her child's mobile phone after it has been confiscated than she is in supporting him with his homework is simply not fulfilling her job as his mother. And it is our duty to tell her this. Otherwise we are failing the child.

Some would say this is lacking in diplomacy. Some would rather pretend to parents that they are doing all the right things, but, for some reason that no one can quite explain, little Korey won't behave. He has special needs. He is black and poor. Or he is white and poor. He is a boy. He is autistic. He has mental health issues. He has anger management issues. It isn't anyone's fault. This is just what happens to children who are like him, with his 'issues.' No one is responsible, so no one should act. We say 'How sad', and move on, leaving the child to spin out of control, fail at school, and take one step closer towards prison.

Truth is supportive

On the wall in my office I have a quote by Thomas Sowell that says, 'When you want to help people, you tell them the truth; when you want to help yourself, you tell them what they want to hear.'

In all organisations, the truth is hard to say and hear. And because people generally want an easier life, they tend to avoid what is hard. It means that in both public and private institutions across the world, people are dishonest with each other, regardless of the consequences.

In schools, the consequences are significant. Thomas Sowell reminds me of this every day and helps Michaela steer the right course when telling the truth is hardest: with parents.

In Britain, it has become so normal to lie to parents that schools don't even think they are doing it. It is considered compassionate. Telling parents the truth, therefore, is considered to be just the opposite. And no one wants to be considered uncompassionate. Why would a school tell parents the truth when all it gives the school is grief? Many parents don't want to hear the truth and are perfectly happy to be lied to by their child's school, by the exam system, by everyone.

Parents receive cut-and-pasted report cards where negatives are always framed as positives, with levels that no parent can understand. (Does anyone know the difference between a 5b and a 6c?) Parents remain in blissful ignorance until their child does poorly at his GCSEs. But by then, it is too late and the connection between what they have been told for years and the failure is never really made. The blame is all laid on the child. Few people realise that a school culture will help to form a child's character and academic success. No one *wants* to think that a school's culture is failing children because it is in no one's interest to do so. The parent likes feeling good about their child and loves to only hear positive feedback. The teacher doesn't want to face a difficult conversation with the parent. Society is happy with the illusion that schools are improving every year and the general lie that our children are just getting cleverer year on year. If we all insist that the emperor is wearing clothes, then who is to say that he isn't?

Not all parents want to be lied to of course. But enough of them do to make it in the interest of schools to continue lying to everyone. So instead of telling them the truth, schools tell parents what they want to hear.

At Michaela we always tell parents the truth, even when it is difficult – *especially* when it is difficult.

The consequence is that most of our parents are better parents thanks to advice we give and expectations we set. Even those who get annoyed benefit. They stomp away and they change for the better because deep down, most parents want to be good parents. It is just that sometimes, in our modern world, it is hard to know what that looks like.

Clarity is supportive

In the same way that being 100% truthful with parents is helpful, so is being clear. We try to be *overly* clear. We send information home via pupils in letters, and via emails and sometimes we even post letters when we suspect the information is not getting home. We warn parents weeks, even months in advance when possible, of expectations and requirements. We then repeat the information to the pupils over and over, at the start of school, at break, at lunch and then via tutors at the end of the day. Our systems allow for this. All the pupils are gathered together in year groups at each one of these intervals. A member of Senior Team speaks to them at the start of the day, at break, and then the lunch leader speaks to them at lunch. The room for miscommunication is slim because we over-communicate. Our systems centralise as much as possible and make everything across the school as consistent as possible. I judge my own success on that: the level of consistency across the school. If we aren't all singing from the same hymn sheet, then that's my fault and it is my job to fix it.

Because our homework is centralised, as Joe Kirby explains, parents understand our expectations. If they don't understand, they are invited in for a one-to-one meeting with a teacher who will talk them through exactly how to support their child at home. I do this myself with parents regularly. We have sheets printed to help support them and we walk them through every step.

If parents don't understand our expectations on equipment (again this is centralised, making it very difficult to get wrong), we have them in to show them what we expect should be in their child's pencil case.

If a parent wants to meet with us, they can meet a member of Senior Team or even the Headmistress within a day of getting in touch. We prioritise parents and we hope they will prioritise their child's education. The plain truth is that not all parents do. And as Sir Michael Wilshaw (Head of Ofsted from 2010) says, 'Society needs to say it is morally wrong to neglect your children. We need to be tougher on parents who don't hold those values. Headteachers should say to a parent, "You're a bad parent," in the same way that we say to a child, "You're a naughty boy."'

And we are not alone. Other schools are doing what we are doing. Recently, I wrote to congratulate the Head who was in the newspapers over holding the line on uniform at his school. Some of his parents were furious. He stood his ground and held on to the school's values. Parents don't always understand, as he did, that the way to run a good school is to demand more from both pupils and parents.

We give huge amounts of support to our parents and in return we expect parents to support their child to meet our very high standards.

Parents who push back

Not all parents manage to be 100% competent. They try, but some just cannot do it. And not all parents manage to be 100% supportive. Some don't even try.

Those who struggle to be the best kind of parent, despite their best efforts, we go on supporting. These parents may never make it to the 100% mark, but they do improve and their children are all the better for it.

The families who are most problematic are the ones who, despite all of our warnings, despite the contract, despite our demand for consistency, will still insist on telling me how to run the school. I often wish the small minority of our unsupportive parents could be in our assemblies and our bootcamp lessons. They would learn about personal responsibility, duty and mindset. They would understand that they, like their child, are master of not only their fate, but of their child's fate too.

So what do you do?

You don't budge.

They complain. I tell them that they need to support us 100%. They complain again. And round it goes. A tiny minority have chosen to pull their children out of the school. These pupils were all well-behaved and were achieving well. We have always been very sad to see these children leave. One parent pulled their child out because they didn't like the food. Another parent pulled their child out because we have a Michaela trouser and she wanted to buy her trousers elsewhere. Another parent pulled her child out because she wanted her boy's mobile phone back. One mum wanted a state of the art building (ours is not) and so when she got a place at another school, off she went. We have yet to get fantastic GCSE and A-level results, so they don't really believe that we are a good school and judge by the architecture instead.

Michaela isn't necessarily for everyone. That goes for staff, pupils and parents. The saddest thing is when the pupil knows how lucky he is to be at Michaela but the parent, knowing little about schools, makes the decision to pull their child out of the school. Once, a year 7 boy came to me in desperation. It was the day his mother was to pick him up to take him for his interview at his new school. He begged me to stop this travesty. He wanted more than anything to remain at Michaela. But his mother wanted him to have lessons in ICT and we don't offer any; we prioritise four hours of Art and Music instead. He knew his behaviour had transformed since attending Michaela. He knew how much he was learning, how his life would be different. She knew nothing except for the mantra that we are in the 21st century so lessons in ICT are necessary. She didn't know that so many ICT lessons are a waste of time. She didn't know that often the pupils know more than the teachers and that one lesson a week is useless when much of that lesson is spent trying to focus the pupils on just sitting still.

I rang her and begged her to pop into the school at the time she was coming to pick him up to go to the interview. Just pop in, I said, give me five minutes of your time. She wasn't interested. 'I've made up my mind,' she said. I tried. The boy's eyes filled with tears. I couldn't do anything. I felt helpless against the world that was working with such might in so many intricate and complex ways to ensure that this boy would remain poor. The Western progressive mind says that it doesn't matter where he goes to school, because the innate talent in him will shine through, whatever the environment. But the Michaela mind says that environment is everything when it comes to forming a child's hopes for a future.

Parents who push back hardest

We had one family that stayed with us for four weeks. Despite the huge success the boy made of his time at Michaela, his mother didn't like the school. What she really disliked was the fact that we insist that families take the notion of personal responsibility seriously.

Amongst other things, she disliked our Family Lunch. As one can read in Michael Taylor's excellent essay, Family Lunch works wonders with our children. Every day we have guests who come to see what is becoming like a wonder of the world: inner-city deprived children, serving each other, cleaning up after each other, holding proper conversations and standing up to give each other 'appreciations.'

In the majority of British schools pupils eat lunch through a canteen system. You either pay for your school lunch on the day, or you pay for lunches in advance. Don't pay? Well it's assumed that you have a packed lunch, but if you don't then quite simply you don't eat. If you are bullied and your money is stolen, no one knows.

At Michaela, we do not accept a situation where children go hungry simply because their parents haven't given them money for lunch. But for Family Lunch to work, it does rely on those who can afford to pay paying their share. Children from the most disadvantaged backgrounds get our Family Lunch meals free, through the free school meals programme. That means the only people we charge for meals are those that are not eligible for free school meals because the Government has determined they have a high enough income to pay for their child's lunches.

If we did not insist on every family paying, at capacity we would spend *twelve thousand pounds* per year covering the costs of lunches for children whose families cannot be bothered to pay. That's why if a family who can pay refuses to pay for the Family Lunch, we give the child a healthy packed lunch in a separate room instead of a healthy vegetarian meal in the dining hall until their parents have paid.

It was this practice that led to a media circus in the summer of 2016, instigated by one unhappy parent, culminating in online death threats directed at me and my teachers.

But the reality is, if a family lands on hard luck, we listen, we support – for uniform or lunch payments – finding a system of payment that they can cope with in their current circumstances.

Is our solution perfect? No. Do we want to have to impose it? No. But if the alternative is letting children go hungry or diverting money from precious teaching resources, then the choice is clear. And the truth is that the policy does ensure that parents who can pay, do pay, the vast majority of the time.

The fact is that when one wants to achieve the extraordinary, difficult decisions are required. One of the responsibilities of a Head is to make difficult decisions and see them through. This is why, no matter what our critics throw at us, we march on ahead, confident that what we are doing is right.

Among our new year 7s, 43 children out of a year group of 120 have siblings in year 8 or 9. The vast majority of our parents are absolutely delighted with the school and are grateful for the difference the school has made not just to their child's academic success, but to the kind of person their child is at home. Children are now thanking their parents for dinner, or helping to tidy the house, or being kind to their siblings. Parents are also grateful because they have learned to be better parents and this has helped them develop a more positive relationship with their child.

Korey is one of those extraordinary successes. We have so many of these, I have lost count. Sure, Korey still gets the occasional detention when he slips back into his old primary school habits, but he is achieving and is totally unrecognisable from who he was at primary school.

The other day Korey passes me as he is leaving at the end of the day. "Good afternoon Miss! Have a good evening!" I smile. "That's right Korey! Looking good!" He grins. "Soft skills Miss!" Korey has been listening to my assemblies. He understands that to be successful, he needs to develop all of himself, not just pass exams: behaviour matters. Now he can do anything he wants with his life. We made Korey's mum a promise. Thanks to the honest, candid way we deal with parents, I know we will deliver.

How I Fell In Love with Teaching Again

William Eastment

I write this chapter having just completed my first week as a Humanities teacher at Michaela Community School and it has been, without question, the best week of my professional career. Just six months ago, I was one of the 43% of state school teachers planning to leave the profession in the next five years. That was before I discovered Michaela.

Throughout my time teaching, it has become a commonly accepted truism that one has two main choices when working as a teacher: either be an 'outstanding' teacher and work all the hours God gives, or be average and have some semblance of a personal life. Neither proposition was particularly attractive to me, and so I found myself questioning my position as teacher just nine months after passing my NQT year.

There are two main ways that working at Michaela addresses that conundrum: a boldness to break the mould of bad ideas that have blighted teachers' (and pupils') lives, and a steadfast commitment to extremely high standards of behaviour.

1: Boldly going where no school has gone before

I had heard about the great things Michaela was doing, but it wasn't until February this year that I began to take a keen interest in exactly what they were doing. I was pointed to a blog post by our Deputy Head, Joe Kirby, that sensibly outlined all the common everyday activities that take up a lot of a teacher's time but that are of questionable impact (so-called hornets) such as individual comments on pupil work, graded observations and whizzy activities like card-sorts or carousels. In this blog post, he goes on to explain how Michaela has done away with all of these distractions in favour of high-impact, low-effort activities (butterflies): no written comments on pupil work, use of high-quality textbooks, centralised homework and centralised detentions.

Every teacher I have met would agree that individual comments on pupil work take up more time than they are worth and that they dread graded observations. However, no school has committed to doing away with these time-intense activities with anything like the vigour that we do at Michaela. Senior leaders in most schools are too in thrall to what Ofsted deem 'good teaching' that they dismiss our ideas as unworkable within the current educational climate.

And they have a point. Our methods subvert the progressive paradigm that currently suffuses our school system. Teaching in the Michaela way involves a lot of direct instruction from the front of the class, and relies on the teacher as the expert in the room. We wholly reject the notion that pupils should be left to 'discover' the answer for themselves, or that they should be encouraged to come up with 'creative solutions' to the problems we set. This stance is anathema to many teachers who trained in England in the last 40 years. Ever since the Plowden Report famously concluded in 1967 that 'finding out is better than being told,' multiple generations of teachers have been brought up on a progressivist diet of Piaget, Dewey and constructivist theories of education. My PGCE essays were judged not on my ability to critically assess the validity of constructivist thinking, but my ability to prove that I had enacted these theories in my classroom practice and to critically evaluate the degree to which I would better enact them next time.

So whilst our methods seem attractive, they do not fit with the constructivist paradigm of education. *Of course* teachers will forever be writing individual comments on pupil work if pupils have been left to 'find out' the answers and get them wrong in countless different ways. Direct instruction solves this problem but too many senior leaders are too terrified to enact these ideas.

Through reading the blogs of the new and founding teachers of Michaela, my eyes were opened to a whole new world of pedagogy that I had not been exposed to before. In the words of one of my colleagues, I felt like Plato's prisoner in the Allegory of the Cave, my eyes hazily opening to a new world of pedagogy that I had not been aware of. The work of cognitive scientists such as Daniel Willingham and the US educator E. D. Hirsch captivated my enthusiasm more than anything on my PGCE reading lists. The problems that seemed to blight my pupils' ability to achieve (low literacy, poor written English, low cultural capital and reading ages way below their chronological age) were all answered within this new literature. I was hooked, and I had to see for myself how this would all work in practice. I arranged my first visit to Michaela.

Needless to say, from the moment I stepped into Jonny Porter's History class on a sunny April morning, I knew I had found the school for me. Pupil recall was exemplary: pupils were drawing on knowledge from multiple disciplines and coped with challenging text with ease. The first activity was a quick recall: put the following events in order (add the dates as an extension). The pupils raced away, most of them easily able to put the events in the right order, with many confidently scrawling the dates too. I sat at the back, genuinely in awe at the ease with which this was being completed. Once Jonny began teaching, he had 30 eyes and minds hanging on his every word. Behaviour was excellent;

pupils diligently listened and made notes when prompted. No one was off task; everyone knew exactly what was expected of them. Once Jonny showed me the quality of the essays produced I knew that Michaela had the right approach. Not only do the essays back this up, but our data on pupils' reading ages cannot be rivalled by any school in the country. Pupils made an average of two years' progress in reading in just one year at Michaela. Many who came in with reading ages below their chronological age are now reading at or above their age. These methods work.

2. Putting it in practice

This week I have finally been able to put these ideas into practice in a fully supportive environment with teachers who are experts at direct instruction and whole-class teaching. I am still working incredibly hard and I am tired at the end of each day. We have a lot of duties to ensure that behaviour standards are upheld all across the school, as Sarah Cullen touches on in her chapter, and the amount we talk and instruct can be tiring. So was I sold on Michaela's promises of reduced workload under false pretences?

No. Everything we do here is so precisely thought about that every minute is used wisely for maximum impact, and the hard work feels worth it. Previously, one would work hard just to keep one's head afloat, just to make sure that the next day was not a disaster. At Michaela, the satisfaction of knowing that not a minute is wasted, and that every minute directly contributes to pupil progress, is incredibly empowering. The knowledge that once I've left school I have actually left work behind is also empowering – we don't mark, as Jo Facer explains in her chapter, so I never have to lug a pile of books home with me when I leave. If we enter data we immediately make use of it with the children and in conversations with our departments – we know it will directly impact our classroom practice. We don't fill in paperwork, and we don't spend lunch breaks chasing pupils for detention. We certainly don't spend five or ten minutes trying to get classes to settle down; they enter in silence and the lesson begins within 30 seconds. The aura of calm is unlike anything I have experienced in any school, from both the pupils and the teachers. I am also told by the established teachers that things get much easier in time, once you've automated Michaela habits and routines.

Behaviour has been a challenge, but not in the way you would expect for a new teacher starting at a new school and trying to establish themselves. The challenge for me has been getting used to having sky-high expectations all the time. It can feel jarring to give a detention for talking in the corridors or for forgetting a pen when these are honest mistakes that any child could make. But then I remember the chaos and the fighting that would occur in the corridors of the schools I have taught in, and the learned helplessness that pupils had become accustomed to. Many pupils in schools simply expect the teacher to provide them with a pen. This attitude helps no one. The pupil learns to expect from others without question. Meanwhile, the stationery budget at some schools could pay for a set of textbooks for each department. So we stay firm: we will *always* give a detention for forgetting a pen because we know it is the kindest thing to do in the long run. And we narrate this to the pupils endlessly. We remind them that if we provided them with pens then we would have less money for high-quality textbooks, and that by remembering a pen each day they are learning habits that will help them later in life. We are ruthlessly consistent on this and on all aspects of behaviour management. This means the pupils arrive in lessons and know exactly what is expected of them.

So much poor behaviour in other schools occurs at the point of disconnect between the teacher's expectations and the pupils' conduct: some teachers may allow low-level chatter, others may insist on silence. Some may insist that all eyes are facing forwards, others may reprimand for daydreaming or not focusing. This is not an issue at Michaela because all our standards are exactly the same. Pupils know exactly what is expected of them. That is not to say that pupils don't break the rules; they do. But when they do they know exactly what form of punishment they will receive and there is no arguing, no bitterness and no resentment. The pupil takes the punishment on the chin and resolves to change their behaviour next time. It is astounding to see how much the pupils value this certainty. Just yesterday I saw a child put their hand up and admit to an infraction without any prompting from the teacher: 'Miss, you just gave Avram a demerit for fiddling but I just wanted to let you know I was doing the same.' I have seen pupils, again without prompting, thanking teachers for demerits and detentions because they know it will help them change their bad habits in the future. The pupils value and recognise that this system helps contribute to the calm and studious atmosphere and that this will ultimately lead to better results and better life chances in the future. They would not want to do anything that jeopardises that.

I believe that the 'Michaela Way' is the solution to so many of the problems facing education today. I have relished every moment of this first week and am looking forward to the challenges ahead as we grow and develop as a school. I have rediscovered my love of teaching. I no longer dread the 'nightmare' class. I no longer work hard just to keep treading water. I know my hard work will be recognised, appreciated and valued by the pupils I teach. I know that I won't be judged by a number once a half-term by a senior leader I barely know, but that

I will be visited daily and given honest and candid feedback on how to improve by several members of staff.

Just like Plato's prisoner, I now have a desire to tell everyone of the brave new world I have seen. Many will disbelieve and many will be sceptical. To the sceptics I say: take the first step out of the cave and see for yourself the impact we are having. We are always open.

Two Years In

Katie Ashford

Our pupils come from a wide variety of cultural backgrounds and live in one of the poorest boroughs in London. The odds are stacked against them right from the start. 55% of our kids are eligible for the Pupil Premium Grant, around 20% arrive with a 'Special Educational Need' label attached to them, 45% speak English as an additional language, 33% read at a standard below their chronological age, and 62% perform below the national expectation in Maths. Many of our kids are subjects of Child Protection or Child In Need Plans, and a number were either temporarily or permanently excluded from their previous schools. They speak hundreds of different languages and come from all corners of the world. Some of them have seen war, famine, crime and violence, and have fled their homes for a better life in Britain. Fit to burst, the borough's housing situation is at breaking point, and many of our poorest families live in temporary accommodation, meaning that several of them have been forced to uproot and move away from the area at a moment's notice. And whilst we fight for every one of those kids to have the chance to stay at our wonderful school, we are not always successful: sometimes, they are relocated to Luton or Birmingham or beyond, and we never see them again.

Every teacher wants to stop deprivation determining destiny, and Michaela teachers are no different. Our relentless, unyielding focus on high expectations of behaviour, a rigorous, stretching curriculum, and an unapologetic 'no excuses' culture has enabled our children to thrive in a world that tacitly accepts that they will fail. By treating every child like they are aiming for Oxbridge, by harnessing the fire and ambition to succeed that everyone has within them, and by never allowing them to settle for anything other than their strongest effort, we are helping our children to overcome the barriers that some say are insurmountable.

Whilst we can feel proud of what our pupils have achieved so far, we know that the biggest climb is yet to come. We hope that we will be able to maintain our children's progress as they move into Key Stage 4. Time will tell. But the story so far looks promising. So far, our pupils on average are making two years' progress in reading in one year, and, on average they make double the normal progress in Maths. Some children have made up to five years reading progress in one year. Visitors to the school are always amazed by their books and essays.

A sample of some of our children's stories are below.

Hasnat's Story

Hasnat arrived at Michaela a middle attainer eligible for free school meals. Her reading age was below average. She has been encouraged to read out loud in class and has joined Reading Club; this has developed a real passion for reading independently. By the end of year 8, Hasnat's reading age had increased by more than five years. She is now reading at the level expected of a 17-year-old. Hasnat also made great progress in Maths. In her first two years at the school she improved her standardised score by 20 points in the subject.

Kamron's Story

Kamron arrived at Michaela in our first cohort with a statement of Special Educational Needs outlining extreme learning difficulties. His statement expressed his inability to consistently count beyond 10, form sentences or behave in an appropriate manner around other children – at times physically lashing out. Kamron had a reading age of 7 years and 9 months on entering the school. Since joining Michaela, he has gone from strength to strength. His behaviour is exemplary and he gets on perfectly well with all of his peers. His reading age improved by over four years in his first two years at the school and is now almost in line with his chronological age. He enthusiastically contributes to every lesson.

Harry's story

Harry arrived at Michaela a middle attainer eligible for free school meals, with a reading age of 9 years and 9 months. He achieved average scores at the end of year 6. Now, Harry is now working at the top of the school, and is a 'Future Leader.' One of our most hardworking pupils, he has read over 1 million words and 30 classic texts this year. He is one of our top performers in Maths, getting into the top 5 pupils on the Maths homework charts nearly every day, sometimes doing over 500 questions in a single evening.

Jayrelle's story

Jayrelle joined us midway through year 8 after exclusion from two secondary schools and spending time at a pupil referral unit. Jayrelle's behaviour was a serious concern when he first joined Michaela. However, intervention and conversations with Senior Leaders at the school coupled with a calm, academic atmosphere and consistent approach to discipline has brought out the best in Jayrelle. He now regularly finds himself invited to join his peers in Friday

Football after school, acknowledging the fact that he has gone from a serious behavioural concern to a pupil with one of the highest number of merits in the year. Jayrelle's progress is also seen in the work he is producing: his end of year assessment in History was particularly impressive.

Hamali's Story

Hamali arrived in year 7 as a high achiever. He has gone from strength to strength in all of his subjects. He recently came second in a national timestable competition (bettered only by Hudson, another Michaela pupil). As well as his success in Maths, his reading age went from 14 years and 11 months at the beginning of year 7 to the maximum score of 17 years by the end of the year.

Fabrizio's Story

Fabrizio arrived in September 2014 with a reading age of 8 years and 4 months and a hatred of reading. In primary school, he was a frequent absentee and struggled with his confidence in reading, writing and arithmetic. His English level was a 3b and his Maths was below a level 2. He could barely construct a sentence in writing and became extremely frustrated and demotivated whenever he came across numbers. He would cry when asked to practise single-digit addition or multiplication sums in one-to-one sessions with his form tutor. In two years, he has made dramatic progress: his reading age reached a staggering 15 years and 10 months in July 2016. He can multiply and divide fractions confidently and is working on complex algebraic sums in Maths. He can write accurately and regularly makes profound contributions in English lessons, most recently commenting on how Shakespeare's *Merchant of Venice* 'offers a challenge to the hypocrisy of the Christian church.' He is no longer on the SEN register and now loves to read.

Hudson's Story

Hudson arrived at Michaela in September 2015 with a statement of Special Educational Needs outlining myriad behavioural and cognitive difficulties. He had particular trouble communicating with adults and his peers and would break down in tears regularly. Since joining Michaela, Hudson has transformed. He is receiving far fewer sanctions for incomplete homework and lack of concentration. June of year 7 saw Hudson take a trip to an educational conference at Oxford University to talk about the key to his success in Maths. In the same month he set a new record and was the outright winner of a national Maths competition. His academic success has had a positive impact on other areas for Hudson. He is much happier and more confident communicating with his peers and adults now than ever before.

The Journey Continues

When I stand in the corridors and watch our kids file by, smiling, proudly wearing their immaculate Michaela uniforms, when I visit lessons and see every single child enraptured by their teacher's words, when I listen to their appreciations at Family Lunch, or read their essays, or chat to them in the library, or spot them saying 'thank you' to the number 83 bus driver, or picking up litter on the streets, or see that they have done extra homework 'just because, Miss,' I can't help but feel hopeful. I feel hopeful that the next stages in our journey will get our pupils to their desired destinations, despite the inevitable challenges that we'll face along the way. I feel hopeful that our kids, who had so many odds stacked against them when they arrived, will leave here and be welcomed into a world that was once closed off to them, a world of success, of opportunities, of wonderful choices and – most importantly – of happiness.

Birbalsingh and Lemov on Michaela

Katharine Birbalsingh

Visitors often ask me how I had this vision, how I knew what I wanted. I always reply that I didn't have this vision. I didn't even know this was possible. I simply gathered similarly-minded people together, and we built what we have: a school that surprises us at every turn.

Whenever I have a visiting Head or Deputy in my office and I tell them some of the things that I think leadership should do, they always look at me as if I've lost my mind. I tell them about our candour chart in the staffroom that encourages staff to give each other stars for having difficult conversations with each other. I describe our dislike of bureaucracy and determination to reduce paperwork as much as possible. I speak of always considering the effort made by the teachers against the impact on the school and pupils. And then I get a bit carried away and start saying how the buck stops with us, how I believe, whatever is wrong in the school – that it's my fault, no one else's. And ultimately it is up to me to fix it.

While visitors tend to love Michaela, if they speak to me during their visit, they always raise an eyebrow. One of the most surprising things I say is that I believe that I am there for the staff, not the pupils. That doesn't mean I don't care about the kids. I do, more than you can imagine. My whole life has been dedicated to trying to change an education system that I believe is not working in their interests. But I also think that it is the role of the Head to consider the welfare of their staff first. If you look after your staff, your staff will look after the kids. And you need them to do just that: there are more of them than you.

I recently put up a Richard Branson quote in my office. 'Train people well enough so they can leave, treat them well enough so they don't want to.' He is spot-on.

One pioneering charter school leader, Doug Lemov, who runs the charter network Uncommon Schools in the US, and wrote *Teach like a Champion*, and who has accomplished so much for disadvantaged children across Uncommon's 49 schools, came to visit us recently. It was an honour to have him in our school. I want to share his write-up extensively because he does a far better job than I could, of explaining some of what we do.

Doug Lemov writes:

> As I walked through London's Michaela School I was struck suddenly by a strong intuition – call it fear maybe – that recalled my days as a teacher

in a high performing urban school. I was in my late twenties then, and my colleagues and I were seeking, like Michaela, to engineer every moment for maximum student benefit. God, we loved those kids. And they needed every ounce of what they had and what we had to have a fighting chance. So we pushed them hard and worked long hours. We were going to do every single thing we could. But the hours were often unsustainably long I can now see.

So when I glimpsed the artful intentionality of every moment in student's lives, the impeccable designed and executed systems, I feared that this was also true of Michaela. I knew this would challenge the long term sustainability of the school. Those brilliant teachers would tire. Many would leave. Organizational memory, the culture, the will to sustain it all would be diluted. The school would regress to the mean.

But happily like many intuitions which we presume are accurate, mine appears to have been in large part unfounded. And this is very good news, not just for Michaela but for every school seeking long-term, sustainable excellence – because one reason teachers at Michaela told me they leave by five is that they do something brilliant, simple and replicable to reduce workload without eroding outcomes.

Doug goes on to talk about our reduced marking, our feedback from the front of the class, that Jo Facer describes in her chapter. So why do we put staff first? Doug Lemov explains:

This is hugely important because workload has historically been an Achilles heel in the high performing urban schools movement. To change the lives of students otherwise cut off from opportunity is an immense job and often presents a brutal choice. Do you reduce the hours for the adults – the adults you love and honor and who give deeply of themselves to help others – and know that the cost will be lesser outcomes for the students and families you also love and have dedicated your professional life to serving? Or do you push for maximum outcomes for kids and know that people you care about will sometimes – often – work too hard and suffer?

In the end the core social good – the expectation shifting inner-city school – will only be as expandable as we need it to be if we can unlock large scale efficiencies- ways to continue to get maximum value for kids at more sustainable cost for adults. Insights into game changing efficiencies and synergies are rare. But Michaela is on to one.

Doug Lemov is very kind. But it is true: we do try to make what we do both sustainable and scalable. We are constantly thinking about what our decisions would look like across a full school, or even across a few schools. Would they work on a larger scale? And I think they would.

In another post, Doug writes about how we teach the children gratitude. Again, this is something people can find surprising. How do you teach children to be grateful or to be kind? It seems unnatural, almost wrong. But kindness, as Brett Williams notes in his chapter, is intrinsically wrapped up in being grateful. As Doug Lemov writes, happiness is too:

> But there was something more to the smiles and later it hit me that part of it was due to the school's strong culture of gratitude. Michaela prizes gratitude. To some degree it requires it of students, which may seem strange at first but being there helps you to see why. It has subtle and far-reaching sinews.
>
> The most palpable expression of gratitude came at lunch when, after eating, the pupils stood and offered 'appreciations.' Allowed the chance to express gratitude in front of half the school, their hands shot into the air. All of them. Everyone wanted to be chosen to say thanks.
>
> Students thanked their classmates for helping them study. They thanked their teachers for expecting a lot and helping them. They thanked them for planning great lessons. One student thanked the lunch room staff for cooking for them. And still the hands shot up into the air. A student thanked his mother for everything she did to provide for him. He was perhaps 13, this young man, and shared his appreciation in front of a few hundred other teenaged boys, speaking haltingly but honestly about how grateful he was for how hard she worked and the sacrifices she made. You don't see 13-year-old boys do that every day.
>
> A student at my table – it's communal meals at Michaela – thanked me. He wasn't really sure who I was and why I was there but it was unusual to eat with a man with a strange accent who said he had come from America to see what they did here and now he could show that he was a man and not a child and understood that it was a good thing and that it was right to show that you appreciated that. 'I want to thank sir for coming to see us,' he said.
>
> I found myself wondering about it. Here were kids from some of the poorest sections of the city, kids who faced difficulty at home and on their way to school. Many had left (or even lived still) in places wracked by violence and despair. But at Michaela, students' days were punctuated not by someone reminding them that they had been hard-done by but by the assumption that they would want to show their gratitude to the world around them.

What did this mean? Well first of all it gave rise to a culture of thoughtfulness. Everywhere I looked students did things for one another. In one class a student noticed another without a pencil and gave her one without being asked. In the hallway a student dropped some books and suddenly three or four students were squatting to pick them up. Students left class and said thank you to their teachers.

Maybe thanking makes it so. Are kids inclined to be good? Many, yes. And when they know that their goodness is seen and valued, not just by their teachers but their peers, it spreads. Maybe at first it's due to the plausibility of appreciation. But after a while it just takes on a life of its own. People are kind and considerate because, at Michaela, it's what they do.

But the gratitude, I think, is as much about the giver as the recipient. Maybe that's the most important point. To show gratitude does two things. It changes your perception of the world. It causes you to look for and then to see the goodness around you, and therefore to perceive a world full of goodness all around you. Which makes you happy. And just maybe optimistic – to think the world is the kind of place that will embrace you when you give your best.

But a second gift is bestowed upon the giver. To express gratitude is to give something to someone. And to give is to be in a place of power. After all you must have something of value to give it away. And so all that thanking – all that valued and honored thanking, all that making a big deal of the moment when you say, 'I appreciate what you've done' and assume this is immensely important – is a way of saying to the students: you have something of value. You have stature. But you also must remember that you derive your strength from your willingness to help others. When you give, you make yourself rich.

Doug Lemov articulates the ideas underpinning our school culture so well that I thought it would be useful for readers to see some of Michaela through his eyes. We are constantly visiting other schools, learning from them, taking ideas and bringing them back to Michaela. We wouldn't exist if it were not for all of the generous schools out there who have invited us in and given us ideas on how to make our school better.

Like them, we are always open to visitors. We love to have guests to eat lunch with our kids. We also learn from our visitors who give us advice on GCSEs and A-levels, on how we can keep our school the way that it is, as we grow. That is our challenge. At the time of writing, we only have 360 kids. The challenge is to retain what we have achieved for 840 when we are full.

Do I have a vision for it? Yes, but I know it will change a thousand times before we get there. We'll sweat the small stuff, hold on to our values and the rest should follow. It feels like we're on a rocket to the moon.

Let's hope we get there.

What Are We Afraid Of?

Jo Facer

A few months ago, an education consultant approached me about a blog I write called readingallthebooks.com. They reached out to express their concerns about the approach to English teaching celebrated in the posts I was sharing, and wanted to help me see that there was another way to teach. Leaving aside the irony that I had in fact taught in just that 'other way' for the majority of my time as a teacher (I was a fan of infinite group work, Philosophy for Children, and card sorts, until a propitious meeting with Joe Kirby and Katie Ashford in 2013 revealed a different way), it was fascinating to hear arguments I myself had made years earlier repeated to me again.

All the standard concerns were present in my questioner: creativity, discovery, 21st century jobs, soft skills, books kids could 'relate to.' When I said we would teach *Skellig* when Eton taught it, the returning riposte was that Wellington College teaches happiness – why don't we? Aren't we denying our children the experiences that rich kids get at private schools? On and on the conversation went with both of us at odds.

I'm not a fan of friction, so I sought to find a compromise ground. The beauty of the free schools policy, I put forward, was that schools like Michaela can exist, but then so can schools with very different ideas to ours. I cited a number of free schools, all innovating, all trying new ideas, all the polar opposite of Michaela.

I went further: we don't know it all at Michaela. If our kids get great outcomes, like they have done so far, at GCSE, A-level and beyond – great. But if they don't, and if progressive, discovery methods yield improved outcomes for children, then of course we would look into that!

My questioner interrupted me there: 'Oh – I don't doubt you'll get brilliant outcomes.'

This admission stunned me. I couldn't understand how someone could accept that what we were doing would lead to 'brilliant outcomes' for children, and still oppose it. As if brilliant outcomes were easy... As if it weren't a national crisis that some 47% of kids in 2015 didn't even achieve five C grades including English and Maths.

What are people afraid of? I can understand a worry that we might be letting down poor kids. If what we do doesn't work and hundreds of children every year are leaving our school with nothing, and nowhere to go, that is a massive problem. But if you accept that our kids are probably likely to leave with results, to leave us with doors open, to leave us with choices for their futures, to leave us as kind, grateful and happy human beings wanting to do good in the world... What is so threatening about that?

Is it that we've become so accustomed to an education system that only works for the middle classes that we've given up on the idea of poor kids achieving great outcomes, so we've decided we don't care about grades? Or is it that we've decided society is so broken, we can't begin to educate these kids but must parent them instead? Or have we shifted the goalposts from academic achievement to vague aspirations like 'happiness,' 'confidence,' 'curiosity'? To argue this is to forget that a child who leaves formal education without academic results, like almost half the country's 16-year-olds do, or who leaves illiterate like 20% of 16-year-olds do, has far fewer opportunities for long-term life happiness.

And as anyone who has visited our school will attest: our children are happy. This is not a Gradgrindian, Victorian school, filled with hateful, overbearing, cane-wielding megalomaniacs. We love our children, and they love being here. One recent visitor shared his experience of interacting with our children, commenting: 'The children note the school's strictness but have already fully internalised and grown to appreciate the importance of the rules and norms. I guess that Aristotelian line about learning to love virtue by practising it is true. They sincerely appear to obey out of a desire to excel, not begrudgingly out of fear of punishment. This in turn has fostered pride in them – completely sans smugness – when they compare themselves to others in the area, who they see poorly dressed or behaving rudely on the public transport out of school hours.'

Why are our children so happy? One: they are safe. In most inner-city schools, bullying occurs, corridors are disorderly, and lunch-halls are filled with the fear of having to sit alone. None of these things are the case at Michaela. Two: they are successful. A knowledge curriculum means even the children who are furthest behind can tangibly see how much they are learning, and experience success in their learning. Three: gratitude. Scientists have shown that the surest route to happiness is to be grateful. As Mike Taylor's chapter on Family Lunch explains, gratitude is the cornerstone to our children's daily experience at Michaela.

But to leave aside their happiness in the moment, consider their happiness in the long run. Strong outcomes means choices for children. The grim reality of hating your job and hating your life comes from limited choices. People in prison are not happy. People permanently on the dole tend not to feel fulfilled. We want long-term happiness for our children, which is why we don't mind if they are a bit upset by a detention. In the long run, will they remember 20 minutes of silent self-quizzing while their peers played? I doubt it. And if they do, in maturity they will understand that so much of their long-term happiness depended on internalising that strict discipline, that key to success.

The reality is that when only 16% of children on free school meals are making it to university, something is horribly wrong with the system. When only 53% of children are getting five C grades, something is horribly wrong with the system. When kids leave school with nothing, the system has broken.

The injustice of state education should be a national outrage; it should be the civil rights issue of our generation. Why can't every kid achieve what private school kids achieve? When I was 11, I won an assisted place to a private school. I was plucked from a state school that would go into special measures when my cousins attended it in later years. At the private school, I was shocked by the standards and discipline, forced to raise my game. At that school, I was subject to rigorous learning, high expectations, and a totally academic education, through sheer luck – luck of timing, luck of having a mother who knew how to apply for these things. Why can't all kids have access to a quality education? Why do we decide for them that they can't do that, that academic subjects are too difficult for them?

Teaching some of the weakest children at Michaela, I have been bowled over by what they know. Our weakest KS3 pupils can *all* spell Shakespeare accurately, can *all* write at length, can *all* use ambitious vocabulary (onomatopoeia, photosynthesis, sovereignty) correctly, and all know who Agamemnon was, and why Marlowe might be alluding to him in *The Jew of Malta*. All of them. They simply *can do it*. They *can* learn, they *can* remember, they *can* read, they *can* write. And anyone who says they can't should come and see what is happening, not just at Michaela, but at other schools around the country who are defying the odds with their kids.

The consultant and I had a lively exchange, which I found enjoyable and interesting enough to still be musing over months later. Towards the close of our discussion, they commented that if we did what we did in Michaela that was fine, but 'you write about it, so other schools are starting to be interested. My worry is that more and more people will do this, and all schools will become like Michaela.'

I couldn't help but chuckle merrily, as I replied: 'That's my dream.'

What do Visitors and Parents Say?

Visitors' quotes

At Michaela, we are frequently host to visitors, often teachers, from all around the country and from as far afield as Australia and the United States. Here is a sample of quotes made by visitors following a visit to the school.

"Without exception the children were engaged, purposeful and clearly enjoying their lessons."

"How lucky the children are to be in a school that places such a high value on learning and behaviour."

Diane Murphy
Thinking Reading

"Amazing how students put themselves forward without fear of ridicule from their peers."

Claire Delaney
Managing Director – Place Group Ltd

"An ethos that balances genuine warmth and care with precisely defined boundaries and standards of behaviour.

"The behaviour of the pupils was always courteous and respectful."

John Roberts
Chief Executive – Edapt

"I was very impressed by my visit to Michaela and I have been enthusing about the school at every opportunity since."

Boris Johnson
Mayor of London

"It was wonderful – and almost surreal – to see pupils behaving so well without exception."

Robert Peal
History teacher

"Appreciations during lunch clearly have a lasting impact on students by the high regard they have for each other."

Laura Wynne
Headteacher – Kingsbury Green Primary

"The corridors on change-over between lessons were calmer than I have ever seen in any school I have ever visited."

Peter Lee
Head of School – Q3 Langley Academy

"The quality of the lessons, the focused concentration of the pupils and the high expectations of the curriculum are everything we dreamed of from the free school programme."

Nick Gibb
Minister of State for School Reform

"A warm environment full of happy and articulate students who evidently love their school."

Mrs Hazell and Mrs Male
Teachers – Severn Vale School

"Genuine joy and excitement around the school and in lessons."

"Before our visit we expected to be impressed by many of your achievements; however we didn't expect to be blown away. We were."

Andrew Wright
Assistant Headteacher – John Hampden Grammar School

"Since visiting your school I haven't stopped eulogising about it to my friends and family."

Saqib Chaudhri
Assistant Headteacher – Burntwood School

"Michaela is showing what is possible for state schools across the country."

"The standards of conduct were second to none."

"Pupils talked with pride about completing several hours of homework each night, supported by a healthy competitive spirit."

Stuart Lock
Principal – Cottenham Village College

"The sense of mission, team work, high expectations and determination of staff... a team of forward-thinking, creative and highly professional teachers."

"To say that we were inspired is an understatement."

"An absolute commitment to learning and a real joy and passion for achievement."

Ruth Robinson
Principal – Swindon Academy

"Students were overwhelmingly welcoming and demonstrated a stellar level of engagement in the classroom."

"I have visited ten schools this year and many more in previous years and Michaela stood out as the most unique."

David James
Director of Operations – UP Academy Olivier, Boston, United States

"Over the years I have visited and worked in many schools, both in the state and in the independent sector, but I have never seen a school with such high expectations of its pupils."

"I was extremely impressed by how knowledgeable and well-mannered your pupils are and by the confidence and maturity they show when interacting with adults."

"The perfect combination of strictness, warmth and humour."

Michele Ledda
Director of Civitas Schools

"Students share [the Headmistress's] passion for their school and the knowledge students have retained is striking."

Dame Sally Coates
United Learning/Ex-Principal – Burlington Danes Academy

"Those who bring sunshine to the lives of others cannot keep it from themselves. Michaela pupils certainly radiate sunshine."

Revd Peter Wolton
Executive Vice Chairman – New Model School

"A calm, purposeful atmosphere is present throughout the school."

"Michaela is going further than private schools typically do, in its determined and admirable creation of a civilised, ordered community."

Anthony Radice
English Teacher

"In due course, I expect children who are now at Michaela to go on to be doctors, barristers, solicitors, high-flying executives and so on and on."

"You are literally transforming lives and making them better, happier and more productive than they would otherwise have been."

James Bartholomew
Journalist and Author

"Michaela Community School is a wonderful example of what can happen when ambition, vision and persistence intersect. For the pupils, an extraordinary educational experience that celebrates learning and achievement in a way that few schools do; for staff, an environment where they are simply allowed to teach as much as possible, free from the toxic solvents of bureaucracy and inconsistency."

Tom Bennett
Behaviour Expert – Department for Education

Some parents' quotes

'Michaela has given my daughter a sense of confidence and pride that were never there before. She used to be so nervous and scared to go to school in primary school. Now she walks out with her head held high. I am relieved and happy I chose Michaela- it is changing our lives.'

'Ok ok ok....I'm smiling....Michaela is the best school ...not only in Brent...not only in London...not only in England...not only in the UK...not only in Europe....not only in the west ....not only in the world but in the UNIVERSE!'

'Thank you for all your hard work, your understanding and your caring for my daughter's future. She has become a better person in the short time she has been in your school. I know now that my daughter will do well in life.'

'There's no other school where you feel your child gets a one to one every day, the teachers here are passionate about teaching, the education is impeccable. The standards and values they teach at is what is missing from schools today'

'The best choice by far for my two sons at Michaela. No school gives so much to each child. They expect top standards yet give top standard (sic) too. There's consistency with rules which gives it more importance. They love it, come home happy and know the work has to be done.'

'I am proud to be part of the Michaela parent team. As a parent in today's society I am concerned about some of the challenges our children faces (sic) for the future. Michaela teaches great discipline and integrity. Giving children the opportunity where they would not have received in other public schools. Children are held accountable for their actions, learning and development which are valuable life lessons for the future.'

'I have seen such extraordinary improvement in my son's attitude, aptitude and his overall work ethic. The past year at Michaela has instilled him with a sense of discipline and pride.'

'Michaela has made my daughter into a young woman. She help (sic) me around the house and is a great influence on her five younger sisters. I was worried about her before she joined the school but now I have no worries about her future.'

'My daughter was (a) shy and reserved person, so much so that I was very worried about her settling in. Now she holds a very good conversation with adults in the family and outside the family. Her vocablary (sic) has expanded so much that she sometimes corrects me when I make grammatical errors! She is more open and is very committed to her school work.'

'The kindness and manners Michaela has taught my sons has been the biggest surprise. They are helpful around the house and I no longer have to worry about leaving them alone. They are mature young men thanks to Michaela's discipline.'

'I am very much impressed with your school and all the staff. I'm thankful to all of it. I can see great progress in my daughter. She is really doing very good. I really appreciate all your hard work thanks a lot.'

'Chosing (sic) Michaela was the best it put children to the test and of course they will come out on top. I would recommend Michaela to any parent it's strick (sic) and that's what I love about it nowadays children need to know right from wrong at a young age. It's also preparing the children for the future. Thanks teachers and staff continue doing what you doing.'

'I am so impressed by the incredible structure and organisation at Michaela. Also the teachers' personal interactions with the pupils each morning are so lovely to see!'

'Michela (sic) has helped my daughter in boosting her comfidence (sic) and making her a strong young woman with good values.'

'I really love Michalea (sic) as its a special school which offers great education, my girl has learnt a lot and the behavior (sic) is brilliant. Eveyday (sic) as I send Fatima to school, I guarantee that she is receiving very good education and that she is 100% safe. Lunch is very special and unique. Thanks for offering which is a great school.'

'I chose a new Free School for my eldest daughter after I heard Ms Birbalsingh talk of her plans for this new school and fell in love with this great new ethos of learning. The school is everything and more than what I expected. My daughter has excelled in learning new subjects for the first time enjoying her learning with great results too! After being so impressed with the Michaela experience I also sent my second daughter to Michaela and have recommended the school to all my friends and family. The teachers and staff at the school are the reason behind the school being so great.'

'I would like to say thank you to this school because my daughter is always happy when she comes back school. She also working really hard and this is all down to the staff. Thank you.'

'I have never had to ask my girls to do their homework, it is done with love automatically and they spend about 2/3 hours on homework every day and enjoy it because they have been given homework in what they have actually been taught. Choosing Michaela as a secondary school for my daughters has been one of the best choices I have made.'

'I believe there is no other school out there like Michaela in the whole of (the) UK. I feel so privileged.'

'I can already see differences in my child. She's more responsible, confident and her attitude is improving all day, more and more and more. She loves her teachers and she's really happy when she's talking about new things learn (sic) at school.'

'My son is more punctual, more disiplined (sic) and eager to work at home. He has also started loving reading books at home.'

'My daughter has changed a lot in the course of just two weeks! She has learnt how to use a knife and fork. She is very pleased to attend Michaela, she says that she's "won the lottery"!'

'The Michaela way of paying attention to detail is really exceptional. I already see the difference in my child. This prepares a pupil for adulthood.'

'Our son attends *The New Michaela Community School* and after many experiences in other schools he is finally really happy and loves school. He is learning and always wants to go to school and I receive lots of feedback from him. This is a great source of relief and joy to us and we are very grateful that schools like Michaela Community School exist. We want our child's school experience to be a happy one and so it is important that choice in schools is possible. The level of support from teachers is truly exceptional. Can't wait for my littke (sic) one to start same school next year!! Keep it up'

'(My son is) arguing less with his younger brother. He will explain or discuss issues rather than argue over them. His confidence has gone up and he is more willing to learn new things.'

'Since starting Michaela I have noticed that my son has begun to take pride in not only his academic work but also in fulfilling his responsibilities.'

'Thank you for all your support and help that you as a school have shown us. I have recommended loads of people to send their children to Michaela, the school has done wonders for my son and I feel they will also benefit from the school in a very positive way.'

'Thanks to all staff for the incredible progress my child has made since joining the school. I am so impressed with all the hard work they put in to everything they do now.'

'(Since joining the school) he helps out more in the house with cleaning, cooking and takes far more responsibility for things. He is becoming a polite young man.'

'We would like to thank Michaela for teaching our daughter that determination and hard work will help her achieve her goals.'

'I am so pleased with my son's table manners since attending Michaela and his attention span has improved so much! I'm very happy I made the chose (sic) to send him to this special school.'

'My son's manners have changed completely since he started school at Michaela. He used to hate reading but he reads all the time now. I recommend Michaela to all my friends.'

'I am really very happy with everything about the school, especially the support I receive. The best thing about the school is that I can leave my son in the morning knowing that he is happy and most importantly safe.'

'Michaela is an outstanding school for my son because I have seen many changes in his attitude at home. He is kind to his sister and is helpful and thoughtful. He has completely changed and I couldn't be more proud.'

'The amount my son know now is incredible! Whenever we watch TV he tells me some facts about whatever is on! He remember so much and feels like he is intelligent. This has made him much brave (sic) and more confident with people.'

'The teachers are the best I've ever met. If I had teachers like them I would have loved scool (sic). They take time to explain everything and the difference in (my daughter) is unbelievable. When I take her to visit relatives, they can't believe how much she has changed!'

'My daughter has grown in self-confidence and has learnt to use her time effectively. I am very proud of the progress she has made at Michaela'

'My son is happy at last at school. Thank you Michaela!'

'My daughter loves the school. She never complains even when she wakes up in the morning. She loves all the lessons and she feels much more clever. Michaela is the best!'

'Michaela is the best school in the country. It changes lives of the pupils every day.'

'My son was rude and always got in trouble at his old school. He needed discipline and rules and Michaela has given him. He still has a long was to go but he is beginning his journey and I see changes in him every day. He is happier and better behaved.'

'My son has improved at Michaela because he is kinder to his brothers, has better table manners and lets people in before him.'

'Since attending Michaela, our daughter is quietly confident, extremely motivated and totally empowered to achieve outstanding results.'

'I really love Michaela as it's a special school which offers great education, (my daughter) has learnt a lot and the behavior (sic) is brilliant. Everyday (sic) I send (my daughter) to school I guarantee that she is receiving very good education and that she is 100% safe. Lunch is very special and unique.'

'The school has far exceeded our expectations. Specifically, we are relieved that our daughter is being educated in an environment that strongly promotes high standards in behavior (sic) and achievement. She is notably more mature, organised and forward-thinking. She is planning her academic future and setting her aims high. Michaela has given her vision and an excitement for learning!'

'Michaela is the perfect blend of stimulation and discipline to give our children the advantage they need to be competitive in society.'

'I have never, ever, been in a school where, without exception, every single pupils (sic) behaves in such a courteous and confident manner.'

'I chose Michaela because of the discipline, which is what he needs and needed. And he is getting it at your school. He is a totally changed boy, since going there.'

'It is not what you do for children, but what you have taught them to do for themselves, that will make them successful human beings.'

Pupil Testimonials

Joe Allan

(All pupil names have been changed to preserve anonymity)

'I understand now that I am the master of my own fate. By working hard and showing kindness, I can choose my future.' – Hanna (Year 8).

In just a few short years, Michaela will have its first set of GCSE and A-level results. Only then will we be able to demonstrate more fully whether our methods work. Whilst we are pretty confident that what we are doing is right, and whilst we have courage in our convictions, we are careful not to grow complacent. As any teacher, senior leader or Head knows, making a school work is an unrelenting task of Herculean effort. And yet, in two short years, I have been astonished at some of the turnaround stories I have witnessed. The hard work, determination, resilience, guts, tenacity and sheer willpower of the senior leaders and teachers, combined with an implacable focus on high standards, have resulted in something that many may consider to be more valuable and important than any exam results.

I began working at the school as a 'Teaching Fellow' when the school opened in 2014. At the time, I saw it as a job – a job I was keen to do well at, of course, but a job nonetheless. I thought I would spend a year here before moving on to some traditional form of teacher training. It wasn't until I got to know the staff and pupils at the school that I realised that Michaela would be so much more than a job for me. Within just a few months, I could see the impact the high standards were having on the children, though I could barely believe it. We had pupils go from reading age 9 years to 15 years within 10 months; pupils who were mute transform into chatty, confident, proud young people; children with appalling behaviour records and exclusions, who'd spent time in a Pupil Referral Unit and on reduced timetables, become eloquent, hardworking, grateful young people. The school seemed to be achieving the impossible. It was something that I knew I had to remain a part of.

But don't just take my word for it. This chapter brings to life the voices of the children we teach every day, their stories and their views. Whilst we are yet to achieve our first GCSE results, we are already beginning to see the fruits of the hard work of our youngsters.

Raheem's Story (Year 7)

'The biggest difference is the high standards. At my primary school I never felt like I was being expected to work my absolute hardest. I didn't realise how hard I could work until I came here. At my old school, the teachers would spend all their time with one or two naughty pupils and we would just have to sit there waiting. That would make everyone else start to mess around because it was so boring. I got in trouble a lot by the end of year 6. I never get detentions at Michaela. I also have improved my writing so much. I always used to do the minimum but now I do the maximum – this has been because of the teachers and because of the self-quizzing I do at home.'

Sarah's Story (Year 7)

'We work hard and are kind to each other here. There is no point in just working hard, or just being kind, we need to do both. I am building much better habits since coming to Michaela. I'm kinder to my parents and they are very happy I came here. I also choose to work harder – I pick more challenging books to read to really improve my knowledge. My parents they are thrilled when I tell them about what I learnt in lessons.'

Tyler's Story (Year 8)

'Michaela is different because we memorise what we need to know. Because we make the most of every single second in the classroom and don't waste time at all, we can achieve perhaps twice as much as at other schools. Even handing out books, we make the most of every second and can get started after eight or ten seconds. I remember things from the beginning of year 7 about Mesopotamia and Mandela and I never could at my primary school. At that school we didn't really learn very much. The teachers were very nice but I have improved my reading so much at Michaela. I used to read books that were easy but now I always choose the classics.'

Aisha's Story (Year 8)

'My biggest change has been my appreciation. I appreciate and am grateful now for Michaela and for my life. Before Michaela I would never show gratitude and take everything for granted but I have stopped that now. Michaela is also the best because there is no bullying. At my primary school even friends bullied each other and teachers couldn't do anything to stop it. I'm proud when I'm out on the streets being Michaela; we are going to achieve. I feel sorry for my friends and cousins who are at really bad schools where they get bullied and teachers get upset and can't even do anything about it.'

The above pupils joined us at the beginning of year 7 and so have no experience of other secondary schools. The following accounts are from several pupils who have left other secondary schools to join us. They have switched schools for a variety of reasons. In some cases, their parents moved to the local area. Some were tormented by bullying. In other cases, they themselves bullied others.

Yasmin's Story (Year 8)

'In my other school, the students could do anything. Even if it was bad the pupils could get away with it because the teachers wouldn't really care about them. Sometimes even the teacher would be scared of the pupils and not trying to stop them doing anything. Like one time I was in class and we heard lots of screaming and shouting. The whole class got up and went to see and there were two boys fighting and there were no teachers around to stop them and we called our class teacher and all she said was "don't worry, that's not our problem" and she just went back to look at her computer. We kept on telling the teacher that they were still fighting but she would ignore us and tell us off. In Michaela, not only do we have a strict policy of no fighting but our teachers care about each and every child. That was the bad part of my old school. The fact that I cannot say even a minority of positives makes me feel like if I had stayed longer I would not go anywhere in the future and I really feel sympathy for my friends that still go there. Now I am able to sit in class and not have distraction – from any corner of the classroom. Being in Michaela is like I am in a safe-zone, somewhere where everyone has strict boundaries and somewhere where the teachers truly care. This experience in Michaela allows me to have the future that could never have happened in any other school. In this school I know that I will be successful in life and have a big future where all the doors will be open for me.'

Michael's Story (Year 8)

'In my old school behaviour was really bad. No one would listen or respect teachers. Students would have water-fights in lessons and they would throw water at teachers. Students would write swear words on the whiteboard. If students were angry or if they didn't want to work they would throw their chairs and leave the classroom. When we used to line up to buy our lunch, the older students would push in the line, and I would to wait for a long time until I ate my lunch which made me only have about ten minutes to eat. I would even have to stand while eating my lunch because all the tables were taken by the older pupils. Corridors were a mess, and moving between classes always took us about 8 minutes, fights always occurred and people would hide in the toilets to skip lessons. This made me feel annoyed, angry and sad at the same time because I wouldn't learn or have a chance to have lunch. Basically the school was a mess. I am happy and grateful that I came to Michaela because everything here was completely different. We make the most of every single second and the teachers care about all of our futures.'

Kaljinder's Story (Year 8)

'The differences between Michaela and my old secondary school are the respect and behaviour to the teachers. In my previous secondary school, there would be students swearing to the adults and keep on disrupting every time they'd like to say something. However, in Michaela not one child would ever disrespect the teacher in any form. Since I've joined Michaela I can feel safe going to classrooms. Now I don't hear a peep or whisper coming out of class instead of hearing someone getting picked on or someone getting physically hurt. Most of the time I would get so mad knowing that I've not learnt anything and people would cry coming out of the exam room because they know they should've started to work before and should have just listened. Now I know that I should never disrupt any teacher.'

Tomasz's Story (Year 7)

'In my old secondary school there was lots of bullying. People would have been bullied because of their skin colour, their weight and their appearance. I had a friend who witnessed someone bullying someone else. He had a talk with the boy and he said the boy was in tears, he said that before this the boy had never been scared of school but now he wanted to leave the school and even leave Brent. Teachers in my old school always said they will sort it out, but the boy said the next day that the bully was still being mean to him. In lessons, in my previous school, the behaviour in class was disgraceful. In assessments children threw paper at each other, they went on their phones, all the teacher could do was to send the child into isolation where they would have to work on their own away from other pupils and then the next day the behaviour got even worse. Teachers were weak – this was one of the reasons I left my previous school. This made me feel like I was not safe at school anymore. Every day I would come home telling my parents that I learnt nothing today but now I have changed my school I feel safer and I learn a lot. My message to all Michaela pupils is to not take this great school for granted.'

An understandable criticism of our image for pupil success and personal growth is that it only works for one kind of pupil. Zero-tolerance discipline and knowledge-rich curricula may very well lead to great character development for the brightest but what about everyone else? We maintain that the Michaela Way does not discriminate. Anyone can take responsibility, develop good habits and break out of bad habits. The following accounts are from a range of pupils with various levels of academic ability and behaviour. They range from pupils who joined us when reading at the level of a six-year-old, to pupils arriving reading at the level of 16-year-olds and targeting Oxbridge. What unites all of these pupils is that they have all clearly come to believe that they can and should hold themselves to a higher standard. They can break the habits that would otherwise limit their options, and broaden their horizons. Below is an account from a high-achieving pupil, who arrived at Michaela with a reputation for disruption.

Cara's Story (Year 8)

'My behaviour at Primary school was turbulent, belligerent and absolutely shambolic. It was rare when I did not get scolded by a teacher at least five times a day, and a teacher always wanted to have a word with my mother. However, there were days when I was a "good girl"... Well, when I wanted to be. Although I had never been in so much trouble that I ended up excluded, or in the Headteacher's office, I was a serious trouble maker that would definitely end up in isolation, or worse, if I had attended Michaela at that time. For example, at Primary school, I loved to wind up the supply teachers and make a complete fool of myself, being the ultimate clown of the class. However, at Michaela, I would never dream of mocking the teachers, who I know sacrifice their time to help us to live the best lives possible. In addition, I especially struggled to control my emotions. Teachers always said that I had "anger issues," but now I know that it was just a problem with self-control. I used to throw outrageous tantrums, hurting those who dared to come near to me. I was the sort of child that parents would tell their children not to hang out with. However, at Michaela, I aspire to be a role model and inspiration to all the future younger years, leaving a positive effect on them.'

The following are two accounts of a pupil who came to the school with a long history of behavioural issues. The first is from before he joined us. The second is after his first term at the school. The third paragraph contains his own views of his journey at Michaela so far.

Darnell's Story (Year 7)

An account from Darnell's primary school from July 2015:

'Darnell has a problem with authority. He has had this problem since Reception, but it has worsened since the beginning of year 6. His problems are emotional. He's typical of boys round here. He gets distracted easily and dislikes detentions. He attends the local Behavioural Unit 2 days per week. The other 3 days, he is in school until 1.30pm because he simply cannot cope with the full school day. On a regular basis, he has tantrums after lunch. He cries and throws himself into the walls. On some occasions, he throws chairs. He struggles to relate to other children, even those who are friendly towards him. Situations often escalate to violence and he often hits other children. He uses abusive language. He sees red daily. In year 6, he has been particularly violent. He regularly uses profanities towards pupils and staff. He has bad reactions when things go wrong and takes punishments very personally. He finds it difficult not to talk or swing on his chair in lessons. In my opinion, Darnell will need a reduced timetable. I think a full timetable from September would be very damaging for him.'

An account from Darnell's Michaela form tutor, December 2015:

'Darnell is focused, hard-working and very enthusiastic in lessons. He always has his hand up in discussion, and he often shares excellent ideas. Just last week, he stood up in front of the class to give an eloquent, impassioned and impromptu "prosecution" speech in an English lesson on Roman rhetoric and the law courts. He started off the year in the first week of school in terrible habits: slouching, overreacting and sulking. He still sometimes doesn't sit up straight in class, he still sometimes rolls his eyes when he gets a demerit, and he still sometimes sulks if he gets a detention. However, his self-control and his behaviour have improved massively since the start of the year. In his interactions with teachers, guests and staff, he is polite, professional and considerate, talking happily about how much he has changed. He still sometimes tries to catch others' eyes in the corridors, but it is unthinkable that he throw a tantrum, let alone a chair. He had not shown any violent behaviour since coming to Michaela. On the contrary, he has behaved like a gentleman, studying hard, succeeding in his subjects and enjoying lunchtimes playing basketball. He has improved his merit balance by 142 points in half-term 2 compared to half-term 1. His attendance is sky-high at 100%. He leaves schools at 4pm every day like every other student, and has not had to take any days or time off in a behavioural unit. Far from being very damaging for him, a full timetable of lessons at Michaela has been the making of him. Today, Darnell is on track to achieve fantastic academic results, and his habits of politeness and consideration are improving every day. He has achieved a complete turnaround within two terms at Michaela; now, the sky is the limit for what he can achieve.'

Darnell's Perspective:

'Since I've started Michaela, the three things I'm most proud of is my behaviour, attitude and reactions. The reason why those three things have changed is teachers such as Mr. Kirby, Mr. Smith and Ms. Facer. I have had lots of talks with Ms. Facer to help improve my habits. Mr. Smith has helped me improve my attitude of how I see things because I would always look at things negatively – now, I try to look at things positively. Mr. Kirby and I have had lots of talks about my balance for merits and demerits I had 30 demerits a week so I practised, practised, practised until I thought I was ready enough to have a positive attitude. At first, the Michaela system of rules was very different from my primary school rules. I have got use to the rules because I choose to make positive choices. In Primary school I would have a problem with my self-control because I would be rude to people and I would just get so emotional or angry I would resort to violence with chairs and other things. Whenever I got sent home or in internal exclusion, I would have a negative attitude towards it. Now I'm in Michaela if I'm in isolation or detention I try and reflect on next time "what would I do differently next time?" I think that I have changed a lot since primary school. I remember one time I had a brilliant week at school I was more on the positives than the negative and every day I came home my Mum felt so happy. I wanted to see that because I don't like to see my Nan or my mum crying. I have also changed because I want a good future.'

The following two accounts are from two high-achieving girls who work diligently, behave impeccably and are confident and courteous with adults and their peers alike. It is easy to assume that such exceptional children would be fine anywhere: perhaps children like this have always been this way, and will continue to be this way wherever they go to school. Their own words suggest this isn't necessarily the case.

Hanna's Story (Year 8)

'In my primary school, behaviour was atrocious. We ran in the corridors and were told off all the time but the teachers couldn't tell us what to do. When we had supply teachers it was like a room full of wild animals. We threw pens at each other and even at the teacher. Some of my classmates were swearing at the teacher and leaving the class whenever they felt like it. By 10.30 the supply teacher had fled our class in tears. This was a typical day when a supply teacher came to my school.

Since I have joined Michaela, I have immensely improved my behaviour, my trust with the teachers and my concentration in classes. In my primary school I rarely got in trouble with my teachers because they did not suspect that I was the one that was the one who was actually disrupting lessons. My behaviour was better than most of the students in my class because I did not lose my temper and get into physical fights. However, I had many verbal fights with most of my classmates; it was seen as normal. Throughout my time in primary school I had quite good grades compared to everyone else even though I did not listen to the teacher most of the time. This made me arrogant and hubristic so I did not work as hard as I do now in Michaela. I have changed many of my bad habits in Michaela because of the strict atmosphere. I used to talk to my friends all the time in class. I did not work as much as I could have because it was not expected of us to get exceptional grades.

In primary school I barely put my hand up because I was not comfortable speaking with large groups of people. This was because many people jeered and made fun of people who answered questions enthusiastically. When I did pay attention to my teacher I usually knew the answer to the questions but I was too anxious and afraid to put my hand up in fear of being bullied. I came to understand that what I do does not ultimately affect my teachers but it affected me. I understand now that I am the master of my own fate. By working hard and showing kindness, I can choose my future. I have older brothers and sisters, who have graduated from university but they were not Russell Group Universities so I am aspiring to get accepted to Oxbridge. I came to Michaela to help me pursue my dream and direct my path to greatness. I have improved in many ways that I did not know that I had to improve in. I have made my family proud in coming to Michaela. I have improved in many ways that I never expected to.'

Naomi's Story (Year 8)

'In my primary school, there were no consequences, there was no detention system. There was no respect. Teachers, pupils and staff would all give excuses and stay off from work or school with no one to stop this from happening. Supply teachers were plentiful and some even had permanent jobs there. No one listened and no one did as they were told. There was no sense of authority. Our teacher would simply tell us she was disappointed in us and then carry on with the day as if nothing had happened.

In primary school, I was deemed trustworthy by my teachers. In a way I was. I could be trusted to do something for my teachers, and to hand in completed homework on time. However, if I could get away with talking in line to my friends, making fun of others with my friends, I would. Most of my friends were not the best of influences. But I knew these things were wrong. My primary school did not have the best of rules and they were not strict. Teachers found it easier to give a warning rather than a deserved detention. In primary school it was normal that even if you did not work hard you could still be top of the class. It was normal that someone at the top of the class was born smart and could understand everything much easier than someone at the bottom of the class. I know now that this is false. Hard work brings you to the top. Even though I was put in top Maths group and had a high reading and English level, I most regret not working harder and truly deserving these titles. I was complacent and put off working hard in any way I could. Michaela changed me. In year 7, I was not completely "Michaela" but I understood the values of Michaela and wanted to work more towards this in year 8.

Miss Birbalsingh's words changed and influenced me for the better. Her assemblies made me think about my life and what I wanted out of it. I now know that I want to study law at Cambridge. I want to become a human rights lawyer. I want to be proud of my achievements in my life. I want to be a role model for aspiring lawyers, doctors and those of all professions. I want my future children to strive for what I hope to achieve, and not to be ashamed of my life. I want to make my mother proud of me, make my entire family proud of me. I want my teachers to remember me for someone who worked hard, who was kind and who was enthusiastic. I want my teachers to remember me as someone who deserved a place at a top university and who deserved her job and career. I want to leave a great and amazing legacy behind. I will not be able to achieve these goals if I had not attended Michaela and won a place at the best secondary school in Britain.'

Of course, not all pupils walk through the doors at Michaela and are immediately transformed, courteous and grateful. In some cases, habit change takes longer. The following deals with the case of a highly achieving pupil who arrived very complacent, and after a year was showing few signs of changing. The first section is a would-be response to a university asking for a character reference at the beginning of year 8 (which we shared with him), the second is the same at the end of year 8. The third is the pupil's own account of his progress.

Lamar's Story (Year 8)

Hypothetical response to a university's reference request for Lamar, September 2015:

'Lamar is complacent and ungrateful. He was involved in a fight in public in year 8, bringing the school into disrepute, the very same day that the Headmistress had a conversation with him about his attitude. His body language is negative and slumped in lessons. He does the minimum of homework and shows the minimum of initiative. He refuses to take responsibility and often blames others for the negative consequences of his poor choices. He hasn't shown any gratitude to his teachers over the years, instead telling one senior leader that her resources were "boring," in spite of the many hours of dedication that she had spent on them. He intentionally distracts others in lessons, and has made rude gestures to other pupils. He avoids interactions with teachers, and comes across as aloof and arrogant. Lamar has not listened or acted on the frequent conversations we have had with him about improving his attitude. I do not recommend that he be given a place at your University.'

Hypothetical response to a university's reference request for Lamar, July 2016:

'Lamar is now focused, dedicated and hard-working in lessons, listening intently, contributing a great deal in class and asking thoughtful questions. His merit balance has changed from -150 in January to +300 in July. From September to January, Lamar got 28 detentions and removed from lessons 7 times. From February to July, Lamar only incurred 4 behaviour detentions and did not get removed from lessons once. He is polite and friendly around school, takes responsibility for his mistakes and tries to improve. He works hard on his homework, often being announced in assembly for being top of the year group for the amount of evening Maths prep he completes. He has joined us in Friday football, our weekly reward for those in the top 25 of the year group for their merit balance, every week for the last 7 weeks from May to July. He is now polite, grateful and happy in his interactions with his teachers. He has been to every Maths club and Debating club since January, and has applied and been accepted to the Michaela Oxbridge preparation programme. He tells me he wants to study Maths or Theology at Oxbridge. In short, Lamar has achieved a complete transformation in his habits in the last six months at Michaela. If he continues on this trajectory, and keeps up the hard work and habit change, I would highly recommend him for a place at Oxbridge, or any of the best Universities in the world.'

Lamar's Perspective:

'I have changed my behaviour significantly throughout the second half of year 8. During most of year seven and half of year 8, I was ungrateful and careless. I showed almost no respect for the amount of hard work my teachers would do for me. I did not reflect on the many conversations and interactions my teachers would have with me, instead telling one English teacher that her resources were boring. I did the bare minimum of homework almost every day. I had reached a point where if I was given even a single demerit, I would be placed in internal isolation and I had to work alone, away from other pupils. I was going nowhere and I decided to change it for the better. I first worked hard on improving my trust with teachers: I would work hard at home attempting to do as many IXL Maths questions as possible a night. It showed teachers that I was very grateful for the Maths resources they set out for me. I then focused on body language. I had asked a very well behaved pupil in my form on how to improve my behaviour in lessons, which helped me to join him in Friday Football multiple times. I was in turn, happy at seeing my mum elated when she opened the reward email at the end of every week where I had acquired over 50 merits in less than five days. My goal of studying theology or computer engineering was now possible as my teachers would write positive references for the universities that I would be applying for, aiming to go to MIT or Cambridge. However, I still have a long way to go. I always aim for one hundred percent and I need to work very hard to achieve this. I have achieved a lot during the last few months, but I still have a long road to go.'

This final account is from one of our biggest success stories. This boy joined us from a Pupil Referral Unit after being expelled from two other schools. It was clear he was on a very dangerous path when he joined us. He is not our only pupil who has been excluded from other schools.

Jerome's Story (Year 8)

'Before I came to Michaela Community School I attended other secondary schools. I have noticed the big difference in behaviour and respect. At my first school I was probably a bully and getting bullied myself. At Michaela, there is such a big difference in terms of the noise level and respect. At other schools you would not be able to walk through a corridor without getting a headache. At Michaela there is a big difference. I was surprised by the respect and how pupils treat their peers and teachers, everyone said "good morning" and asked how I was, and what brought me to Michaela; and they gave good eye contact. In other schools they don't bother to give eye contact, say good morning or ask about your day. They will either walk past and give you a dirty look or ask "who are you?" in a rude way. Sometimes it is very intimidating. In lessons the noise level in other schools is very loud sometimes we don't even learn anything, but at Michaela all of that is different. We learn so much more than I expected.

Since the day I was told I was accepted into Michaela Community School I have changed. Although I occasionally get into minor incidents, I have changed for the best and now it is time to see where I go from here. Before I came to Michaela I watched 42 hours of TV – six hours a day. Now I only watch two hours a week so I have more time to help my siblings with their homework and tidying their room. I always used to have flaming arguments with my Mum. Since I've started Michaela we don't argue, we actually bond more, we laugh together. My sisters and I were always fighting but now we don't as much, my anger has calmed down a lot. I used to fight every day but now I haven't fought in a year and a half. That is a big improvement on my behaviour and self-control.'

What unites all of these pupils is that they feel like they can learn. Children remember. They remember the feeling of sitting in a classroom and wasting time. They remember being unable to recall anything about a topic after six weeks of learning about it. They remember hours wasted while a teacher tried to negotiate with the naughtiest child, day after day. A zero-nonsense, zero-tolerance, zero-excuses policy is enabling these children to flourish. Their pride, enthusiasm and excitement shines out of them, even as they stand in the freezing cold yard and chant 'Invictus' at the top of their lungs each morning. It is remarkable to witness, and knowing that the pupils can see the impact the school has had on their lives makes us even more committed to maintaining the ethos as we grow.

Reading the preceding chapters of this book, you might find plenty of what we are writing hard to believe. But these words are directly from the pupils themselves. These children have not been made to write these words – they have written these words themselves, alone, and from the heart. Those who visit are amazed by a great variety of aspects of what we do, but every single one is amazed by our wonderful, happy children.

Two years ago, I came to Michaela to earn a paycheque and get some experience of a London school. Within months, I not only realised that Michaela could change my life, altering my course from traditional teacher training to Michaela training, but I learned that our collective commitment had the power to transform the habits – and lives – of some of the most vulnerable pupils from one of London's poorest boroughs.

Appendices

Examples of Humanities Work

This essay was produced in January of year 8 from memory and without notes. At the beginning of year 7, the pupil's work was rife with spelling errors and they were unable to use dates accurately. By virtue of being explicitly taught the points of analysis, recapping on previous lessons, being drilled on key dates and tested on key spellings, the pupil is able to produce a rich and analytical essay. The pupil makes an independent historical judgement: 'the barons were a minor challenge to the king's power and authority because the Magna Carta was overstated.' The pupil uses precise examples of people, places and date to inform their explanation: 'King John...had lost much of his land such as Anjou.' The conceptual vocabulary used to explain their point is much more sophisticated: 'The cultural, spiritual and political hegemony of the Church meant that it was the most significant rival to the king's power in medieval England.'

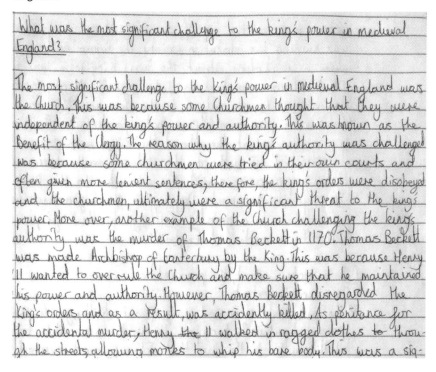

What was the most significant challenge to the king's power in medieval England?

The most significant challenge to the king's power in medieval England was the Church. This was because some Churchmen thought that they were independent of the king's power and authority. This was known as the Benefit of the Clergy. The reason why the king's authority was challenged was because some churchmen were tried in their own courts and often given more lenient sentences; therefore, the king's orders were disobeyed and the churchmen, ultimately were a significant threat to the kings power. More over, another example of the Church challenging the kings authority was the murder of Thomas Beckett in 1170. Thomas Beckett was made Archbishop of Canterbury by the King. This was because Henry II wanted to overrule the Church and make sure that he maintained his power and authority. However, Thomas Beckett disregarded the King's orders and as a result, was accidentally killed. As penitance for the accidental murder; Henry the II walked in ragged clothes to through the streets, allowing monks to whip his bare body. This was a significant ~~threat~~ challenge to his power and authority because the peasants would have judged the king when he was in the streets and ultimately, threatened his status in the social society. The cultural, spiritual and political hegemony of the Church meant that it was the most significant rival to the king's power in medieval England.

The Barons were a minor challenge to the king's power and authority because the Magna Carta was overstated. When King John was crowned, society did not support him. This was because ~~his more~~ he had lost much of his land such as Anjou in which his more successful brother Richard the lionheart had won. King John did not live to the ~~same ex~~ same standards as his brother, ruining his reputation and deceiving most people's expectations. Moreover, his poor performance in battles granted him the name of softsword This was, a significant threat because the king, who was to some extent.

The following examples are from a lower-ability pupil with limited English, who arrived in September of year 7 with a reading age of 7 years and 4 months. Unsurprisingly, they were unable to spell or produce a well-constructed sentence.

By January of year 7, after being regularly taught, tested and recapped on the unit content and key spellings, the pupil is familiar and confident with some difficult spellings, though there are some grammatical and syntactical mistakes. The pupil still struggles to recognise when to use capital letters but the construction of sentences is vastly improved.

Explain three factors that were important to the development of Ancient Egyptian ~~Civil~~ civilisation

One factor that was important to the development of Egyptian Civilisation was Geography. This was important because the River Nile allowed people to trade and transport their goods. This was important because the River Nile provided water for Irrigation, so they can create an agricultural surplus. This was important because the ~~deserts~~ Sahara deserts surrounding Egypt protected it from invasion until Hyksos invade ~~in 1640 BC~~ in 1640 BC. Additionally, such as pharaohs king khufu and Hatshepsut build impressive monuments I such as Obelisks, pyramid and ~~sphinkes~~ sphinxes to reinforce their power and authority and they left their Legacy for us.

Farming was another important factor in the development of Egyptian Civilisation. This was important because the pharaohs were able to ~~create an agricultural surplus to produce~~ organise create an agricultural surplus and produce farmworkers. This was important because, if there incase was ~~at~~ a famine the people go to ~~pharaohs~~ farmers and ask them for food and ~~pharaohs~~ farmers ~~power increased slowly.~~ became more powerful. The pharaoh ~~pay to soldiers~~ s were able to pay soldiers to protect them.

Finally, another important factor was Writing. This was important because it helps farmers to write down how many crops they have grewn. This was important because the pharaohs the only one were able to read and write ~~and~~ so this increased their power. This was important because

By January of year 8, the same pupil is demonstrating excellent spelling of challenging words: 'lenient', 'Canterbury', 'cultural', 'spiritual', 'hierarchical' and 'feudal.' Precise examples of people, places and dates deployed to bolster analysis: 'Thomas Becket,' '1170' and '1348.' The pupil has developed sophisticated judgements: 'both of these examples illustrate the cultural, spiritual and political power [of the Church]. This continued independence was [the] most significant challenge to the king's power in [the] medieval period.' By focusing on a strong grasp of chronology, testing and recapping of previous lessons along with simple lessons filled with reading, and deliberate, focused practice of comprehension and analysis, pupils are able to make remarkable progress in just two years.

What was the most significant challenge to the king's power in medie
val England?

One of the most significant challenges to king's power was
the ~~Church, they~~ Church, the churchmen's thought they were independen
t of the king's power. One example of this was the 'Benefit of the
Clergy'. Benefit of the Clergy' is ~~when~~ the ^process ^when churchmen are allowed
to give trials in courts with more lenient sentences. Another exa
mple of this was the murder of Thomas Bechet in 1170. Th
omas Bechet was made Archbishop of Canterbury by Henry II
because the king wanted to gains control over the church.
Thomas Bechet resist his attempts and restricts his
power. Henry II's knights accidentally murder Thomas Beche
t N King Henry II walked bared foot to ^Archbishop ^of Canterbury and ^the ^water; wh
ip by monks. Both of these examples illustrate that
the cultural, spiritual and polictical power, this ~~continued~~ cont
inued independence was most significant ~~and~~ challenged ki
ng's power in medieval period.

Another challenge that was most significant to the king's
power was~~t~~ the Peasant's Revolt, because these new class
of landowners called the 'yeoman farmers' disrupted the trad
itional, hierarchical stratified feudal system. In 1348, the Bla
ck Death killed between a third and a half of England's
population. Land owners found it increasingly difficult to
find peasants to work on their land. Peasant's were nowe
able to move farm to farm and ask for higher wages. In
addition, some peasants gained more money than others and
they were able to buy land from their ^own plague victims in
^are cheaper prices. This ~~was~~ because of the new class of land
owners called the 'yeoman farmers', disrupted tradition feudal
system. This was important because the king relied on bard
ns to maintain his power throughout England. The new class

Here is another example of a low ability pupil. This is his assessment in January of year 7. His assessment demonstrates some knowledge of the importance of farming and geography to the development of Egyptian civilisation, but his understanding is superficial. His ability to express his ideas is limited: 'Farming was another important factor in the development of...' His handwriting is haphazard and he makes frequent mistakes.

> Explain the factors that were important to the development of Ancient Egyptian civilisation
>
> One factor that was important to the development of Ancient Egyptian civilisation was farming. This was important because the Egyptians the river Nile is part of geography - famers there urys for gods as they grew an agricultural surplus. This lead to people not having to be famers farmers would irrigate (there) crops with a black silt which was on the bottom of the nile. If anyone did not have to be farmers and nomadic, they could build advanced societies because the people who were still farmers had or was growing an agricultural surplus so then they would sell it and
>
> Farming was another important factor in the development of Egyptian civilisation Because famers could have more crops than they need, which is an agricultural surplus, this ment that they would grow sell there food of trade it. Famers irrigated crops by using the Nile that would flooded land leave a black silt.
>
> Finally, another (important) factor was geography. This was important because the Sahara Desert and the river nile helped them for example the Sahara Desert protected the Egyptions until the Hyksos invaded it. The Nile helped them transport goods such as limestone and basalt to build impressive monuments mostly for their leaders pharaohs.

Here is the same pupil's assessment on the challenges to the king's power in the medieval period in January of year 8 – 12 months later. His handwriting, spelling and grammar is hugely improved: 'peasants,' 'hierarchical,' 'Runneymede' and 'traditional' are all spelt correctly. He uses precise dates, people and places committed to memory to bolster explanation: 'c.2 million,' '1215,' 'King John,' 'Runneymede' and 'Magna Carta.' Importantly, his conceptual understanding is much more advanced and he expresses himself clearly: 'This [the yeoman farmer] was important because it challenged the traditional landlord and the hierarchical society and also the feudal system' and 'the Magna Carta, which was an important document which restricted the king's power and made him subject to the law.'

> What was the most significant challenge to the king's power in the medieval period?
>
> The peasants were a significant challenge to the king's power because after the Black Death there, which killed c.2 million people, in the medieval period there were not many peasants left. The peasants who survived would have have demand for higher wages for from the land lord and if the land lord said no the peasants u would have of gone to work on another farm. This new class of peo meanwhile other peasants were by buying and for rock bottom prices, which had to once belonged to a plague victim for f rock bottom prices, this new class of land owners were called the yeoman yeoman farmer. The This was important because it challenged the traditional landlord and the hierarchical feudal society system and also the fueldal system.
>
> The barons were a challenge to the king's power because f in 1215 they had made king John sign the magn.

> Another challenge the to the king's power in the medieval period was the barons because in 1215 they ~~met~~ met king John at Runneymede hill hill to sign the Magna ~~Carter~~ Carta, which was an important document which restricted the kings power and made him a subject to the law. Before the Magna Carta king John could ~~e~~ throw people into jail without a trial by ~~dory~~ jury and he could raise taxes for his disastrous military

Here is the same pupil's assessment on the causes of the Civil War at the end of year 8 – just under two years after he arrived at Michaela. We can see his handwriting has improved, almost beyond recognition, as have his spelling and grammar: 'profligate,' 'Parliament,' 'Arminian' and 'debt' are all spelled correctly. He has remembered precise dates, people and places, which he has committed to memory to bolster explanation: '£2 million,' '1215,' '1625' and 'Arminian, William Laud'. He writes at greater length and he expresses himself with much more sophistication, even if he doesn't always choose the bon mot: '...this emboldened Parliament and had made them think they have a higher authority than the King' and 'These examples are important because they clearly illustrate the financial enmity between the Crown and the King.'

> ## Why did civil war break out in 1642?
>
> One reason civil war ~~bree~~ broke out in 1642 was ~~of~~ because of Charles' profligate, lavished and extravagant spending. In 1625, Charles had asked Parliament for £2 million to ~~have a war~~ fund a war against the Spanish but Parliament only voted to give him £250,0 this ~~had~~ led to Charles brutally loosing the war. Charles had inherited debt from his father leading him to build up a debt of £1 million ~~pan~~ and during the period of 'Personal rule', where he had made an unpopular tax called the 'ship money' tax this had led him to be deeply unpopular because he did not have Parliament agreement which was against the Magna

Carta which King John had to sign in 1215. Charles and Parliament had ~~na~~ built up financial tension because Charles would spend his money on his favourites, ~~er~~ (George Villiers), art and war and would have to keep on going back to Parliament and ask them for money this emboldened Parliament ~~and had~~ and had ~~made~~ them think that they have a higher authority than the king. These examples are important because they clearly illustrate the financial enmity between the crown and ~~the~~ the King. This was important because this was one of the crucial reasons of why civil war broke out in 1642.

Another reason civil war broke out was because of the religious ~~tension~~ division between the Arminian crown and the Puritan Parliament. In 1625, Charles had married a French Catholic princess named Henrietta ~~Maria~~ Maria this was important because it led Parliament to believe that Charles was a secret ~~P~~ papist. In 1633, during the period of 'Personal rule' Charles ~~had~~ appointed an Arminian, William Laud, the Archbishop of Canterbury this was problematic as Laud was an Arminian and Parliament where Puritan. In 1637, Laud tried to impose his prayer book ~~on Scotland~~ ~~this plan~~ ~~to~~ and uniformity in Scotland this plan backfired and the Scottish invaded demanding £25,000 every month. Laud attacked ~~back~~ Puritans and banned their books so when William Prynne (a puritan) said that Laud grew up in a dung hill, which was very offensive in those days, Laud had Prynnes ears cut off for

Examples of English Work

The following high-ability pupil joined Michaela with promising but inconsistent, and often structurally confused, written work. At Michaela, we test pupils on complex vocabulary, spelling and grammar. In lessons pupils read and write a great deal. The results of this simple method can be seen in the year 8 essay below. This pupil's essay is remarkable in terms of her insightful comments, extensive quotations, and clear links between high-level context, and the content. She skilfully combines her knowledge of the play- which has been previously taught, tested and recapped – with advanced vocabulary explicitly taught in previous units: 'Macbeth is unambiguously culpable for his own downfall... His arrogance, deceptiveness and false sense of security are his hamartia...' The Michaela commitment to consistently revisiting prior knowledge has allowed this pupil in her conclusion to make a comparison to Julius Caesar, a play she has not studied since year 7.

Who is most responsible for Macbeth's tragic downfall?   23

The witches in Shakespeare's tragedy, Macbeth, are majorly responsible for Macbeth's tragic downfall. Shakespeare introduces them with pathetic fallacy of 'Thunder' and 'lightning' to give the audience a clear idea of their nature and intentions. It is clear from the start of the play that the witches are planning Macbeth's downfall when they say "when the hurly burly is done," when the battle's lost and won" & using rhyme, antithesis of 'lost' and 'won' and satanic language. This quotation demonstrates that the witches are aware of Macbeth's destiny and downfall and crypticly foretell his fate through prophesies, however Macbeth is unaware that their prophecies are leading to his decapitation, instead of his rise of power. The witches' first three prophecies state that Macbeth will be the 'thane of Cawdor' and 'Hail Macbeth, all hail to you, that shall be king hereafter' combining repetition and later on, Macbeth's hamartia. These prophesies lure Macbeth into a false sense of security which is one of the main reasons for his downfall. However, when the witches tell Banquo that his 'sons will be kings', it seems like this is the point where Macbeth is beginning to feel challenged and growingly suspicious. Straight after when Macbeth does become the thane of Cawdor, he along with Banquo are questioning 'does the devil speak true? This could have alarmed the Royal Court because in 1604 they became fiercely religious Protestants and would have completely rejected that Satan woul d speak any truth. However, this challenged James' because the witches had actually prophecised his reign, even though in 1597 he wrote Demonology, a book stating that he was against witchcraft and saw it as evil. James I had no choice but so silently agree with the witches or else he would be interrogating his place on the throne. The witches continuously use rhyming couplets in their chantings such as "fair is foul and foul is fair" ~~so~~ to ~~almost~~ captivate the audience and make them complicit with their diabolical ~~meant~~ incantations. We can see this when Macbeth says "So foul and fair a day I have not seen," demonstrating repetition and antithesis of 'foul' and 'fair' to showcase the effect that the witches⁴ already have on him, and

⁴ because he how they're already infecting his psychology. In the witches' last
   assume's   set of prophecies, about Macduff, himself and Dunsinane, he is cert
   everyone is   ain that he is invincible and invulnerable. The witches tell Ma
   of woman-born cbeth to 'beware Macduff' and that 'none of woman-born shall harm Macbeth'. However, Macbeth ~~does not~~ completely ~~reject~~ disregards the prophecy about Macduff*, leading to his downfall. The witches say that 'Macbeth shall never vanquished be until Great Birnam Wood to Dunsinane Hill shall move him', however Macbeth thinks it is imp ossible, so he does not take much advice. When Dunsinane does mov e, Macbeth realises that the witches have tricked him and known for his downfall all along. What supports this is when Macduff says, 'I was from my mothers womb untimely ripped', a Macbeth's anagnore sis. So although the witches plant a seed in Macbeth's mind, h is the one who commits ~~the~~ regicide of Duncan and ~~so~~ ~~completes~~ Pushes his fulfils fate.

Lady Macbeth is also partially to blame for the downfall of Mac beth because she is his 'fiend-like queen' who challenges Mac beth and persuades him to commit regicide. Lady Macbeth is clearly ~~a~~ close ~~person~~ to Macbeth as he sends the letter, a prop, to her telling her about the witches' prophecies. She tells Macbeth to "look like the innocent flower, but be the serpent under it," ~~containing antithesis~~ ~~encouraging~~ Macbeth to be deceptive and a traitor. ~~This~~ This would have connected to the 17th century Jacob eans because in 1605, ~~to~~ to celebrate the discovery of the Gu

Fantastic research ✓

powder Plot, James I had a medal made of a snake conceal
ed within flowers. This would have made the audience feel a
if Lady Macbeth almost represented and symbolised the Catholic
conspirators. "I will pour my spirits into your ear" demonstrate po
ssessive pronouns which demonstrate how Lady Macbeth is a
culprit in his downfall. The Jacobeans would have disliked this be
cause it would have subverted the predictions of the patriarchy. W
-hen Macbeth decides not to murder Duncan, Lady Macbeth challenge

his masculinity, 'if you were a man' and bravery until he eventually co
mmits the regicide of Duncan. However, after this, Macbeth completely
shuts her out of his murderous campaigns, including the murder of
~~Duncan~~ Banquo and Lady Macduff and her son, which is why Macduff behead
him So, for this reason, we cannot say that she is the ~~pr~~ most res
ponsible for Macbeth's downfall. "What's done cannot be undone", show
antithesis and chiasmus and this scene demonstrates Lady Macbet
's guilty conscience playing with her mind, leading to her suicide. Th
could have corroborated with the Jacobeans ^worldview^ to prove that women cou
not be in control, for they were not mentally stable enough

Macbeth ~~is the~~ is unambiguously culpable for his own downfall in
'Macbeth'. His arrogance, deceptiveness and false sense of security
are his hamartia, leading to his death. At first Macbeth appears
as a humble man ^and^ "full of the milk of human kindness" demonstrating
~~simile~~ personification and symbolism. After the witches' prophecies
Macbeth takes his fate in his own hands and murders Duncan ^in 1045^
After he suspects Banquo, "our fears in Banquo stick deep", he murders
Banquo and attempts to kill his son Fleance. As he believed he was
Banquo's descendant, James I would have immediately disliked Mac
beth, as would the fiercely religious Protestant audience for committi
ng regicide, an act of damnation. Macbeth cannot seem to be
able to control killing people and instead murders more people to
make up for his guilty conscience; "I am in blood stepped so deep,
should I wade no more, for to go back would be tedious as go over"
demonstrating blood imagery. Macbeth thinks he is invincible as
he thinks that everyone is of "woman-born" so he will continue to
reign. After Lady Macbeth's death and Dunsinane begins to move, Macbe
th realises how he has challenged his own destiny and played with

his own fate. He fights until he is decapitated and Malcolm is restored as King. The 'dead butcher' demonstrating inhuman imagery showing Macbeth's desire for murder, is dead; a ~~man~~ catharsis for both the audience and the characters in the play. ~~The~~ Macbeth tried to take control

of his fate, leading to his downfall. He could of chosen not to listen to the witches or Lady Macbeth, but instead he allows his psychology to be plagued by their desires.

In conclusion, the eponymous, tyrannical protagonist, Macbeth, is most to blame for his downfall. The witches did plant a seed in his mindset, however Macbeth chose to coerce his destiny and almost ~~be~~ turn desperate for more of their prophecies. Lady Macbeth does persuade Macbeth to commit regicide by emmasculating him, but she is shut out from Macbeth's further ~~ambitions~~ lust for ambition Macbeth compares himself to Caesar "Mark Antony to my Caesar" and Shakespeare stages this so that the audience can compare the themes of the two plays: power, ambition and tyranny. However, Caesar does not allow himself to be persuaded by his wife, Calpurnia, and augers. Macbeth is most culpable for his downfall because his false sense of invincibility, his hamartia, leave him blind to the further consequences his tyranny would have on him: his beheading

How does Shelley present the themes of hubris and nemesis in 'Frankenstein?

The theme of hubris and nemesis in the novel, Walton is presented supercilious and a explore that wants to go to the North Pole. Walton is we willing to sacrifice his men for glory to the North Pole. 'You seek for knowledge wisdom as I once did' this illustrates that Frankenstein and Walton are doubling because they both wants to be re glory and 'seeking for' knowledge *they are* this emphasises that Walton is transforming to Frankenstein because Walton is focus to go to the North Pole and doesn't care about the men and fra when Frankenstein made the creatu he didn't care about the creature's feelings or that the creature is going to be lonely. 'do not not deserve to accomplish some great purpose? this demonstrates that Walton is questing that is that do he deserve to reach glory' This links the period of the Enlightenment creates the french terror and guillotine in 1793. How?

The theme of hubris and nemesis nemesis in the novel, Frankenstein is presented as a scientist scientist that wants to discover the secrets of life and death and creates a creature, the imply that he is playing God part and it is hubris he and he eat from the tree of knowledge and become god-like able to create life and this hightlights that he chooses glory than his wealth. 'so much has been done more, far more will I achieve' this demonstrates

that he is only thinking about himself and
~~that~~ he is only thinking about to have glory
and to ~~or~~ create use and achieve it. This
illustrates that Frankenstein is not thinking, before
he creating of creature and doesn't know whats
going to happen to when the creature comes
alive. The soul both of hope and fear Justine
died she rested and I was alive 'this ~~emphas~~
emphasises that ~~Fransten~~ Frankenstein is not
taking responsibility and that he is still thinking
about himself and that he saying that Justine
is lucky she is dead because Frankenstein
have to carry the guilt, this links to the
Rime of Ancient Mariner when the Mariner
told self guilty when he shot the bird and
starved on the ship and have to carry the
guilt for eternity.

(15)

This lower-ability year 8 pupil entered Michaela with a reading age of 8 years and has benefitted from additional reading tuition in a small group after school. Key spellings from the unit have been identified and explicitly taught; key concepts have been drilled and committed to memory. In her essay, the pupil uses high-level vocabulary and her spelling is impressive. Her command of complex concepts like 'hubris' and 'nemesis' is evident, as is her contextual knowledge. She uses her broader study to draw on Shelley's allusion to 'Rime of the Ancient Mariner,' which, as with all Michaela pupils, she has learned to recite off by heart.

Examples of Artwork

This pupil had very limited knowledge of colour theory when starting at Michaela. He is now able to identify contrasting colours and as a result has produced a skilful representation of Van Gogh's 'The Siesta.'

Note: You can see the full colour version of this artwork on the inside back cover.

This pupil had no experience of working with oil pastels when starting at Michaela. He has learned how to blend oil pastels effectively and as a result has produced excellent contrast in this still life.

Note: You can see the full colour version of this artwork on the inside back cover.

This pupil was unable to draw 3D shapes accurately when starting Michaela. He has learned how to draw accurately from observation using his observational skills and is now able to produce highly skilful tonal studies such like this.

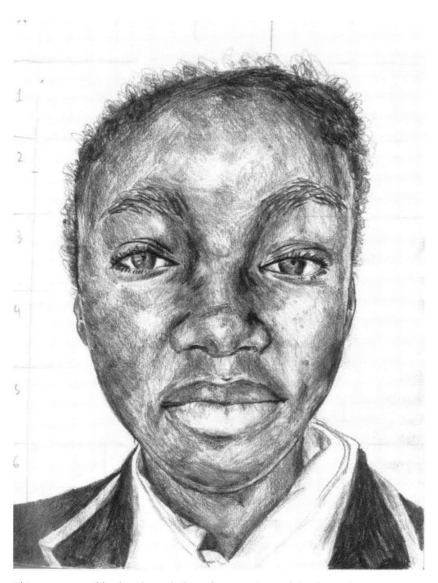

This year 8 pupil had no knowledge of proportions of the face when starting at Michaela; she would draw the eyes to high on the forehead and was unable to draw the features accurately. Now she is able to draw with correct proportions and add such realist details and texture to the features to achieve a striking likeness.

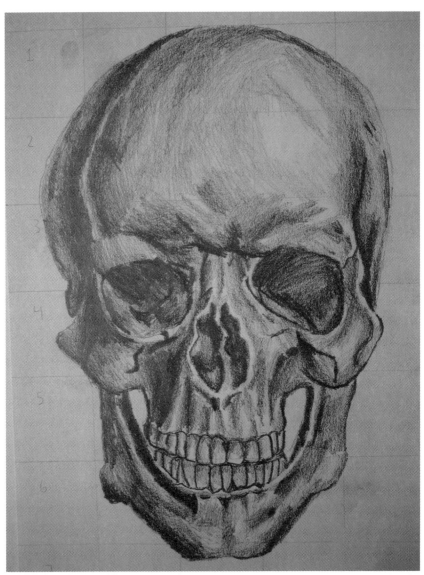

Before Michaela, this year 8 pupil had never used the grid method. She would work at a painstakingly slow pace and would rarely resolve outcomes within the given time. This was completed in a one hour exam. She has been able to apply graduated tone and produce effective contrast through an extended range of tone.

This pupil was unable to achieve a range of tone when using chalk and charcoal when starting Michaela. At first she first demonstrated very limited skills. She has learnt how to blend the media carefully whilst always considering the direction of the form and, as a result, demonstrates fluent skills.

This year 7 pupil was unable draw the body in correct proportions and demonstrate different textures when starting Michaela. She has since learned about the structure and proportion of the body and mastered different mark-making techniques, and as a result is able to produce a highly skilful drawing of the human body including a range of textures.

This pupil was unable to produce a range of tone when using pen (cross-hatch technique) when starting at Michaela. Her outcomes were both unrealistic and flat. She has since learnt how to vary the density of line and, as a result, is able to produce a skilful replica of Henry Moore's hand drawing.

This pupil was unable to reproduce shapes and textures with accuracy when starting at Michaela. He has mastered the grid method and as a result is able to reproduce photographs with skill and confidence.

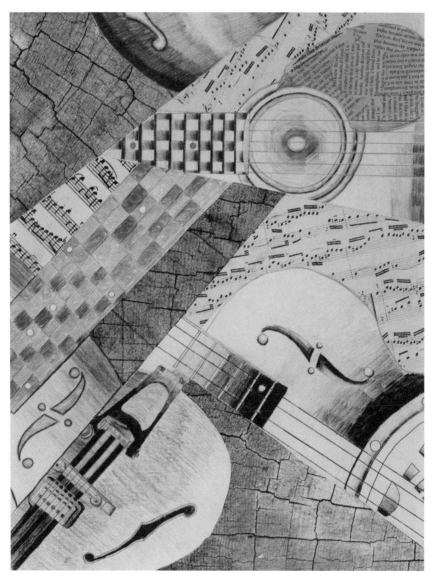

This pupil had no knowledge or understanding of Cubism when starting at Michaela. He learned all of the key terms, characteristics and history of the movement and, as a result, he was able to make direct connections to the movement through design, composition choice and selected media to suit his intentions. (Note: You can see the full colour version on the inside front cover)

Examples of French Work

All pupils join us with very little or no French. We use a literacy and phonics first approach, with lots of reading out loud and analysing the written word. As a result, even pupils who join us half-way through the year are, after just a few months, able to produce highly accurate and complex written and spoken French.

Normalement j'aime aller au ciné mais vendredi soir c'était vraiment ennuyeux. Je suis sorti avec mon frère et ma soeur comme d'habitude. En général, on s'entend plutôt bien mais vendredi soir c'était un peu différent. Mon frère ne parle pas beaucoup normalement mais il était vraiment agaçant vendredi soir. Je ne sais pas pourquoi mais mon frère m'a grondé sans cesse. Quoi que je fasse et quoi que je dise il dit que je suis ennuyeux. Lundi soir je voudrais aller à la patinoire avec mes amis mais malheureusement j'ai beaucoup de devoirs donc ce ne sera pas possible.

Samedi prochain je vais a faire mes devoirs dans ma chambre bien sûr. Il faut que je fasse mes devoirs avant de sortir avec mes amis. Je trouve ça normal en fait parce que si on veut réussir il n'y a pas de raccourci. Est-ce que vous avais une remède miracle? Est-ce que vous avais une baguette magique? non! Pourquoi? Parce que ça réciste pas, en fait. Si on veut réussir il faut tout simplement

All of our pupils begin year 7 learning PROFS – past, reasons, opinions, future and subjunctive. Even pupils with low literacy levels in English become familiar with a range of grammatical structures and vocabulary more commonly seen at A-level. Everything is translated using 'dodgy English' – literal translations – so that they have everything they need to understand and master these phrases.

9 il est rare que

Je ne dis pas que je sois f-
ainéante, mais quand même il faut que
je bosse bien comme le dit le dicton

16. Bien que mes parent soisant Francais
ils habite aux états-uni états unis
17. normalement je n'aime pas pendant la semaine j'ai trop de devirs
18. Je voudrais aller à la plage avec mon oncle
et ma tante
19. Bien que je sois sportif je n'aime pas
nager
20. en fait je préfère lire et de la ma chambre
21. en écoutant de la musique
21. Il est rare que faire to mes devoirs en
regardant la télé
22. pendant la semaine j'aime trop lire et
j'aime faire mes devoirs

il est rare que je fasse mes devoirs en
écoutant de la musique ou en regardant la
télé car ça me distant distrait

1. Je suis allé au château
2. il est allé à la plage.
3. elle est allée à la piscine
4. ils est allé à la patin ou oire
5. ils est allé

1. Je suis allé au château ✓
2. il est allé à la plage ✓
3. elle sonest allée à la piscine ✓
4. elles est allés à la piscine ✓
5. elles sont allées à la musée ✓
6. est-ce que aime allé à la boulangerie ✓
7. est-ce que vous aime allé à la pâtisserie
8. Est-ce que tu aimes lire ✓
9. Est-ce que vous aimez faire de la natation ✓
10. Est-ce que tu aime aménager.
11. Est-ce que vous êtes sportif.
12. Est-ce que tu est chauve
13. je vais aller au château

À mon À avis, et évidemment c'est un avis très personnel, la langue française est plus ou moins logique c'est du hahan

tom Je ne suis pas convaincu(s) qu'il ait raison. Je ne suis pas convaincu(s) qu'il
raison ait raison, je ne suis pas convaincu(s) qu'il ait, je ne suis pas convaincu (s) qu'il ait raison, Peu importe, il n'y a pas de remède miracle, Peu importe, il n'y a pas de remède miracle, peu importe, il n'y a pas de remède miracle. si on veut réussir dans la vie, si on veut réussir dans la vie, si on veut réussir dans la vie, il faut tout simplement persévérer, il faut tout simplement pe se

We don't start with single words of vocabulary, building to longer sentences, as is common practice in MFL classrooms. We begin with PROFS and a wide range of proverbs and idioms, in lengthy texts with parallel translations. As a result, pupils learn to write extensively and are consistently provided with models of interesting, real-life French. This pupil, after a year and a half, writes fluidly using idiomatic French, the subjunctive and a wide range of complex structures.

*) Je ne dis ~~que~~ pas que je suis fainéante mais quand même il faut ~~dire~~ que je bosse bien Comme le dit le dicton ≪ Au boulot ! ≫

*) À ~~mon~~ avis, `Ca vie` des jeunes `n'est` ~~ne~~ pas du tout compliquée ! Certains diraient ça, mais ~~moi~~, je ne suis pas d'accord. Selon Moi, les jeunes sont tout à fait paresseux et égoïste ! Bien que je m'entende `bien` avec ma mère, elle dit parfois que je ne travaille pas assez, et elle a raison. Je viens d'acheter un nouveau portable, et hier je j'ai passé sept heures ~~heures~~ ~~à~~ jouant. Donc aujourd'hui, mes notes ne sont pas très bonnes, et il faut que je travaille ~~bosse~~ beaucoup plus. Ça crève les yeux ! Si on veut vraiment maîtriser une matière, il faut ~~bosse~~ bosser !

J'ai seize ans, et mon anniversaire est le vingt-et-un juillet

A mon avis, et évidemment c'est un avis personnel, la vie des jeunes n'est pas du tout compliquée :

1) Je voudrais aller à la salle de sport, une fois par semaine.
2) Mais, malheureusement, ce n'est pas possible tout le temps.
3) Je me sens toujours mieux après être allée à la salle de sport.
4) donc j'aime aller tous les jours, étant allée au collège.
5) Bien sûr, parfois, je n'ai pas envie d'y aller après le collège,
6) mais, comme le dit le dicton personne n'est parfait ! Certainement pas moi.
7) Cependant il faut dire ~~qu'il faut~~ que j'aille à la salle de sport.
8) parce que franchement je suis plutôt ~~gou~~ ~~si~~ gourmande surtout les week-ends.

J'habite à Wembley mais j'ai habité en France et je voudrais habiter au Sénégal parce qu'il fait vraiment chaud là-bas.

`Vocab`
~~Each month~~ chaque mois, semaine, année, personne, oublier, vrai, souvent
d'élèves, j'oublie

Les riches deviennent plus riches et les pauvres deviennent plus pauvres. Ceux qui travaillent réussissent et ceux qui retravaille pas s'appauvrissent.

1) En général je préfère aller à la plage.
2) parce que j'aime faire de la planche et voile
3) L'année dernière je suis allé à Montpellier
4) avec mes parents. C'était incroyable.
5) J'ai fait beaucoup de sport. surtout du foot.
6) Comme je viens de dire, je suis plutôt sportive sportif.
7) Je tiens ça de mon père. Il est très sportif aussi
8) Malheureusement il il y a eu un accident
9) quand on était à la plage et
10) Mon père s'est cassé la jambe
11) donc il a fallu aller à l'hôpital
12) En fait j'ai fait m'est arrivé à peu près la même chose

This pupil joined Michaela with no French. As a result of our intense focus on the written word, a huge amount of reading out loud and reading complex texts, after eight months this pupil is using PROFS with aplomb – again, a level of French more commonly seen employed by much older pupils.

H45

French
1. Je suis allé(e) au château
2. Il est allé à la plage
3. Elle est allée à la piscine
4. Ils sont allés à la patinoire
5. Elles sont allées au musée
6. Est-ce que tu aimes aller à la boulangerie?
7. Est-ce que vous aimez aller à la pâtisserie?
8. Est-ce que tu aimes lire?
9. Est-ce que vous aimez faire de la natation?
10. Est-ce que vous êtes sportive?
11. Est-ce que tu aimes nager?
12. Est-ce que tu es chauve?
13. Je vais au château
14. Demain je vais aller au château
15. Je vais au collège
16. Demain je vais aller à la piscine
17. Ce sera génial parce que je suis sportive
18. Ce sera génial parce que je suis très sportive
19. Ce sera fantastique parce que je suis plutôt sportive
20. Bien que je sois sportive je n'aime pas le foot
21. Bien que je sois qu'il soit sportif il n'aime pas le tennis
22. Il faut que je fasse mes devoirs
23. Il faut qu'il fasse ses devoirs
24. Il est rare que j'aille au théâtre
25. Il est rare qu'il aille au théâtre
26. Il est rare que je sorte le soir
27. Il est rare qu'il sorte le soir
28. Il est rare qu'ils aille au cinéma
29. Aimez-vous sortir le soir?
30. Aimes-tu aller au cinéma
31. J'aime aller en France
32. Il aime aller en Espagne
33. Elle aime aller en Allemagne

Examples of Music Work

A Year 8 pupil's work. The majority of pupils arrive with no prior knowledge of music theory or notation. We begin with basics.

At Michaela, we place a high value on all music pupils having a good sense of internal pitch. They use solfege to help them 'hear' the notes mentally from reading them on paper. All pupils are able to use solfege by the end of the first year.

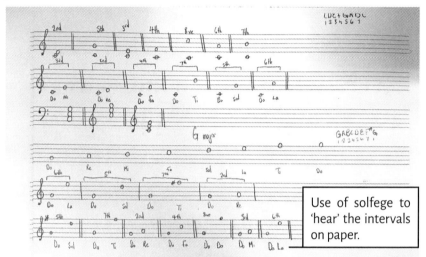

Use of solfege to 'hear' the intervals on paper.

By the end of one term in Notation and Harmony lessons, all pupils are able to use notation comfortably and use that skill to identify all major intervals in a variety of keys.

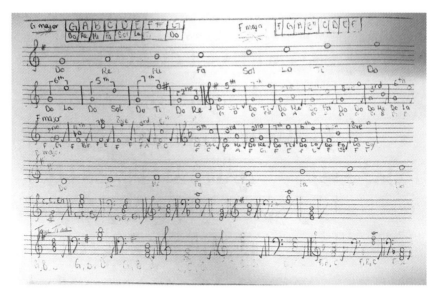

By the time they do their final exams for the first year, pupils are well above Grade 1 theory level, with the additional help of solfege. Pupils can use solfege in any key they have learnt, and identify all of their tonic triads.

Pupils learn about rhythm notation. They work on counting out and subdividing correctly. This also helps to support their learning in Maths in year 7.

Pupils are equipped to be able to hear simple pieces of music and write them down, starting with simple rhythm and pitch dictation, and building up to short melodies.

Examples of Appreciation

At Michaela, pupils are taught and encouraged to be grateful. At lunch-time, in assemblies and in every interaction, practising gratitude is central to Michaela life. One way in which pupils share their gratitude is by writing appreciation postcards to their teachers, parents and peers. Some examples are shared below.

NAME: Ms Cullen

TUTOR GROUP: 7 Athena

Dear Ms cullen,
      I would like to thank you because you are a great and enthusaistic form teacher and when I was sick you brightened my day and you are very caring.

NAME: Ms Speller.

TUTOR GROUP: Thank you so much for the wonderful art lessons. I really enjoy them and I always learn something new! I would also like to thank you because you always record how to do paintings step by step. It is very helpful! Best wishes,

NAME: Ms. Speller

TUTOR GROUP: 8 Athena

Thank you for taking the time to teach me about traditional drawing techniques and about the history of art. I have also improved a lot since I started attending your lessons. It is also true what they say "The Earth without art is Eh".

NAME: Miss Speller

TUTOR GROUP:

Thank you for being an enthusiastic form tutor who always pushes us to do our best and it works, and it always wants me to work had, to get merits and to make my teachers proud. Tutor time is always fun with a lively atmosphere and a time to help me to reflect on what I had done that was good and what I could do that could have been better, and that is largely due to your hard work to help us suceed.

NAME: MICHAELA !!!

WE LOVE YOU!!!

TUTOR GROUP: Thank you Michaela. You have been so inspiring for everyone at Michaela. You have been so courageous when having cancer. Because of you Ms Birbalsingh open this incredible school. We have learnt a lot from you and we will never forget YOU!!! Your LEGACY will never be forgotten.

Yours Sincerely

NAME: Ms Birbalsingh

TUTOR GROUP: —

Dear Ms Birbalsingh, thank you very much for being the best headteacher anyone could ask for. Since attending Michaela, I have reformed into a polite young lady and I have learnt more than I could ever imagine. My family and I would thank you for your support and kindness beyond measure. I hope you have a lovely and relaxing holiday.

NAME: Miss Lund

TUTOR GROUP: 8A

I would like to appreciate you for the kind things you do for our form and all the enthusiam you put in lessons and by helping me during the hard times this week. And for correcting me on my behaviour
                                        from

NAME: Ms Ashford

TUTOR GROUP:

Dear Miss Ashford,
Thank you for leading a great, persuasive and philosophical assembly.

NAME: Ms Bettahar

TUTOR GROUP: 7 Zeus

I would like to appreciate you because even though you had a cold you still come to school and for chosen the best books to read in form class.

NAME: Mr. Smith

TUTOR GROUP: Michaela Community School

I have always wanted to thank you for giving us motivational speeches and advice on living a happy and Successful life. You may have not actually taught my form a specific lesson but I've learnt so many things from you. — Yours Sincerely

NAME: To All The Teachers

TUTOR GROUP:

I would like to appreciate all the teachers for helping me change my behaviour and making me positive by the day. I may not show it But I am really grateful so thankyou.

YOURS SINCERLY

NAME: Mr. Allan

TUTOR GROUP: 7P

Thank you for your kind words when ever im upset or if there is something wrong you would ask me if im alright which shows me you care even more than I thought you did.
I hope this made you smile!

NAME: Mr Rees

TUTOR GROUP:

I would like to thank you for always reading with great expression in form. I enjoy reading very much and the book makes more sense to me.
Thank you very much.

From

NAME: Mr Kirby

TUTOR GROUP:

Thank you for always taking the time to talk with me about school and the future as well. I really appreciate your considera-tion about how I'm getting on. I know that I can tell you about things that are bothering me and that if I need any help, you are always willing to listen. Thank you for teaching me not to suffer in silence, because it is much better to confront the issues so that they will be resolved and I will always be happy in school.

I hope you enjoy your holiday :)

NAME: Ms Rizvi

TUTOR GROUP: MATHS / SCIENCE

Dear miss. Rizvi,
Thank you for your postcard, but the only reason I got 100% in my maths quiz was because I had an amazing math's teacher (YOU).
from

NAME: Mr Eastment

TUTOR GROUP:

Dear Mr Eastment,
    I would like to thank you for being such a hard - working, positive teacher. I appreciate the fact that you mark our practice books and it must be difficult to read some of our handwriting (mine included)!
    Yours sincerely

9 A

NAME:

TUTOR GROUP: Thank you for helping me become a better person, for supporting and encouraging me to get home early. and to be 100% michaela. :)

Thank you so much

NAME: Mr Taylor

TUTOR GROUP:

I would just like to thank you for your enthusiasm in our history lessons. I have really & enjoyed learning this half-term. You have helped me and given useful advice to me in terms of my writing skills which I am sure will improve throughout the years to come.
Thank you,

NAME: Miss Birbalsingh

TUTOR GROUP: Dear Miss,

Thankyou very much for creating this wonderful and unique school, of which I am very proud to attend. Michaela has truly changed me into a better person and has transformed me into a more ambitious pupil, that has absorbed the characteristics of integrity, perseverance and sympathy. I always look forward to your inspiring words of wisdom in assembly and I always aspire to be such an insightful orator and powerful woman like you in the future.

NAME: Ms Newman

TUTOR GROUP:

For always testing me on my religion and history knowledge which helps me get 100% in my weekly quizzes and for all the work you do in the humanities department.

Thank you,
From

NAME: Mr Porter

TUTOR GROUP:

Thank you for all the hard work you have put in our Religion lessons. I have found them very insightful and interesting. You have helped me understand many people around me in my life. I'm looking forward to the next half term.

From:

NAME: Miss Speller

TUTOR GROUP:

Dear Miss Speller, I am extremely grateful to have you as a form tutor because you are always so supportive and you really encourage us to improve in everyway. You inspire me to work harder in all my subjects and I am really grateful for you.

Best wishes

Twitter handles and blog links

	Twitter handles	Blogs
Katharine Birbalsingh	@Miss_Snuffy	tomisswithloveblog.wordpress.com
ENGLISH		
Katie Ashford	@katie_s_ashford	tabularasaeducation.wordpress.com
Jo Facer	@jo_facer	readingallthebooks.com
Lia Martin	@liaesthermartin	whathappensnextmiss.wordpress.com
Joe Kirby	@joe__kirby	pragmaticreform.wordpress.com
HUMANITIES		
Jonathan Porter	@JHC_Porter	tolearnistofollow.wordpress.com
William Eastment	@WilliamEastment	
Lucy Newman	@MsLNewman	educationlucille.wordpress.com
Joe Allan	@JoeAllan9	
Mike Taylor	@mike_taylor11	aienaristeuein.wordpress.com
MUSIC		
Sarah Clear	@sclear_29	michaelaartsblog.wordpress.com
Chashe Musarurwa	@chashemusic	michaelaartsblog.wordpress.com
SCIENCE		
Cassandra Cheng	@casscheng2	chengreaction.wordpress.com
Olivia Dyer	@oliviaparisdyer	edudyertribe.wordpress.com
Jake Plastow	@JakePlastow	
MATHS		
Brett Williams-Yale	@BrettWYale	
Hin-Tai Ting	@HinTai_Ting	mathagogy.wordpress.com
Naveen Rizvi	@naveenfrizvi	conceptionofthegood.co.uk
Tom Kendall	@tkendalluk	
Dani Quinn	@danicquinn	missquinnmaths.wordpress.com
FRENCH		
Barry Smith	@BarryNSmith79	hackingattheroots.wordpress.com
Jessica Lund	@jessicalundx	jlmfl.wordpress.com
Fadila Bettahar	@FadilaF11	
ART		
Elizabeth Speller	@Lizzie_Speller	michaelaartsblog.wordpress.com